Better Homes and Gardens®

PRIZEWINNING RECIPES

200 of the best dishes from Better Homes and Gardens® Prize Tested Recipe® Contest

Meredith® Books

Des Moines, Iowa

Better Homes and Gardens® Books
An imprint of Meredith® Books

Prizewinning Recipes
Editor: Kristi M. Thomas
Contributing Editors: Shelly McConnell, Spectrum
  Communication Services Inc.
Associate Art Director: Lynda Haupert
Photographers: Mike Dieter, Scott Little
Food Stylists: Dianna Nolin, Charles Worthington
Copy Chief: Catherine Hamrick
Copy and Production Editor: Terri Fredrickson
Managers, Book Production: Pam Kvitne,
  Marjorie J. Schenkelberg
Contributing Copy Editor: Sheila Mauck, Jennifer Speer
  Ramundt
Contributing Proofreaders: Marcia Gilmer, Susan J. Kling,
  Beth Popplewell
Indexer: Sharon Duffy
Electronic Production Coordinator: Paula Forest
Assistants: Judy Bailey, Mary Lee Gavin, Karen Schirm
Test Kitchen Director: Lynn Blanchard
Test Kitchen Product Supervisor: Marilyn Cornelius

Meredith® Books
Editor in Chief: James D. Blume
Design Director: Matt Strelecki
Managing Editor: Gregory H. Kayko
Executive Food Editor: Jennifer Dorland Darling

Director, Retail Sales and Marketing: Terry Unsworth
Director, Sales, Special Markets: Rita McMullen
Director, Sales, Premiums: Michael A. Peterson
Director, Sales, Retail: Tom Wierzbicki
Director, Sales, Home & Garden Centers: Ray Wolf
Director, Book Marketing: Brad Elmitt
Director, Operations: George A. Susral
Director, Production: Douglas M. Johnston

Vice President, General Manager: Jamie L. Martin

Better Homes and Gardens® Magazine
Editor in Chief: Jean LemMon
Executive Food Editor: Nancy Byal

Meredith Publishing Group
President, Publishing Group: Christopher M. Little
Vice President, Finance & Administration: Max Runciman

Meredith Corporation
Chairman and Chief Executive Officer: William T. Kerr

In Memoriam: E. T. Meredith III (1933–2003)

All of us at Better Homes and Gardens® Books are dedicated to providing you with the information and ideas you need to create delicious foods. We welcome your comments and suggestions. Write to us at: Better Homes and Gardens Books, Cookbook Editorial Department, 1716 Locust St., Des Moines, IA 50309-3023.

If you would like to purchase any of our books, check wherever quality books are sold. Visit our website at bhg.com.

Our seal assures you that every recipe in *Prizewinning Recipes* has been tested in the Better Homes and Gardens® Test Kitchen. This means that each recipe is practical and reliable, and meets our high standards of taste appeal. We guarantee your satisfaction with this book for as long as you own it.

Pictured on front cover: Grecian-Style Chicken
  (recipe, page 125)
Pictured on page one: Chocolate-Praline Squares
  (recipe, page 216)

Cover Photo:
Photographer: Jay Wilde
Food Stylist: Dianna Nolin

Sharing recipes is one of a cook's greatest pleasures. How many of your favorites came from friends or family? Probably quite a few. I love thumbing through my own files of treasured recipes and fondly remembering the people who passed along these gems to me.

Better Homes and Gardens® Prizewinning Recipes—filled with contest-winning recipes that have appeared in *Better Homes and Gardens®* magazine during the past eight decades—celebrates these sentiments. Recognizing the joy cooks get from sharing recipes, in 1923 the magazine's food editors began the annual Better Homes and Gardens® Prize Tested Recipes Contest. Top winners were awarded $5, a sum worth a week's worth of groceries for a family in the 1920s.

The contest left an indelible mark on modern cooking—a standard of exactness and taste appeal. Early editors of the magazine noted, "Since the beginning of cookery, the evils in housewives' recipes have been the words 'scant,' 'heaping,' 'rounding,' and 'pinch.' Unless a recipe is accurate as to measurements and clear as to method, it is not dependable for other women to follow." So in 1934, *Better Homes and Gardens* magazine issued "the stamp of recipe endorsement," a symbol ensuring that the featured recipes were clear enough to be duplicated in anyone's kitchen. It was recognized as "the mark of an accurate, dependable recipe by homemakers in suburbs and cities from coast to coast."

The popularity of the contest continues. Today's winning recipes earn $400, with the annual grand prize worth $5,000. The contest also celebrates a priceless legacy: generations of cooks—both men and women—who love to invent and share recipes. With *Prizewinning Recipes* you'll have a chance to glimpse into kitchens nationwide and sample blue-ribbon recipes from America's best hometown cooks—all tested and endorsed with the red plaid seal of approval by the Better Homes and Gardens® Test Kitchen.

Kristi Thomas

Kristi Thomas
Food Editor
Better Homes and Gardens® Prizewinning Recipes

Contents

Ricotta Puffs, page 32

Appetizers & More

CHAPTER INDEX

Spiced-Tea Special

Prep: 15 minutes **Chill:** Several hours

1955

Mrs. Richard Selander
Aurora, IL

A mellow blend of spices and three fruit juices make this warm-weather tea as delicious as it is refreshing. During cold weather, try it warmed to chase away the chills.

4 tea bags	2 cups cranberry juice
¼ teaspoon ground allspice	1½ cups cold water
¼ teaspoon ground cinnamon	½ cup orange juice
¼ teaspoon ground nutmeg	⅓ cup lemon juice
2½ cups boiling water	Lemon slices (optional)
½ to ¾ cup sugar	

1 Place tea bags and spices in a heat-proof glass bowl. Pour the boiling water over tea bags and spices. Cover; let stand 5 minutes. If desired, to remove spices, line strainer with coffee filter or 100% cotton cheesecloth; strain tea mixture over a bowl. Discard spices.

2 Stir sugar into brewed tea; cool. Stir in cranberry juice, cold water, orange juice, and lemon juice. Cover and chill thoroughly. If desired, garnish with lemon slices. Makes six 9-ounce servings.

Nutrition Facts per serving: 125 calories, 0 g total fat (0 g saturated fat), 0 mg cholesterol, 7 mg sodium, 32 g carbohydrate, 0 g fiber, 0 g protein. Daily Values: 77% vit. C, 1% calcium, 1% iron.

White Sangria Punch

Prep: 25 minutes **Chill:** 2 to 24 hours

1 small honeydew melon, halved,
    seeded, and cut into chunks
1 small pineapple, peeled and cut into
    chunks
4 medium peaches, cut into thin
    wedges
1 lemon, thinly sliced
1 lime, thinly sliced
2 750-ml bottles dry white wine,
    chilled

½ cup sugar
2 tablespoons lime juice
1 1-liter bottle carbonated water,
    chilled
1 cup loosely packed small fresh mint
    leaves
  Fresh pineapple spears

Norma F. Keleher
Pacific Grove, CA

Because it's filled with fresh fruit, this party punch can double as a beverage and an appetizer.

 In a large punch bowl combine melon, pineapple chunks, peaches, lemon slices, and lime slices. Add wine, sugar, and lime juice. Stir well to dissolve sugar. Cover and chill for at least 2 hours or up to 24 hours. Just before serving, stir in carbonated water and mint leaves. Serve with pineapple spears. Makes 16 servings.

Nutrition Facts per serving: 123 calories, 0 g total fat (0 g saturated fat), 0 mg cholesterol, 20 mg sodium, 16 g carbohydrate, 1 g fiber, 1 g protein. Daily Values: 2% vit. A, 35 % vit. C, 2% calcium, 9% iron.

spanish sipper

Sangria, a traditional Spanish beverage, was originally made with red wine, fruit juices, fruit slices or chunks, carbonated water, and occasionally a splash of brandy. The name comes from the Spanish word for blood because of the concoction's deep red color. The drink burst onto the American scene when it was introduced at the Spanish Pavilion of the 1964 New York World's Fair. During the 1960s and 1970s, Sangria appeared at parties across the nation. Over the years, the concept of Sangria has evolved. White Sangria Punch, above, is a 1990s variation that replaces red wine with white wine and more traditional fruits, such as apples and oranges, with melon, pineapple, and peaches.

Cranberry Cheesecake Shake

Start to finish: 10 minutes

1985

Marilyn Mueller
Fayetteville, AR

This thick and luscious drinkable version of cheesecake earned top ranking in the appetizers and beverages category of our 1985 Holiday Recipe Contest.

1 3-ounce package cream cheese, softened
1 cup milk
2 cups vanilla ice cream

½ of a 16-ounce can jellied cranberry sauce
1 cup fresh cranberries
Sugared cranberries (optional)*

1 Place cream cheese and milk in a blender container. Cover and blend until combined. Add ice cream, cranberry sauce, and the 1 cup cranberries. Cover and blend until nearly smooth, stopping to scrape down sides if necessary. Serve immediately. If desired, garnish with sugared cranberries. Makes four 8-ounce servings.

*Note: For sugared cranberries, freeze whole fresh cranberries; roll in sugar until coated.

Nutrition Facts per serving: 385 calories, 21 g total fat (13 g saturated fat), 73 mg cholesterol, 163 mg sodium, 45 g carbohydrate, 2 g fiber, 6 g protein. Daily Values: 25% vit. A, 8% vit. C, 18% calcium, 2% iron.

yuletide fare '80s-style

In 1985, Better Homes and Gardens® magazine sponsored a contest asking readers to share their cherished holiday recipes. Thousands responded, submitting ideas for main dishes, appetizers and beverages, food gifts, side dishes, cookies and candies, homemade baked goods, and recipes from kids. The letters proved without a doubt that real holiday traditions are built on family recipes. The 35 winners, which included Cranberry Cheesecake Shake, above, provided a snapshot of what America was cooking in the 1980s.

Hazelnut-Praline Dream

Start to finish: 5 minutes

1994

Kristine Feher
Passaic, NJ

Kristine recommends keeping the ingredients for this easy ice cream drink on hand so you can whip it up whenever you want a refreshing adult treat.

1 pint caramel-swirled vanilla ice
   cream with pralines or
   butter brickle ice cream

1⅓ cups milk
⅓ cup hazelnut liqueur

1 In a blender container combine ice cream, milk, and liqueur. Cover and blend until smooth. Serve immediately. Makes four 6-ounce servings.

Nutrition Facts per serving: 414 calories, 26 g total fat (12 g saturated fat), 111 mg cholesterol, 181 mg sodium, 30 g carbohydrate, 1 g fiber, 8 g protein. Daily Values: 15% vit. A, 1% vit. C, 25% calcium, 2% iron.

brewing up a storm

Although coffee has always been part and parcel of American cuisine, it has had its ups and downs. Coffee drinking was so important during World War II, the government considered it essential for the soldiers' morale. After the war, coffee drinking tapered off as Americans began to favor soft drinks. In the 1970s, new innovations in automatic drip coffee makers prompted Americans to rediscover coffee, but plain brew just wouldn't do. Java fanatics began buying whole bean coffees and grinding them themselves—trying myriad flavors from vanilla to mint to hazelnut to Irish cream. And in the 1990s, the espresso craze hit. Coffee shops sprang up everywhere, and Americans dropped by to enjoy coffee creations of all kinds—both hot and cold. It didn't take long for cooks to begin experimenting at home. Soon sippers, such as Frothy Mocha Seville, right, were winning accolades.

Frothy Mocha Seville

Start to finish: 15 minutes

½ cup packed brown sugar
4 ounces semisweet chocolate, cut up
2 ounces unsweetened chocolate, cut up
1 tablespoon finely shredded orange peel
½ teaspoon ground cinnamon

4 cups hot brewed coffee
1 cup half-and-half or light cream, warmed
1 recipe Whipped Honey-Orange Topping
Shredded orange peel (optional)

Josephine B. Piro
Easton, PA

Friends visiting on a wintry night inspired Josephine to create this chocolate-and-orange-flavored coffee sensation.

1 Place brown sugar, semisweet chocolate, unsweetened chocolate, the 1 tablespoon orange peel, and the cinnamon in a blender container. Cover and blend until chocolate is finely chopped. Remove half of the chocolate mixture; set aside. Add 2 cups of the hot coffee to blender container; cover and blend at medium speed until chocolate is melted. Add ½ cup of the half-and-half or light cream; cover and blend until frothy. Pour into 4 coffee mugs or cups.

2 In a blender container combine reserved chocolate mixture and remaining coffee. Cover and blend at medium speed until chocolate is melted. Add remaining half-and-half or light cream; cover and blend until frothy. Pour into 4 more coffee mugs or cups. Top each serving with a spoonful of Whipped Honey-Orange Topping and, if desired, additional shredded orange peel. Makes eight 6-ounce servings.

Whipped Honey-Orange Topping: In a chilled bowl combine ½ cup whipping cream, 1 tablespoon honey, and 1 tablespoon orange liqueur or orange juice. Beat with chilled beaters of an electric mixer on medium speed until soft peaks form.

Nutrition Facts per serving: 245 calories, 17 g total fat (7 g saturated fat), 32 mg cholesterol, 24 mg sodium, 27 g carbohydrate, 1 g fiber, 3 g protein. Daily Values: 10% vit. A, 2% vit. C, 5% calcium, 8% iron.

Hawaiian Lemonade

Start to finish: 10 minutes

1959

*Martha Johnson
Boston, MA*

Lemonade goes Hawaiian with the addition of pineapple. Ginger ale and apricot add to the intriguing blend of flavors.

½ of a 12-ounce can (¾ cup) frozen lemonade concentrate, thawed
¾ cup water
1 12-ounce can (1½ cups) apricot nectar, chilled

1 12-ounce can (1½ cups) unsweetened pineapple juice, chilled
Ice cubes
Chilled ginger ale (about 1¼ cups)
Lemon slices (optional)

1 In a pitcher combine lemonade concentrate and water; add apricot nectar and pineapple juice. Place ice cubes in six 12-ounce glasses. Pour juice mixture over ice cubes. Fill glasses with ginger ale. If desired, garnish with lemon slices. Makes six 8-ounce servings.

Nutrition Facts per serving: 138 calories, 0 g total fat (0 g saturated fat), 0 mg cholesterol, 8 mg sodium, 35 g carbohydrate, 1 g fiber, 1 g protein. Daily Values: 9% vit. A, 20% vit. C, 2% calcium, 4% iron.

hawaiian improvisation

Cooks across the U.S. have been hearing the call of the Hawaiian Islands ever since the early days of the 20th century. In the 1920s and 1930s, any dish that simply contained pineapple was considered Hawaiian—even pineapple on baked ham. In the 1940s and 1950s, restaurants such as Don the Beachcomber's and Trader Vic's presented an Americanized blend of Polynesian and Chinese foods that was dubbed "Hawaiian." By the late 1950s, with tourists flocking to visit the islands and the popularity of the movie *South Pacific,* the Hawaiian party or luau became a fashionable way to entertain. Rather than authentic Hawaiian cuisine, the menu typically featured dishes with a Polynesian influence, such as rumaki, shrimp tempura, and Hawaiian Lemonade, above.

Dried Tomato Spread

Prep: 35 minutes   **Chill:** 4 to 24 hours   **Stand:** 30 minutes

De Anne Pearson
Austin, TX

Fresh basil puts a summer spin on this make-ahead cream cheese spread that's welcome at any party.

1 to 2 cloves garlic, minced
1 tablespoon olive oil
½ cup dried tomatoes (not oil-packed), snipped
⅓ cup dry white wine
1 8-ounce package cream cheese, softened

⅓ cup snipped fresh basil
3 tablespoons grated Parmesan cheese
Baguette-style French bread slices, toasted
Fresh basil leaves (optional)

1 In a medium skillet cook garlic in oil until light brown. Add dried tomatoes and wine. Cook, uncovered, over low heat for 15 minutes. Remove from heat; let stand 10 minutes. Drain off liquid.

2 Meanwhile, in a food processor bowl or blender container combine cream cheese, snipped basil, and Parmesan cheese. Cover and process or blend until smooth. Add tomato mixture; process until almost smooth. Transfer to a serving bowl. Cover and chill for at least 4 hours or up to 24 hours. Let stand at room temperature for 30 minutes before serving. Serve with toasted baguette slices. If desired, garnish with fresh basil leaves. Makes 1 cup.

Nutrition Facts per teaspoon spread: 25 calories, 2 g total fat (1 g saturated fat), 6 mg cholesterol, 36 mg sodium, 1 g carbohydrate, 0 g fiber, 1 g protein. Daily Values: 2% vit. A, 1% calcium.

Artichoke-Chili Dip

Prep: 10 minutes **Bake:** 20 minutes

1 14-ounce can artichoke hearts, drained and chopped

1 4½-ounce can chopped green chili peppers, drained

1 cup light mayonnaise dressing or salad dressing or regular mayonnaise or salad dressing

½ cup grated Parmesan cheese (2 ounces)

Toasted pita chips, vegetable dippers, tortilla chips, and/or breadsticks

1981

*Mary Bergeron
Seattle, WA*

To keep this rich dip warm during your party, place it on a warmer tray or in an electric fondue pot.

1 Combine the artichoke hearts, chili peppers, mayonnaise dressing or salad dressing, and Parmesan cheese. Spread mixture in a 9-inch pie plate. Bake in a 350° oven about 20 minutes or until heated through. Serve warm with pita chips, vegetable dippers, tortilla chips, and/or breadsticks. Makes about 2⅔ cups.

Nutrition Facts per tablespoon dip: 28 calories, 2 g total fat (1 g saturated fat), 3 mg cholesterol, 94 mg sodium, 2 g carbohydrate, 0 g fiber, 1 g protein. Daily Values: 4% vit. C, 2% calcium, 1% iron.

dips never die

Some food historians claim party dips were born in the 1950s with a mixture of sour cream and dry onion soup mix that was called California Dip. The truth is, dips are actually much older. Cookbooks of the 1940s refer to chips with dips. By the 1950s, however, cocktail parties had become an institution and appetizers that were easy to eat standing up, such as dips, were de rigueur. Even though times and tastes have changed, people are still hosting cocktail parties and are still relying on versatile dips, such as Artichoke-Chili Dip, above, to tide guests over until dinner or to offer as a snack.

Olive Cheese Ball

Prep: 35 minutes **Chill:** 4 to 24 hours **Stand:** 15 minutes

- 1 8-ounce package cream cheese
- 8 ounces blue cheese, crumbled
- ¼ cup butter or margarine
- ⅔ cup chopped pitted ripe olives, well drained (one 4½-ounce can)
- 2 tablespoons snipped fresh chives
- ⅓ cup coarsely chopped walnuts or almonds, toasted
- Fresh parsley (optional)
- Assorted crackers or apple slices

1959

Mrs. Edith Weller, Strehle Litchfield, IL

Standing the test of time, this delightful combo of cream cheese, blue cheese, ripe olives, and walnuts still makes a terrific nibble for modern-day parties.

1 Place cream cheese, blue cheese, and butter or margarine in a large bowl; let stand until room temperature. Beat cheeses and butter with electric mixer on low speed until smooth. Stir in olives and chives. Cover and chill for at least 4 hours or up to 24 hours.

2 Shape mixture into a ball; cover and chill until serving time. To serve, roll in nuts. Let stand for 15 minutes. If desired, garnish with parsley. Serve with assorted crackers or apple slices. Makes 3 cups.

Nutrition Facts per tablespoon: 50 calories, 5 g total fat (3 g saturated fat), 11 mg cholesterol, 106 mg sodium, 1 g carbohydrate, 0 g fiber, 2 g protein. Daily Values: 4% vit. A, 3% calcium, 1% iron.

cheese balls catch on

Nobody knows exactly when the first cheese ball appeared at a party, but miniature morsels of cheese have been part of ladies' luncheons since the turn of the 20th century. In the 1940s, bite-size balls of cheese coated in nuts, parsley, or chipped beef were common fare at cocktail parties. By the 1950s, the full-size version was becoming popular. Early cheese balls often were based on processed cheese spreads spiked with Worcestershire sauce or bottled hot pepper sauce and rolled in pecans or walnuts for crunch. As the decade passed, cooks varied the cheese ball theme and came up with unique combinations, such as Olive Cheese Ball, above.

Garlic-Feta **Cheese Spread**

Prep: 15 minutes **Chill:** 1 to 24 hours

Joanne Spencer
Brookfield, CT

Feta cheese supplies a new flavor to the ever-popular cream cheese spread. Garlic and a variety of dried herbs add gusto.

4 ounces feta cheese, crumbled
½ of an 8-ounce package cream cheese
    or reduced-fat cream cheese
    (Neufchâtel), softened
⅓ cup mayonnaise or salad dressing or
    light mayonnaise dressing or
    salad dressing

1 clove garlic, minced
¼ teaspoon dried basil, crushed
¼ teaspoon dried oregano, crushed
⅛ teaspoon dried dillweed
⅛ teaspoon dried thyme, crushed
    Fresh thyme (optional)
    Assorted unsalted crackers

1 In a food processor bowl or mixing bowl combine feta cheese, cream cheese, mayonnaise or salad dressing, garlic, and dried herbs. Cover and process or beat with an electric mixer on medium speed until combined. Cover and chill for at least 1 hour or up to 24 hours. If desired, garnish with fresh thyme. Serve with assorted crackers. Makes 1½ cups.

Nutrition Facts per tablespoon: 51 calories, 5 g total fat (2 g saturated fat), 11 mg cholesterol, 84 mg sodium, 0 g carbohydrate, 0 g fiber, 1 g protein. Daily Values: 2% vit. A, 2% calcium.

whirlwind discovery

The food processor had its beginnings in the restaurant kitchens of France where chefs found the machine invaluable for chopping, slicing, shredding, and even kneading bread dough. Before long, the food processor was redesigned for home use and introduced to home cooks in 1975 at the National Housewares Exposition in Chicago. When culinary professionals began singing its praises, the food processor was on its way to becoming a home kitchen basic. With a food processor, recipes such as Garlic-Feta Cheese Spread, above, whirl together in seconds.

Herbed Leek Tart

Prep: 15 minutes **Bake:** 15 minutes **Stand:** 5 minutes

1 10-ounce package refrigerated pizza dough
6 medium leeks, thinly sliced
3 cloves garlic, minced
2 tablespoons olive oil
1 teaspoon dried herbes de Provence or dried basil, crushed

2 tablespoons Dijon-style mustard
1 tablespoon water
1 cup shredded Gruyère or Swiss cheese (4 ounces)
¼ cup pine nuts or chopped almonds, toasted
   Fresh savory (optional)

1 Grease a baking sheet. Unroll pizza dough onto prepared baking sheet; press to form a 12×9-inch rectangle. Bake in a 425° oven for 7 minutes.

2 Meanwhile, in a large skillet cook leeks and garlic in olive oil about 5 minutes or until tender. Remove from heat. Stir in herbes de Provence or basil. Stir together mustard and water; spread over prebaked crust. Top with leek mixture, cheese, and nuts.

3 Bake about 8 minutes more or until cheese is bubbly. Let stand 5 minutes before serving. Cut into 24 squares. If desired, garnish with fresh savory. Makes 24 squares.

Nutrition Facts per square:
74 calories, 4 g total fat
(1 g saturated fat), 5 mg
cholesterol, 88 mg sodium,
7 g carbohydrate, 1 g fiber,
3 g protein. Daily Values:
1% vit. A, 2% vit. C,
5% calcium, 5% iron.

1998

Mary-Jane Stanton
Rehoboth Beach, DE

Mary-Jane relies on ready-made dough to save time when she makes this Swiss cheese-and-nut-laden appetizer. Herbes de Provence, a classic French combination of basil, fennel seed, lavender, marjoram, rosemary, sage, summer savory, and thyme, seasons the tart. The blend also nicely flavors cooked meat, poultry, or vegetables.

Asparagus Spring Rolls

Start to finish: 45 minutes

Colleen Gardner
Plano, TX

Colleen adds a creative twist to company-special meals by serving these fresh and fun appetizers of lasagna noodles wrapped around smoked salmon and asparagus spears.

1	8-ounce package reduced-fat cream cheese (Neufchâtel)	3	quarts water
2	tablespoons snipped fresh chives	1	tablespoon olive oil
2	tablespoons milk	¼	teaspoon salt
1	to 2 tablespoons snipped fresh dill	8	dried lasagna noodles
1	clove garlic, minced	24	fresh asparagus spears
1	tablespoon lemon juice	6	ounces thinly sliced smoked salmon
½	teaspoon freshly ground black pepper	8	long fresh chives

1 In a small bowl combine cream cheese, snipped chives, milk, dill, garlic, lemon juice, and pepper; set aside.

2 In a 4-quart Dutch oven combine the water, oil, and salt; bring to boiling. Add lasagna noodles; cook for 10 to 12 minutes or until noodles are nearly tender.

3 Meanwhile, snap off and discard woody bases of asparagus spears. If necessary, trim asparagus to 5-inch lengths. Add asparagus to pasta; cook 3 minutes more. Drain; rinse with cold water. Drain again. Pat lasagna noodles dry with paper towels.

4 Spread about 2 tablespoons of the cream cheese mixture evenly over each lasagna noodle. Divide salmon evenly among the noodles, placing a single layer of salmon on each noodle. Place 3 asparagus spears on one end of each noodle, letting the tips extend beyond the edge. Roll up each noodle. Tie with a fresh chive. If desired, stand spring rolls upright to serve. Makes 8 spring rolls.

Nutrition Facts per spring roll: 196 calories, 10 g total fat (5 g saturated fat), 27 mg cholesterol, 350 mg sodium, 17 g carbohydrate, 1 g fiber, 10 g protein. Daily Values: 13% vit. A, 14% vit. C, 3% calcium, 8% iron.

Dale's Baja-Derves

Prep: 15 minutes **Microwave:** 1 minute per platter

1989

Dale L. Studebaker
Long Beach, CA

Dale created and named (taking a little poetic license) these cheddar-and-shrimp hors d'oeuvres while camping in Baja, Mexico in a motor home. Who said camping can't include cocktail party snacks?

1½ cups shredded cheddar cheese
      (6 ounces)
1 4½-ounce can diced green chili
      peppers, drained
1 2¼-ounce can sliced pitted ripe
      olives, drained

¼ cup thinly sliced green onions
¼ cup mayonnaise or salad dressing
1 4-ounce can tiny shrimp, rinsed and
      drained
36 to 40 tortilla chips

1 In a large bowl combine cheese, chili peppers, olives, green onions, and mayonnaise or salad dressing. Gently stir in shrimp. Arrange about half of the tortilla chips on a 12-inch microwave-safe platter.* Top chips with half of the cheese-shrimp mixture. Microwave, uncovered, on 100% power (high) for 1 to 2 minutes or just until cheese is melted, giving platter one half-turn halfway through cooking. Repeat with remaining chips and cheese-shrimp mixture. Makes 12 servings.

*Note: To bake in a conventional oven, use two 12-inch pizza pans. Bake in a 350° oven for 7 to 8 minutes or just until cheese is melted.

Nutrition Facts per serving: 144 calories, 11 g total fat (4 g saturated fat), 29 mg cholesterol, 320 mg sodium, 6 g carbohydrate, 1 g fiber, 6 g protein. Daily Values: 5% vit. A, 12% vit. C, 12% calcium, 4% iron.

south-of-the-border serendipity

Nachos were first served in the 1950s by Ignacio Anaya, owner of the Victory Club in Piedras Negras, Mexico. At that time, women from south Texas cities, such as San Antonio, Abilene, and San Angelo, often crossed the border into Piedras Negras to shop and have lunch. One day a group stopped by the Victory Club. Because the restaurant was low on supplies, Ignacio improvised an appetizer: He put cheese on toasted tortillas and added slices of jalapeño pepper. Because his nickname was Nacho, he christened his creation a "Nacho special." Tex-Mex snack food hasn't been the same since. Dale's Baja-Derves, above, is a 1980s adaptation of the old standard.

Mushroom-Crepe Lasagna

Prep: 40 minutes **Bake:** 20 minutes

1 7-ounce jar roasted red sweet
   peppers, rinsed and drained
⅓ cup half-and-half or light cream
1 teaspoon balsamic vinegar
1 8-ounce package cream cheese,
   softened
3 tablespoons snipped fresh parsley
1 teaspoon bottled minced roasted
   garlic

¼ teaspoon ground black pepper
3 cups sliced crimini, button, and/or
   shiitake mushrooms
1 medium onion, chopped (½ cup)
2 tablespoons margarine or butter
4 ounces thinly sliced prosciutto or
   ham, chopped (about ¾ cup)
5 purchased crepes

1999

Jennifer Spencer
Alpharetta, GA

Layered bliss describes
this elegant appetizer.
Purchased crepes, a
modern-day boon for
busy cooks, reduces the
prep time. Round or
square crepes work
equally well.

1 For sweet pepper sauce, in a blender container or food processor bowl combine roasted peppers, half-and-half or light cream, and vinegar. Cover; blend or process until smooth. Pour into a small bowl. Cover; set aside.

2 In another small bowl stir together cream cheese, parsley, garlic, and black pepper; set aside. In a large skillet cook mushrooms and onion in hot margarine or butter over medium-high heat for 4 to 5 minutes or until mushrooms are tender and most of the liquid evaporates. Remove from heat; stir in prosciutto or ham.

3 Place one crepe in the bottom of a lightly greased 9-inch pie plate. Spread about one-fifth of the cream cheese mixture over crepe; sprinkle with about one-fifth of the mushroom mixture. Add a second crepe (if using square crepes, set second crepe at a slight angle to the first crepe so points are staggered). Add another one-fifth of the cream cheese and mushroom mixtures as before. Repeat with the remaining crepes, cream cheese mixture, and mushroom mixture, ending with mushroom mixture. Cover loosely with foil.

4 Bake in a 350° oven about 20 minutes or until heated through. Cut into wedges to serve. Pass sweet pepper sauce. Makes 6 to 8 servings.

Nutrition Facts per serving: 285 calories, 24 g total fat (12 g saturated fat), 65 mg cholesterol,
509 mg sodium, 9 g carbohydrate, 1 g fiber, 10 g protein. Daily Values: 35% vit. A, 122% vit. C,
5% calcium, 11% iron.

Mushroom **Croustades**

Prep: 40 minutes **Bake:** 25 minutes

Beth Labant
Elk Grove Village, IL

No dough to roll here. Instead, press sliced bread into muffin cups to create the crusts for these appetizers.

24 slices firm-textured white bread
3 tablespoons chopped shallots or onion
¼ cup margarine or butter
3 cups finely chopped fresh mushrooms
2 tablespoons all-purpose flour
1 cup whipping cream
2 tablespoons snipped fresh chives

1 tablespoon snipped fresh parsley
½ teaspoon lemon juice
¼ teaspoon salt
⅛ teaspoon ground red pepper
Dash ground black pepper
2 tablespoons grated Parmesan cheese
Dairy sour cream (optional)
Snipped fresh chives (optional)

1 Lightly grease twenty-four 2½-inch muffin cups. Cut a 2½-inch round from each slice of bread.* Carefully press each bread round into one of the prepared muffin cups to form a shell. Bake in a 400° oven about 10 minutes or until golden brown.

2 Meanwhile, for filling, in a medium saucepan cook shallots or onion in hot margarine or butter for 4 minutes. Stir in mushrooms; cook, uncovered, about 15 minutes or until most of the liquid has evaporated. Stir in flour. Add whipping cream all at once. Cook and stir until thickened and bubbly. Cook and stir for 1 minute more; remove from heat. Stir in the 2 tablespoons chives, the parsley, lemon juice, salt, ground red pepper, and black pepper.

3 Remove bread shells from muffin cups. Place bread shells in a shallow baking pan. Spoon filling into shells; sprinkle with Parmesan cheese. Bake, uncovered, in a 350° oven for 15 minutes. If desired, top with sour cream and additional chives. Makes 24 appetizers.

*Note: You can use the bread scraps to make soft bread crumbs for casserole toppings or meat stuffings.

To Make Ahead: Prepare the baked bread shells as directed. Place in a freezer container or bag and freeze for up to 3 months. To serve, thaw bread shells. Fill and bake as directed.

Nutrition Facts per appetizer: 93 calories, 6 g total fat (3 g saturated fat), 14 mg cholesterol, 126 mg sodium, 8 g carbohydrate, 0 g fiber, 2 g protein. Daily Values: 8% vit. A, 1% vit. C, 2% calcium, 4% iron.

Mushroom-Spinach Pinwheels

Prep: 30 minutes **Chill:** 30 minutes + 1 hour **Bake:** 20 minutes

1 8-ounce package reduced-fat cream cheese (Neufchâtel), softened
⅔ cup butter, softened
1 cup all-purpose flour
1 cup self-rising flour
1 10-ounce package frozen chopped spinach
2 tablespoons butter
2½ cups chopped fresh mushrooms
1 large onion, chopped (1 cup)
1 tablespoon all-purpose flour
½ teaspoon salt
½ teaspoon dried oregano, crushed
½ teaspoon lemon juice
⅛ teaspoon garlic powder
¼ cup grated Parmesan cheese
1 egg white
1 tablespoon water

1998

Patricia Marallo
Bay St. Louis, MS

For a head start on these appetizers, prepare them in advance and freeze the unbaked slices in freezer-safe containers up to 3 months. To serve, bake the frozen slices as directed.

1 In a large mixing bowl beat together cream cheese and the ⅔ cup butter. Add the 1 cup all-purpose flour and the self-rising flour; beat well. Divide dough into two balls; wrap and chill 30 to 60 minutes or until dough is easy to handle.

2 For filling, cook spinach according to package directions; drain well, squeezing out excess liquid. Set aside. In a large skillet melt the 2 tablespoons butter. Add mushrooms and onion. Cook and stir over medium heat about 3 minutes or until onion is tender. Add spinach, the 1 tablespoon flour, the salt, oregano, lemon juice, and garlic powder. Cook and stir until mixture thickens. Stir in Parmesan cheese; set aside to cool.

3 On a floured surface, roll one pastry ball to a 12×7-inch rectangle. Spread dough with half the spinach mixture, leaving a ½-inch border around edges. Starting from a short side, roll up dough and filling. Moisten edges with water; pinch to seal. Cover and chill for 1 hour. Repeat with remaining pastry and spinach mixture.

4 Slice logs into ½-inch slices. Place slices on ungreased baking sheets. Combine egg white and water. Brush slices with egg white mixture. Bake in a 400° oven about 20 minutes or until golden brown. Transfer to wire racks; let cool. Makes 28 pinwheels.

Nutrition Facts per pinwheel: 101 calories, 7 g total fat (4 g saturated fat), 19 mg cholesterol, 190 mg sodium, 8 g carbohydrate, 1 g fiber, 2 g protein. Daily Values: 11% vit. A, 2% vit. C, 2% calcium, 4% iron.

Mexican Shrimp Cocktail

Prep: 20 minutes **Chill:** 2 to 4 hours

1 pound fresh or frozen shrimp	¼ cup chopped onion
¼ cup catsup	¼ cup snipped fresh cilantro
¼ cup lime juice	2 avocados, seeded, peeled, and chopped
1 to 2 teaspoons bottled hot pepper sauce	Lime wedges (optional)
½ cup chopped tomato	Purple flowering kale (optional)

1 Thaw shrimp, if frozen. Peel and devein shrimp; cook shrimp in a large amount of boiling water for 1 to 2 minutes or until shrimp turn pink, stirring occasionally. Drain; rinse under cold running water.

2 In a large bowl stir together catsup, lime juice, and hot pepper sauce. Add shrimp, tomato, onion, and cilantro; toss to coat. Cover and chill for at least 2 hours or up to 4 hours.

3 Just before serving, add avocados; toss to coat. If desired, garnish with lime wedges and flowering kale. Makes 8 servings.

Nutrition Facts per serving: 113 calories, 6 g total fat (1 g saturated fat), 65 mg cholesterol, 183 mg sodium, 9 g carbohydrate, 2 g fiber, 8 g protein. Daily Values: 8% vit. A, 20% vit. C, 1% calcium, 9% iron.

1997

*Gail Popham
Donna, TX*

Living near the U.S. border to Mexico gives Gail a familiarity with the area's special ingredients. She used three of them—avocados, fresh cilantro, and shrimp—to create this zesty seafood cocktail.

the saga of shrimp cocktail

Shrimp cocktail is a cousin of the oyster cocktail, which was supposedly invented by a San Francisco miner who enjoyed his oysters with catsup. Throughout the first half of the 20th century, shrimp cocktail usually consisted of cooked shrimp served with a tomato-based sauce seasoned with horseradish, lemon juice, and hot pepper sauce or another hot seasoning. In the 1960s, Americans left traditional shrimp cocktail behind in favor of marinated shrimp, which was often as simple as cooked shrimp tossed with bottled Italian salad dressing. Over the years both recipes have undergone numerous transformations. Mexican Shrimp Cocktail, above, is a 1990s example. Featuring shrimp marinated in a cocktail sauce that's seasoned with a touch of old Mexico, it blends the two recipes.

Chicken-Spinach **Phyllo Rolls**

Prep: 25 minutes **Bake:** 15 minutes **Stand:** 5 minutes

Marline Schinderwolf
Granger, IN

For the ultimate in convenience, assemble and chill the phyllo rolls hours before your party. Then, just before your guests arrive, heat the rolls in the oven.

1 10-ounce package frozen chopped spinach, thawed and well drained
1 5-ounce can chunk-style chicken, drained and flaked
1 cup shredded cheddar cheese (4 ounces)
½ of an 8-ounce tub cream cheese with chive and onion
½ cup chopped walnuts
1 tablespoon dry sherry
½ teaspoon Worcestershire sauce
¼ teaspoon ground nutmeg
8 sheets phyllo dough, thawed
⅓ cup margarine or butter, melted

1 Drain spinach well, pressing out excess liquid. For filling, in a medium bowl combine spinach, chicken, cheddar cheese, cream cheese, walnuts, sherry, Worcestershire sauce, and nutmeg; set aside.

2 Lightly brush one sheet of phyllo with some of the melted margarine or butter. Place another phyllo sheet on top; brush with some margarine or butter. (Cover the remaining phyllo with clear plastic wrap to prevent it from drying out.)

3 Spoon one-fourth of the filling (about ½ cup) evenly down the long side of phyllo, about 2 inches from a long side and 1 inch from a short side. Fold 2 inches of the long side over filling; fold in the short sides. Starting from the side with filling, loosely roll up. Place roll, seam side down, on an ungreased baking sheet. Repeat with remaining phyllo, margarine or butter, and filling. (If desired, cover and chill rolls for up to 6 hours before baking.)

4 Brush tops of rolls with any remaining margarine or butter. With a sharp knife, score rolls at 1½-inch intervals. Bake in a 400° oven about 15 minutes or until golden brown. Let stand for 5 minutes before slicing where scored. Serve warm. Makes about 36 appetizers.

Nutrition Facts per appetizer: 71 calories, 5 g total fat (2 g saturated fat), 9 mg cholesterol, 96 mg sodium, 3 g carbohydrate, 0 g fiber, 3 g protein. Daily Values: 8% vit. A, 1% vit. C, 2% calcium, 2% iron.

Greek-Style Party Pizzas

Prep: 15 minutes **Bake:** 8 minutes

4 6-inch pita bread rounds
1 7-ounce container hummus
1 medium tomato, seeded and
  chopped
½ of a 6-ounce jar marinated artichoke
  hearts, drained and chopped
½ cup crumbled feta cheese (2 ounces)

½ cup shredded mozzarella cheese
  (2 ounces)
2 teaspoons olive oil (optional)
1 teaspoon sesame seed (optional)
8 pitted ripe olives, quartered
  (optional)
Fresh oregano leaves (optional)

Marietta A. Montuori
Sweet Valley, PA

Be adventurous and serve
these feta-and-hummus-
topped mini pizzas at your
next gathering.

1 Place pita rounds on a large baking sheet. Spread each round with one-fourth of the hummus, leaving a 1-inch border. Sprinkle each with one-fourth of the tomatoes, artichoke hearts, feta, and mozzarella. If desired, drizzle with oil and sprinkle with sesame seed.

2 Bake in a 450° oven for 8 to 10 minutes or until cheese has melted and edges are lightly browned. If desired, top with olives and oregano. Cut into quarters. Makes 16 appetizer servings.

Nutrition Facts per serving: 87 calories, 3 g total fat (1 g saturated fat), 5 mg cholesterol, 184 mg sodium, 12 g carbohydrate, 0 g fiber, 3 g protein. Daily Values: 1% vit. A, 6% vit. C, 5% calcium, 4% iron.

m-m-m hummus

In the 1970s, hummus, a classic Middle Eastern dip, came onto the appetizer scene. This exotic dip quickly became popular, perhaps because more Americans were traveling to the Middle East or maybe because the vegetarian movement was gaining converts. Made from mashed chickpeas and flavored with lemon juice, plenty of garlic, and a drizzle of olive or sesame oil, it is traditionally served with pita bread wedges or vegetables for dipping. But many cooks are pushing the culinary envelope, and in Greek-Style Party Pizzas, above, it's used in place of pizza sauce.

Ricotta **Puffs**

Prep: 30 minutes **Bake:** 20 minutes

1997

Lisa D. Gillett
Aurora, CO

Using puff pastry makes it easy to prepare these flaky appetizers oozing with Italian ricotta cheese. (Pictured on page 6.)

1 17¼-ounce package (2 sheets) frozen puff pastry, thawed
½ cup ricotta cheese
½ cup chopped roasted red sweet pepper
3 tablespoons grated Romano cheese

1 tablespoon snipped fresh parsley
1 teaspoon dried oregano, crushed
½ teaspoon ground black pepper
   Milk
   Grated Romano cheese

1 Unfold the pastry on a lightly floured surface. Using a sharp knife, cut each pastry sheet into nine 3-inch squares.

2 For filling, in a medium bowl stir together the ricotta cheese, roasted red pepper, the 3 tablespoons Romano cheese, the parsley, oregano, and black pepper.

3 Moisten the edges of each pastry square with milk. Spoon about 2 teaspoons filling onto one-half of each pastry square. Fold the other half of the pastry over the filling, forming a rectangle. Seal edges by pressing with the tines of a fork. With a sharp knife, cut slits in the top of each pastry bundle. Brush with milk; sprinkle with additional Romano cheese.

4 Arrange pastry bundles on an ungreased baking sheet. Bake in a 400° oven about 20 minutes or until golden brown. Transfer to a wire rack; cool for 5 minutes before serving. Makes 18 puffs.

Nutrition Facts per puff: 137 calories, 10 g total fat (1 g saturated fat), 3 mg cholesterol, 137 mg sodium, 10 g carbohydrate, 0 g fiber, 3 g protein. Daily Values: 3% vit. A, 19% vit. C, 3% calcium.

Cheese Puffs

Prep: 30 minutes **Bake:** 12 minutes

1 3-ounce package cream cheese, softened
1 egg yolk
1 teaspoon lemon juice
1 teaspoon snipped fresh chives
   Dash pepper
½ cup shredded white cheddar cheese (2 ounces)

2 slices bacon, crisp-cooked, drained, and crumbled
1 17¼-ounce package (2 sheets) frozen puff pastry, thawed
   Milk

1974

Mrs. Harold W. Cogger
Newburyport, MA

These flaky morsels boast a savory filling accented with white cheddar cheese and crisp-cooked bacon.

1 For filling, in a small mixing bowl combine cream cheese, egg yolk, lemon juice, chives, and pepper; beat with an electric mixer on medium speed until nearly smooth. Stir in cheddar cheese and bacon.

2 On a lightly floured surface, roll one of the pastry sheets to a 12-inch square. Cut into sixteen 3-inch squares. Top each square with about 1 teaspoon of the filling. Brush edges with milk. Fold in half diagonally. Seal edges by pressing with tines of a fork or fingers. Place on an ungreased baking sheet. Repeat with remaining pastry sheet and filling. (If desired, cover and chill for up to 4 hours before baking.) Bake in a 400° oven for 12 to 15 minutes or until golden brown. Makes 32 puffs.

Nutrition Facts per puff: 87 calories, 7 g total fat (1 g saturated fat), 12 mg cholesterol, 83 mg sodium, 6 g carbohydrate, 0 g fiber, 1 g protein. Daily Values: 2% vit. A, 2% calcium.

appetizer tally

How do you calculate the number of appetizers you'll need for a party? Start by deciding what types of appetizers you'd like to serve. Plan more if they're light; fewer if they're hearty. Next, consider the timing. If a meal will be served shortly after the appetizers, figure you'll need four or five per guest. If a late meal is on the agenda, allow six or seven per guest. If appetizers will be the meal, eight or nine per guest is realistic.

Smoked Salmon Cheesecake

Prep: 15 minutes **Bake:** 35 minutes

1996

Joseph A. Divita
Tonawanda, NY

2 cups soft bread crumbs	½ cup evaporated fat-free milk
2 tablespoons margarine or butter, melted	4 ounces smoked salmon, skin and bones removed and finely flaked
3 eggs	1 teaspoon dried dillweed
1 15-ounce carton ricotta cheese	⅛ teaspoon salt
1½ cups shredded Swiss cheese (6 ounces)	⅛ teaspoon ground white pepper
	Dairy sour cream (optional)

Joseph keeps last-minute party preparations to a minimum by making the crust and filling for this savory cheesecake ahead. He then bakes it at party time and serves it warm.

1 For crust, in a small bowl combine the bread crumbs and melted margarine or butter. Press the crumb mixture onto the bottom of a 9-inch quiche dish; set aside.

2 For filling, in a large bowl use a fork to beat eggs slightly. Stir in ricotta cheese and Swiss cheese. Stir in evaporated fat-free milk, salmon, dillweed, salt, and white pepper. (If desired, cover and chill for up to 6 hours.)

3 Pour filling into prepared crust. Bake in a 350° oven for 35 to 40 minutes or until the center is nearly set when shaken. Cool slightly in pan on a wire rack.

4 To serve, cut warm cheesecake into wedges. If desired, top with sour cream. Cover and store any leftovers in the refrigerator for up to 3 days.* Makes 16 servings.

*Note: To reheat a slice of chilled cheesecake in a microwave oven, place slice on a microwave-safe plate. Cover loosely with microwave-safe plastic wrap. Microwave on 50% power (medium) about 40 seconds or until warm.

Nutrition Facts per serving: 33 calories, 8 g total fat (4 saturated fat), 60 mg cholesterol, 200 mg sodium, 6 g carbohydrate, 0 g fiber, 10 g protein. Daily Values: 10% vit. A, 17% calcium, 3% iron.

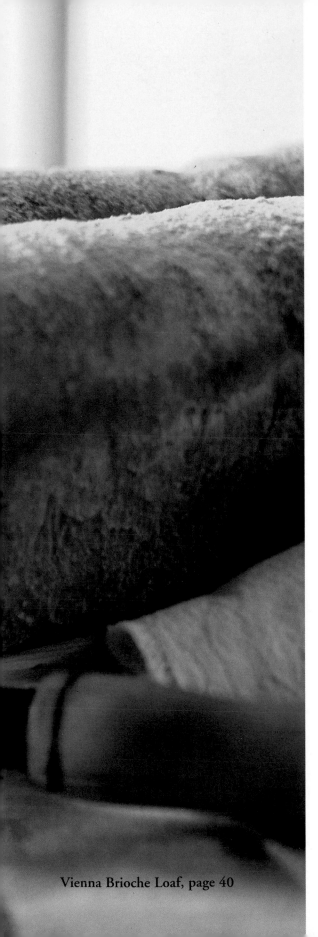

Vienna Brioche Loaf, page 40

Breads

Peppery Cheese Bread

Prep: 15 minutes **Bake:** 45 minutes

1998

Lorette Lambert
Cedar Crest, NM

Spicy brown mustard, plenty of pepper, and cheddar cheese, and yogurt provide luscious contrasts in this loaf.

2½ cups all-purpose flour	1 8-ounce carton plain low-fat yogurt
1 tablespoon sugar	½ cup cooking oil
1½ to 2 teaspoons cracked black pepper	¼ cup milk
1 teaspoon baking powder	1 tablespoon spicy brown mustard
¾ teaspoon salt	1 cup shredded cheddar cheese
½ teaspoon baking soda	(4 ounces)
2 beaten eggs	¼ cup thinly sliced green onions

1 Grease the bottom and ½ inch up the sides of an 8×4×2-inch loaf pan; set aside. In a large bowl combine flour, sugar, pepper, baking powder, salt, and baking soda. Make a well in center of flour mixture; set aside.

2 In a medium bowl combine eggs, yogurt, oil, milk, and mustard. Add egg mixture to flour mixture; add cheese and green onions. Stir just until moistened (batter should be lumpy). Spread batter into prepared pan.

3 Bake in a 350° oven for 45 to 50 minutes or until a toothpick inserted near the center comes out clean. Cool in pan on a wire rack for 10 minutes. Remove from pan; cool for 1 hour on wire rack. Serve warm. Wrap any leftovers and store in refrigerator for up to 3 days. Makes 1 loaf (16 servings).

Nutrition Facts per serving: 179 calories, 10 g total fat (3 g saturated fat), 35 mg cholesterol, 239 mg sodium, 16 g carbohydrate, 1 g fiber, 5 g protein. Daily Values: 4% vit. A, 1% vit. C, 9% calcium, 7% iron.

Cheesy Whole Wheat Fingers

Prep: 15 minutes **Rise:** 1½ hours **Bake:** 18 minutes

1   16-ounce loaf frozen whole wheat
       bread dough, thawed
1   teaspoon dried oregano, crushed
½   teaspoon garlic salt
½   teaspoon paprika

¼   teaspoon celery seed
¼   teaspoon onion powder
1½ cups shredded cheddar cheese
       (6 ounces)

1979

Mary Anita Gamberoni
Butler, PA

Mary Anita points out that white bread dough works equally well in these full-flavored cheese-topped bread sticks.

1 Grease a 15×10×1-inch baking pan. On a lightly floured surface, roll thawed bread dough into a 15×10×1-inch rectangle. (For easier rolling, partially roll out dough. Cover dough; let rest for 10 minutes. Finish rolling.) Place dough in prepared pan. Cover; let rise in a warm place until nearly double (about 1½ hours).

2 In a medium bowl combine oregano, garlic salt, paprika, celery seed, and onion powder; add cheese and toss. Sprinkle cheese mixture evenly over dough. Bake in a 375° oven for 18 to 20 minutes or until golden brown. Cool slightly. Cut into 3×1½-inch pieces; serve warm. Makes 30 pieces.

Nutrition Facts per piece: 62 calories, 2 g total fat (1 g saturated fat), 6 mg cholesterol, 144 mg sodium, 7 g carbohydrate, 1 g fiber, 3 g protein. Daily Values: 2% vit. A, 4% calcium, 1% iron.

fresh from the oven

During the late 1960s and 1970s, Americans who had grown up on fluffy-textured, store-bought bread rediscovered the appeal of home-baked breads. Whole-grain loaves with a chewy, nutty goodness were definitely "in." But as the pace of life accelerated in the late '70s, cooks had less and less time to bake from scratch, so they looked for recipes that tasted down-home good but took less work. Recipes such as Cheesy Whole Wheat Fingers, above, were just the ticket because they started with a prepared product that cut prep time to a minimum.

Vienna **Brioche Loaf**

Prep: 45 minutes **Rise:** 3 hours **Chill:** 6 hours to overnight **Bake:** 35 minutes

Betsy Anderson
Mount Vernon, OH

This European-style sweet bread, brimming with walnuts, is rich and flavorful. Serve it with afternoon tea, or warm and top with orange butter for breakfast. (Pictured on page 36.)

1 package active dry yeast	⅔ cup packed brown sugar
½ cup warm water (120° to 130°)	2 beaten egg yolks
1 cup butter, softened	6 tablespoons butter, melted
4 cups granulated sugar	2 tablespoons milk
1 teaspoon finely shredded lemon peel	¼ teaspoon vanilla
1 teaspoon salt	2 cups chopped walnuts
4¼ cups all-purpose flour	Sifted powdered sugar (optional)
6 eggs	

1 In a small bowl stir yeast into warm water; let stand for 5 to 10 minutes to soften. In a large mixing bowl beat the 1 cup butter, the granulated sugar, lemon peel, and salt with an electric mixer on medium to high speed until fluffy. Add 1 cup of the flour, the whole eggs, and softened yeast. Beat well. Stir in remaining flour. Place dough in a greased bowl; turn once to grease surface. Cover; let rise in a warm place until double (about 2 hours). Chill dough for 6 hours. (Or, omit 2-hour rise; chill dough overnight.)

2 Grease two 9×5×3-inch loaf pans; set aside. For filling, in a medium bowl combine brown sugar, egg yolks, and 3 tablespoons of the melted butter. Stir in milk and vanilla; set aside.

3 Punch down dough. Divide dough in half. Return half of dough to refrigerator. Turn other half out onto a floured surface. Roll into a 14×9-inch rectangle. Brush with 1 tablespoon of the melted butter; spread with half of the filling. Sprinkle with half of the nuts. Beginning at short sides, roll each side up into a spiral to center. Seal each end of the loaf.

4 Repeat with remaining dough, 1 tablespoon of the melted butter, remaining filling, and remaining nuts. Place, rolled sides up, in prepared pans. Brush with remaining melted butter. Cover; let rise in a warm place until double (about 1 hour).

5 Bake in a 350° oven about 35 minutes or until bread sounds hollow when lightly tapped. (If necessary to prevent overbrowning, cover with foil for the last 15 minutes of baking.) Cool in pans on wire racks for 10 minutes. Remove from pans. Serve warm, or cool on wire racks. If desired, sprinkle with powdered sugar. Makes 2 loaves (32 servings).

Nutrition Facts per serving: 223 calories, 14 g total fat (6 g saturated fat), 76 mg cholesterol, 174 mg sodium, 20 g carbohydrate, 1 g fiber, 4 g protein. Daily Values: 10% vit. A, 1% vit. C, 2% calcium, 7% iron.

Orange-Nut Loaf

Prep: 25 minutes **Bake:** 50 minutes

3 cups all-purpose flour	2 to 3 teaspoons finely shredded
¾ cup sugar	orange peel
4 teaspoons baking powder	¼ cup orange juice
1 teaspoon salt	2 tablespoons butter or margarine,
1 beaten egg	melted
1 cup milk	¾ cup chopped walnuts

1 Grease the bottom and halfway up the sides of an 8×4×2-inch loaf pan; set aside. In a medium bowl combine flour, sugar, baking powder, and salt; set aside.

2 In another medium bowl combine egg, milk, orange peel, orange juice, and melted butter or margarine. Add flour mixture to egg mixture. Stir just until moistened (batter should be lumpy). Fold in nuts. Spoon batter into prepared pan.

3 Bake in a 350° oven for 50 to 60 minutes or until a toothpick inserted near the center comes out clean. Cool in pan on a wire rack for 10 minutes. Remove from pan; cool on wire rack. Wrap in plastic wrap and store overnight before slicing. Makes 1 loaf (16 servings).

Nutrition Facts per serving: 177 calories, 6 g total fat (2 g saturated fat), 19 mg cholesterol, 273 mg sodium, 28 g carbohydrate, 1 g fiber, 4 g protein. Daily Values: 3% vit. A, 5% vit. C, 9% calcium, 6% iron.

1943

Elizabeth Nixon
Huron, SD

Bring out the best in this citrus-accented bread by serving it with honey butter or whipped cream cheese.

eggs-traordinary delight

French brioche and Jewish challah are credited as the two recipes that introduced American cooks to egg breads. Brioche gets its rich flavor not only from eggs, but from lots of butter, too. It traditionally is baked in a flared, fluted pan and has a topknot. The origin of the name is said to date back to the beginnings of opera in Paris when musicians were fined if they made a "brioche" or silly mistake. The money from the accumulated fines was used to buy tasty treats from a local bakery for the rest of the musicians. The quaint name has stuck to this delightful sweet yeast bread.

Quick Swedish Rye Bread

Prep: 20 minutes   **Rise:** According to package directions   **Bake:** 30 minutes

Mrs. Albert Turner
Loomis, NE

Because it starts with a hot roll mix, this caraway seed loaf is an easy way to fill your kitchen with the wonderful aroma of freshly baked bread. No kneading required! It's perfect sliced for sandwiches or served warm with a meal.

1 16-ounce package hot roll mix	1 to 2 teaspoons caraway seed
¾ cup rye flour	2 tablespoons molasses
1 tablespoon brown sugar	2 eggs

1 Grease two 8×4×2-inch loaf pans or dishes; set aside. Prepare hot roll mix according to package directions, except stir the rye flour, brown sugar, and caraway seed into the flour-yeast mixture; stir the molasses in with the water called for; and use 2 eggs. Let dough rest according to package directions.

2 Divide dough in half; shape each half into a loaf.* Place in the prepared pans or dishes. Let rise according to package directions. Bake in a 350° oven about 30 minutes or until bread sounds hollow when tapped. Remove from pans and cool on a wire rack. Makes 2 loaves (32 servings).

*Note: Shape each portion of dough into a loaf by patting or rolling. To shape dough by patting, gently pat and pinch each portion into a loaf shape, tucking edges beneath. To shape dough by rolling, on a floured surface, roll each portion into a 12×8-inch rectangle. Starting from a short side, roll up dough. Seal with fingertips as you roll.

Nutrition Facts per serving: 75 calories, 1 g total fat (0 g saturated fat), 13 mg cholesterol, 95 mg sodium, 14 g carbohydrate, 0 g fiber, 2 g protein. Daily Values: 1% vit. A, 3% iron.

Good Seed Bread

Prep: 15 minutes **Bake:** Per bread machine directions

1¼ cups water	¼ cup pumpkin seeds
2 tablespoons honey	¼ cup sesame seed
4 teaspoons canola oil or cooking oil	2 tablespoons poppy seed
1½ cups whole wheat flour	2 teaspoons flax seed*
1¼ cups bread flour	¾ teaspoon anise seed
⅓ cup rolled oats	¾ teaspoon salt
4 teaspoons gluten flour*	1¼ teaspoons active dry yeast
¼ cup shelled sunflower seeds	

K. Janiene Oliver
Golden, CO

Janiene gives this loaf a wonderful crunch by incorporating six different kinds of seeds.

1 Using a bread machine with a capacity of at least 10 cups, add ingredients to bread pan according to manufacturer's directions. Select the basic white bread or whole wheat cycle and the medium color setting. Remove hot bread from pan as soon as it is done. Place loaf on a wire rack; cool completely. Makes one 1½-pound loaf (16 servings).

*Note: Health-food stores typically carry these items.

Nutrition Facts per serving: 150 calories, 6 g total fat (1 g saturated fat), 0 mg cholesterol, 103 mg sodium, 21 g carbohydrate, 3 g fiber, 5 g protein. Daily Values: 2% calcium, 12% iron.

Cheese Batter Rolls

Prep: 25 minutes **Rise:** 1 hour 20 minutes **Bake:** 15 minutes

Mrs. Herman C. Andrus
Ashville, NY

**Delicious with soups or
salads, these golden
no-knead yeast rolls have a
pleasant cornmeal crunch.**

3½ cups all-purpose flour
1 package active dry yeast
1¾ cups milk
¼ cup sugar
2 tablespoons shortening
1¼ teaspoons salt

1 beaten egg
4 slices sharp American cheese,
     chopped, or 4 ounces shredded
     cheddar cheese (1 cup)
½ cup cornmeal

1 In a large mixing bowl combine 2 cups of the flour and the yeast; set aside. In a
medium saucepan heat and stir milk, sugar, shortening, and salt just until warm
(120° to 130°) and shortening almost melts. Add milk mixture to flour mixture; add egg.
Beat with an electric mixer on low to medium speed for 30 seconds, scraping sides of
bowl constantly. Beat on high speed for 3 minutes. Using a wooden spoon, stir in
cheese, cornmeal, and remaining flour. Cover; let rise in a warm place until nearly
double (50 to 60 minutes).

2 Generously grease twenty-four 2½-inch nonstick muffin cups. Stir dough down.
Spoon dough into prepared muffin cups, filling each about three-fourths full. Cover
and let rise until double (30 to 40 minutes). Bake in a 375° oven for 15 to 20 minutes or
until golden brown. Cool in pan for 5 minutes. Remove from pan; serve warm, or cool
on wire racks. Makes 2 dozen rolls.

Nutrition Facts per roll: 119 calories, 3 g total fat (2 g saturated fat), 15 mg cholesterol, 201 mg sodium,
18 g carbohydrate, 1 g fiber, 4 g protein. Daily Values: 3% vit. A, 5% calcium, 5% iron.

no-knead sensation

In 1960, Leona P. Schnuelle set the bread-baking world on its ear by
winning the Pillsbury Bake-Off Contest with a casserole bread that did
not require kneading. The recipe made the rounds of kitchens
everywhere. Homemakers loved the idea of fresh-baked bread with no
kneading. Before long, inventive cooks were adapting the technique to
their favorite breads, such as Cheese Batter Rolls, above.

Pesto Pinwheels

Prep: 25 minutes **Rise:** 45 minutes **Bake:** 30 minutes

- 1 cup packed fresh basil
- ¾ cup pine nuts or almonds
- 3 tablespoons olive oil
- 2 large cloves garlic, minced
- ½ teaspoon salt
- ¼ teaspoon pepper
- ½ cup grated Parmesan cheese
    (2 ounces)
- ½ cup grated Romano cheese
    (2 ounces)
- ⅓ cup diced pimiento
- 2 16-ounce loaves frozen bread
    dough, thawed
    Fresh basil sprigs (optional)

1997

Grace A. Eckstorm
Chandler, AZ

For the best flavor, Grace always makes these distinctive rolls with freshly grated Parmesan and Romano cheeses.

1 For filling, in a blender container or food processor bowl combine the 1 cup basil, the pine nuts or almonds, 2 tablespoons of the olive oil, the garlic, salt, and pepper. Cover and blend or process until mixture is finely minced. Place mixture in a bowl; stir in Parmesan cheese, Romano cheese, and pimiento. Set aside.

2 Lightly grease a 13×9×2-inch baking pan. Roll each of the loaves into an 8×8-inch square. Brush squares lightly with the remaining olive oil. Spread half of the filling on each of the squares. Roll up each square. Seal seam. Slice each roll into 8 pieces (16 total). Place, cut sides up, in the prepared pan. Cover and let rise until nearly double (45 to 60 minutes).

3 Bake in a 375° oven about 30 minutes or until golden brown. Cool slightly; remove from pan. Serve warm. Makes 16 pinwheels.

Nutrition Facts per pinwheel: 224 calories, 8 g total fat (1 g saturated fat), 5 mg cholesterol, 147 mg sodium, 26 g carbohydrate, 0 g fiber, 7 g protein. Daily Values: 1% vit. A, 5% vit. C, 9% calcium, 5% iron.

Cucumber Buns

Prep: 25 minutes **Rise:** 1¼ hours **Bake:** 20 minutes

- 3¼ to 3¾ cups all-purpose flour
- 1 package active dry yeast
- 2 tablespoons snipped fresh chives or 1 tablespoon dried chives
- 1 teaspoon snipped fresh dill or ¼ teaspoon dried dillweed
- 1 medium cucumber, peeled and cut up (1½ to 2 cups)
- ½ cup dairy sour cream
- ¼ cup water
- 1 tablespoon sugar
- 1¼ teaspoons salt

1992

Philip B. Mohr
Schaumburg, IL

Cucumber, dill, and chives give these fluffy yeast rolls garden-fresh flavor.

1 In a large bowl combine 1¼ cups of the flour, the yeast, chives, and dill. In a food processor bowl or blender container process or blend the cucumber until smooth (you should have ¾ cup).

2 In a saucepan heat and stir the cucumber puree, sour cream, water, sugar, and salt until warm (120° to 130°). (Mixture may look curdled.) Add to the flour mixture. Beat with an electric mixer on low to medium speed for 30 seconds, scraping the sides of the bowl constantly. Beat on high speed for 3 minutes. Using a wooden spoon, stir in as much of the remaining flour as you can.

3 Turn out onto a lightly floured surface. Knead in enough of the remaining flour to make a moderately stiff dough that is smooth and elastic (6 to 8 minutes total). Shape into a ball. Place in a lightly greased bowl; turn once to grease surface. Cover; let rise in a warm place until double (about 45 minutes).

4 Grease a 13×9×2-inch baking pan; set aside. Punch dough down. Turn out onto a lightly floured surface. Cover; let rest for 10 minutes. Divide dough into 12 pieces. Shape each piece into a ball; arrange in prepared pan, allowing space between balls. Cover; let rise in a warm place until nearly double (about 30 minutes). Bake in a 350° oven for 20 to 25 minutes or until lightly browned. Serve warm or cool. Makes 12 buns.

Nutrition Facts per bun: 140 calories, 2 g total fat (1 g saturated fat), 4 mg cholesterol, 248 mg sodium, 26 g carbohydrate, 1 g fiber, 4 g protein. Daily Values: 2% vit. A, 3% vit. C, 2% calcium, 9% iron.

Raspberry-Almond Rolls

Prep: 20 minutes   **Rise:** Bread machine rise + 30 minutes   **Bake:** 18 minutes

1997

Nancy Cersonsky
Oxford, CT

Nancy mixes the dough in a bread machine so she can get a quick start on these colorful spirals full of almond flavor.

1 cup water
1 egg
2 tablespoons cooking oil
3½ cups bread flour
¼ cup granulated sugar
½ teaspoon salt

½ teaspoon almond extract
1 package active dry yeast
3 tablespoons raspberry or blackberry jam
1 8-ounce can almond paste*
1 recipe Powdered Sugar Icing

1 Using a bread machine with a capacity of at least 10 cups, add first 8 ingredients to bread pan according to manufacturer's directions. Select dough cycle. When cycle is complete, remove dough from machine. Punch down. Cover; let rest for 10 minutes.

2 Grease baking sheets or a 13×9×2-inch baking pan; set aside. On a floured surface, roll dough into a 12×10-inch rectangle. Spread jam over dough. Crumble almond paste; sprinkle over dough. Starting from a long side, roll up dough; seal seams. Cut into twelve 1-inch slices. Place rolls, cut sides down, 2 inches apart on prepared baking sheets for individual rolls or arrange in prepared baking pan. Cover; let rise until nearly double (about 30 minutes).

3 Bake in a 350° oven until golden brown (allow 18 minutes for individual rolls or about 30 minutes for rolls in pan). Cool on a wire rack for 5 minutes; transfer to a serving platter. Drizzle with Powdered Sugar Icing. Serve warm. Makes 12 rolls.

Powdered Sugar Icing: In a medium bowl stir together 1 cup sifted powdered sugar, 1 tablespoon milk, and ¼ teaspoon vanilla. Stir in enough additional milk, ½ teaspoon at a time, to make icing of drizzling consistency.

*Note: For best results, use an almond paste made without syrup or liquid glucose.

Nutrition Facts per roll: 321 calories, 9 g total fat (1 g saturated fat), 18 mg cholesterol, 99 mg sodium, 54 g carbohydrate, 1 g fiber, 8 g protein. Daily Values: 4% calcium, 15% iron.

French Chocolate Coffee Cake

Prep: 25 minutes **Rise:** 2½ hours **Bake:** 45 minutes

4 to 4½ cups all-purpose flour	1 cup semisweet chocolate pieces (6 ounces)
2 packages active dry yeast	
¾ cup sugar	2 tablespoons sugar
⅔ cup water	½ teaspoon ground cinnamon
½ cup butter, cut up	¼ cup all-purpose flour
1 5-ounce can (⅔ cup) evaporated milk	¼ cup sugar
	1 teaspoon ground cinnamon
½ teaspoon salt	¼ cup butter
4 egg yolks	¼ cup chopped walnuts or pecans

Elena Eritta
Puebla, Mexico

A buttery dough rolled around a luscious chocolate filling and topped with a chocolate, cinnamon, and walnut streusel—what could be better in a coffee cake?

1 In a large mixing bowl stir together 1½ cups of the flour and the yeast; set aside. In a medium saucepan heat and stir the ¾ cup sugar, the water, the ½ cup butter, ⅓ cup of the evaporated milk, and the salt just until warm (120° to 130°) and butter almost melts. Add milk mixture to flour mixture; add egg yolks. Beat with an electric mixer on low to medium speed 30 seconds, scraping the sides of bowl constantly. Beat on high speed 3 minutes. Using a wooden spoon, stir in as much remaining flour as you can.

2 Turn dough out onto a lightly floured surface. Knead in enough of the remaining flour to make a moderately soft dough that is smooth and elastic (3 to 5 minutes total). Shape dough into a ball. Place in a lightly greased bowl, turning once to grease surface. Cover and let rise in a warm place until double (about 1½ hours). Punch dough down. Turn dough out onto a lightly floured surface. Cover; let rest for 10 minutes.

3 Meanwhile, in a small saucepan combine ¾ cup of the chocolate pieces, the remaining evaporated milk, the 2 tablespoons sugar, and the ½ teaspoon cinnamon. Cook and stir over low heat until chocolate is melted. Remove from heat; cool.

4 Grease a 10-inch tube pan; set aside. Roll dough into an 18×10-inch rectangle. Spread chocolate mixture to within 1 inch of the edges. Starting from a long side, roll up dough. Pinch seam to seal. Place, seam side down, in prepared pan. Pinch ends together.

5 In a small bowl combine the ¼ cup flour, the ¼ cup sugar, and the 1 teaspoon cinnamon. Using a pastry blender, cut in the ¼ cup butter until mixture resembles coarse crumbs. Stir in remaining chocolate pieces and nuts. Sprinkle over dough in pan. Cover; let rise in a warm place until nearly double (about 1 hour). Bake in a 350° oven 45 to 50 minutes or until bread sounds hollow when lightly tapped. Cool in pan on a rack 15 minutes. Remove from pan; cool 30 to 45 minutes. Serve warm. Serves 12 to 16.

Nutrition Facts per serving: 455 calories, 21 g total fat (11 g saturated fat), 108 mg cholesterol, 240 mg sodium, 56 g carbohydrate, 4 g fiber, 7 g protein. Daily Values: 15% vit. A, 1% vit. C, 6% calcium, 13% iron.

Peanut Butter-**Banana Bread**

Prep: 25 minutes **Bake:** 50 minutes

Kelly Thornberry
La Porte, IN

Peanut butter lovers will enjoy the flavorful mix of banana, chocolate, and peanut butter in this loaf. For a simpler, unadorned bread, skip the Peanut Butter Frosting.

2½ cups all-purpose flour
½ cup granulated sugar
½ cup packed brown sugar
1 tablespoon baking powder
¾ teaspoon salt
¼ teaspoon ground cinnamon
2 large bananas, mashed (1 cup)
1 cup milk

¾ cup chunky peanut butter
3 tablespoons cooking oil
1 teaspoon vanilla
1 slightly beaten egg
1 cup milk chocolate pieces
1 recipe Peanut Butter Frosting
Crushed peanuts (optional)

1 Grease two 8×4×2-inch loaf pans; set aside. In a large bowl stir together flour, sugars, baking powder, salt, and cinnamon. Make a well in the center of flour mixture; set aside.

2 In another large bowl combine mashed bananas, milk, peanut butter, oil, vanilla, and egg. Add banana mixture to flour mixture; stir just until moistened. Stir in chocolate pieces. Spoon batter evenly into prepared pans.

3 Bake in a 350° oven for 50 to 55 minutes or until a toothpick inserted near the center of each loaf comes out clean. Cool in pans on wire racks for 10 minutes. Remove from pans; cool on wire racks. Wrap in plastic wrap and store overnight before slicing. Before serving, frost with Peanut Butter Frosting. If desired, top with crushed peanuts. Slice to serve. Makes 2 loaves (32 servings).

Peanut Butter Frosting: In a small saucepan heat and stir 3 tablespoons chunky peanut butter and 2 tablespoons margarine or butter until melted. Remove from heat; stir in 1 cup sifted powdered sugar and 1 teaspoon vanilla. Stir in 1 tablespoon milk. If necessary, stir in enough additional milk, ½ teaspoon at a time, to make frosting of spreading consistency.

Nutrition Facts per serving: 177 calories, 8 g total fat (2 g saturated fat), 8 mg cholesterol, 149 mg sodium, 24 g carbohydrate, 1 g fiber, 4 g protein. Daily Values: 2% vit. A, 2% vit. C, 5% calcium, 4% iron.

Island-Style Banana Bread

Prep: 20 minutes **Bake:** 50 minutes

2 cups all-purpose flour
1½ teaspoons ground cinnamon
1 teaspoon baking powder
½ teaspoon baking soda
¼ teaspoon salt
½ cup butter, softened
½ cup packed brown sugar
2 slightly beaten eggs
1 teaspoon vanilla

1 cup mashed ripe banana
   (2 to 3 medium)
½ cup chopped pecans
1 8-ounce package reduced-fat cream
   cheese (Neufchâtel)
1 egg
¼ cup packed brown sugar
½ cup coconut

*Helena Schaefer
Lafayette, LA*

Helena boasts that one
nibble of this tropical teaser
is all it will take to wow
your taste buds.

1 Grease the bottom and ½ inch up the sides of two 7½×3½×2-inch loaf pans; set
aside. In a large bowl combine flour, cinnamon, baking powder, baking soda, and salt;
set aside.

2 In a large mixing bowl beat butter with an electric mixer on high speed for
30 seconds. Add the ½ cup brown sugar, the 2 eggs, and the vanilla; beat until
combined. Add flour mixture and mashed banana alternately to beaten mixture, beating
on low speed after each addition until combined. Stir in pecans.

3 In a medium mixing bowl beat the cream cheese, the 1 egg, and the ¼ cup brown
sugar with an electric mixer on medium speed until almost smooth. Stir in coconut.

4 Pour one-fourth of the banana mixture into each loaf pan. Spoon one-fourth of the
cream cheese mixture over each loaf. Using a thin metal spatula or a table knife, cut
through the batter to marble. Repeat the two layers, but do not marble.

5 Bake in a 350° oven about 50 minutes or until a toothpick inserted near the center
comes out clean. Cool in pans on wire racks for 10 minutes. Remove from pans; cool
on wire racks. Wrap in plastic wrap and store overnight before slicing. Makes 2 loaves
(20 servings).

Nutrition Facts per serving: 191 calories, 11 g total fat (5 g saturated fat), 53 mg cholesterol,
180 mg sodium, 21 g carbohydrate, 1 g fiber, 4 g protein. Daily Values: 9% vit. A, 2% vit. C,
3% calcium, 7% iron.

Heart-Healthy Apple Coffee Cake

Prep: 25 minutes **Bake:** 30 minutes

Nonstick cooking spray
⅔ cup all-purpose flour
½ cup whole wheat flour
1 teaspoon baking soda
½ teaspoon ground cinnamon
¼ teaspoon salt
1½ cups finely chopped, cored, peeled
    apple (such as Jonathan or
    Granny Smith) (about 2 large)
¼ cup refrigerated or frozen egg
    product, thawed

¾ cup granulated sugar
¼ cup chopped pecans or walnuts
¼ cup applesauce
¼ cup packed brown sugar
1 tablespoon all-purpose flour
1 tablespoon whole wheat flour
½ teaspoon ground cinnamon
1 tablespoon butter
¼ cup chopped pecans or walnuts

*Kathleen Fishman
Scottsdale, AZ*

With only 5 grams of fat
per serving, Kathleen's
delectable coffee cake can
be served to fat-conscious
guests with no regrets.

1 Lightly coat a 9×1½-inch round baking pan with cooking spray; set aside. In a small bowl combine the ⅔ cup all-purpose flour, the ½ cup whole wheat flour, the baking soda, the ½ teaspoon cinnamon, and the salt; set aside. In a medium bowl toss together the apple and egg product. Stir in the ¾ cup granulated sugar, ¼ cup nuts, and the applesauce. Add flour mixture; stir just until combined. Pour batter into prepared pan.

2 For topping, stir together the brown sugar, the 1 tablespoon all-purpose flour, the 1 tablespoon whole wheat flour, and ½ teaspoon cinnamon. Using a pastry blender or two knives, cut in butter until crumbly. Stir in ¼ cup nuts. Sprinkle topping over batter in pan. Bake in a 350° oven for 30 to 35 minutes or until golden brown. Remove from pan; serve warm. Makes 10 servings.

Nutrition Facts per serving: 200 calories, 5 g total fat (1 g saturated fat), 3 mg cholesterol, 209 mg sodium, 37 g carbohydrate, 2 g fiber, 3 g protein. Daily values: 2% vit. A, 2% vit. C, 2% calcium, 6% iron.

Braided Cranberry Bread with a Twist

Prep: 30 minutes **Rise:** 1½ hours **Bake:** 25 minutes

1997

*Stefin Preboski
Snohomish, WA*

Chockfull of cranberries, pecans, and spices, this bread is a favorite of Stefin's for a holiday breakfast or brunch. It will fill your kitchen with a captivating aroma.

2¾ to 3 cups all-purpose flour
1 package active dry yeast
½ cup milk
¼ cup water
2 tablespoons granulated sugar
2 tablespoons butter or margarine
½ teaspoon salt
1 egg
½ cup finely chopped cranberries
¼ cup packed brown sugar

2 tablespoons finely chopped pecans
1½ teaspoons finely shredded orange peel
¼ teaspoon ground cinnamon
¼ teaspoon ground nutmeg
⅛ teaspoon ground cloves
1½ teaspoons butter or margarine, melted
1 recipe Orange Icing

1 In a large mixing bowl combine 1 cup of the flour and the yeast; set aside. In a medium saucepan heat and stir milk, water, granulated sugar, the 2 tablespoons butter or margarine, and the salt until warm (120° to 130°) and butter or margarine almost melts. Add milk mixture to flour mixture; add egg. Beat with an electric mixer on low to medium speed for 30 seconds, scraping sides of bowl constantly. Beat on high speed for 3 minutes. Using a wooden spoon, stir in as much of the remaining flour as you can.

2 Turn dough out onto a floured surface. Knead in enough of the remaining flour to make a soft dough that is smooth and elastic (3 to 5 minutes total). Shape into a ball. Place in a lightly greased bowl; turn once. Cover and let rise in a warm place until double (1 to 1½ hours).

3 Meanwhile, for filling, in a small bowl stir together the cranberries, brown sugar, pecans, orange peel, cinnamon, nutmeg, and cloves; set aside.

4 Punch dough down. Turn out onto lightly floured surface. Cover and let rest for 10 minutes. Grease a baking sheet. Roll dough into a 14×10-inch rectangle. Brush with the melted butter or margarine. Spread filling over dough. Starting from a long side, roll up dough. Seal seam. Cut roll in half lengthwise. Turn cut sides up. Loosely twist halves together, keeping the cut sides up. Pinch ends to seal. Place loaf on the prepared baking sheet. Cover; let rise in a warm place until nearly double (about 30 minutes).

5 Bake in a 375° oven about 25 minutes or until golden brown. Remove from baking sheet; cool on a wire rack. Drizzle with Orange Icing. Makes 18 servings.

Orange Icing: In a small bowl combine ½ cup sifted powdered sugar and enough orange juice (1 to 3 teaspoons) to make icing of drizzling consistency.

Nutrition Facts per serving: 67 calories, 2 g total fat (1 g saturated fat), 10 mg cholesterol, 47 mg sodium, 12 g carbohydrate, 1 g fiber, 2 g protein. Daily Values: 1% vit. A, 1% vit. C, 1% calcium, 3% iron.

Creamy Cinnamon Rolls

Prep: 20 minutes **Rise:** 1 hour **Bake:** 25 minutes

1 16-ounce loaf frozen sweet bread dough, thawed	½ cup chopped walnuts
2 tablespoons butter or margarine, melted	1 teaspoon ground cinnamon
	½ cup whipping cream
⅔ cup packed brown sugar	⅔ cup sifted powdered sugar
	Milk

1972

Mrs. R. W. McLuckie
Grand Haven, MI

When you yearn for old-fashioned cinnamon rolls warm from the oven, make your wish come true in almost no time with this easy recipe. It starts with frozen sweet bread dough.

1 Lightly grease two 8×1½-inch round baking pans; set aside. On a lightly floured surface, roll dough into a 20×8-inch rectangle. Brush with melted butter or margarine. In a small bowl combine brown sugar, nuts, and cinnamon; sprinkle evenly over dough. Starting from a long side, roll up dough. Moisten edges and seal. Cut into 20 slices. Place rolls, cut sides down, in prepared pans. Cover and let rise in a warm place until nearly double (1 to 1½ hours).

2 Slowly pour whipping cream over rolls. Bake in a 350° oven about 25 minutes or until golden brown. Let stand 1 minute. Loosen edges; invert onto serving plates. Scrape any caramel mixture left in pan onto rolls.

3 In a small bowl combine powdered sugar and enough milk (2 to 3 teaspoons) to make a glaze of drizzling consistency. Drizzle glaze over warm rolls. Makes 20 rolls.

Nutrition Facts per roll: 157 calories, 7 g total fat (3 g saturated fat), 25 mg cholesterol, 59 mg sodium, 22 g carbohydrate, 1 g fiber, 2 g protein. Daily Values: 5% vit. A, 3% calcium, 5% iron.

Cinnamon **Fantans**

Prep: 30 minutes **Rise:** 2 hours **Bake:** 12 minutes

1959

Mrs. Almous Austin
Newbern, TN

The unique shaping
of these cinnamon rolls
makes them company-
special. Serve them with
your favorite flavored
coffee or tea.

2½ to 3 cups all-purpose flour	1 egg
1 package active dry yeast	2 tablespoons butter or margarine,
¾ cup milk	melted
¼ cup sugar	½ cup sugar
¼ cup butter or margarine	⅓ cup chopped walnuts
1 teaspoon salt	1½ teaspoons ground cinnamon

1 In a large mixing bowl combine 1¼ cups of the flour and the yeast; set aside. In a small saucepan heat and stir the milk, the ¼ cup sugar, the ¼ cup butter or margarine, and the salt just until warm (120° to 130°) and butter or margarine almost melts. Add milk mixture to flour mixture; add egg. Beat with an electric mixer on low to medium speed for 30 seconds, scraping sides of bowl constantly. Beat on high speed for 3 minutes. Using a wooden spoon, stir in as much of the remaining flour as you can.

2 Turn dough onto a floured surface. Knead in enough of the remaining flour to make a moderately soft dough that is smooth and elastic (2 to 3 minutes total). Shape dough into a ball. Place dough in a lightly greased bowl; turn once to grease surface. Cover and let rise in a warm place until double (about 1½ hours).

3 Grease baking sheet; set aside. Punch dough down. Turn out onto a lightly floured surface. Cover and let rest for 10 minutes. Roll out into a 20×10-inch rectangle. Brush with the melted butter or margarine.

4 In a small bowl combine the ½ cup sugar, the chopped walnuts, and cinnamon; sprinkle evenly over dough. Starting from a long side, roll up dough. Cut into eight 2½-inch slices. With slices sitting on edge, snip or cut each slice in thirds without cutting all the way through. Place 3 inches apart on the prepared baking sheet, seam sides down; spread each slightly to form a fan. Cover; let rise until almost double (30 to 45 minutes). Bake in a 350° oven for 12 to 15 minutes or until golden brown. Serve warm. Makes 8 fantans.

Nutrition Facts per fantan: 338 calories, 14 g total fat (6 g saturated fat), 53 mg cholesterol, 405 mg sodium, 48 g carbohydrate, 2 g fiber, 6 g protein. Daily Values: 11% vit. A, 1% vit. C, 5% calcium, 12% iron.

Key Lime Danish Pastries

1995

Mr. Courtney Sikes
Wilmington, NC

Save some of these tangy cream cheese-filled buns for later. Just freeze a few and reheat them in your microwave oven.

Prep: 45 minutes **Rise:** 1 hour **Bake:** 18 minutes

6¼ to 6¾ cups all-purpose flour
1½ cups granulated sugar
2 packages active dry yeast
1½ teaspoons salt
1 cup milk
1 cup water
½ cup butter or margarine
1 egg

1 8-ounce package cream cheese, softened
½ teaspoon finely shredded lime peel
3 tablespoons lime juice
½ cup sifted powdered sugar
1 teaspoon butter or margarine, melted

1 In a medium mixing bowl combine 2 cups of the flour, ½ cup of the granulated sugar, the yeast, and salt; set aside. In a small saucepan heat and stir milk, water, and the ½ cup butter or margarine just until warm (120° to 130°) and butter or margarine is almost melted. Add to flour mixture; add egg. Beat with an electric mixer on low to medium speed for 30 seconds, scraping sides of bowl constantly. Beat on high speed for 3 minutes. Using a wooden spoon, stir in as much of the remaining flour as you can.

2 Turn dough out onto a lightly floured surface. Knead in enough of the remaining flour to make a moderately stiff dough that is smooth and elastic (6 to 8 minutes total). Shape into a ball. Place in a greased bowl; turn once to grease surface. Cover and let rise in a warm place until double (about 1 hour). Punch dough down. Turn out onto a floured surface. Divide in half. Cover; let rest for 10 minutes.

3 For filling, in a small bowl stir together the cream cheese, lime peel, 2 tablespoons of the lime juice, and ½ cup of the granulated sugar; set aside.

4 For icing, in another small bowl stir together the powdered sugar, the remaining lime juice, and the 1 teaspoon butter or margarine; set aside. Lightly grease baking sheets; set aside.

5 On a floured surface, roll each half of dough into a 14×9-inch rectangle. Top each with ¼ cup of the granulated sugar. Starting from a long side, roll up dough; seal seams. Cut each roll into 12 slices; arrange slices 2 inches apart on prepared baking sheets. Make an indentation in each slice; fill each indentation with slightly less than 1 tablespoon of the filling. Bake in a 375° oven for 18 to 20 minutes or until golden brown. Remove pastries from baking sheets; cool slightly. Drizzle warm pastries with icing. Serve warm. Makes 24 pastries.

Nutrition Facts per pastry: 245 calories, 8 g total fat (5 g saturated fat), 31 mg cholesterol, 225 mg sodium, 38 g carbohydrate, 1 g fiber, 5 g protein. Daily Values: 9% vit. A, 1% vit. C., 3% calcium, 9% iron.

Baked Doughnut Twists

Prep: 25 minutes **Bake:** 10 minutes

2 cups packaged biscuit mix	2 tablespoons butter or margarine,
2 tablespoons sugar	melted
2 teaspoons instant coffee crystals	1/3 cup sugar
1/4 cup milk	1/2 teaspoon ground cinnamon
1 beaten egg	1/8 teaspoon ground nutmeg
1 teaspoon finely shredded	
orange peel	

Mrs. Joe Twomey
Phoenix, AZ

Packaged biscuit mix makes these cinnamon-and-coffee-flavored twists simple to stir together.

1 In a medium bowl combine biscuit mix and the 2 tablespoons sugar; set aside. Dissolve coffee crystals in milk; stir in egg and orange peel. Add coffee mixture to biscuit mixture all at once; stir just until moistened.

2 Turn dough out onto a well-floured surface; knead gently for 10 to 20 strokes or until nearly smooth. Pat or lightly roll dough to 1/2-inch thickness. Cut dough with a floured 2½-inch doughnut cutter. Holding opposite sides of the doughnut, twist once, forming a figure 8. Place on an ungreased baking sheet. Bake in a 400° oven for 10 to 12 minutes or until golden brown. Brush each twist with melted butter or margarine. In a shallow dish combine the 1/3 cup sugar, the cinnamon, and nutmeg. Dip each twist into sugar mixture. Serve warm. Makes 8 to 10 doughnuts.

Nutrition Facts per doughnut: 213 calories, 8 g total fat (3 g saturated fat), 35 mg cholesterol, 407 mg sodium, 31 g carbohydrate, 0 g fiber, 3 g protein. Daily Values: 4% vit. A, 1% vit. C, 5% calcium, 6% iron.

dining car discovery

The first packaged biscuit mix was introduced by General Mills in 1931. The birth of the mix was pure happenstance. One of the company's executives boarded a train late one night without having had dinner. He went to the dining car with little hope of getting a hot meal. To his surprise he was served a warm dinner complete with fresh hot biscuits. Later, he asked the chef how he made the biscuits on such short notice. The chef told the company executive that he kept a blended mixture of lard, flour, baking powder, and salt on ice (there were no refrigerators at that time) for emergencies. The rest is history.

Nutty Snails

Prep: 40 minutes **Rise:** 1½ hours **Bake:** 12 minutes

3½ to 4 cups all-purpose flour	½ teaspoon salt
1 package active dry yeast	2 beaten eggs
1 cup milk	1 recipe Powdered Sugar Icing
¼ cup sugar	½ cup chopped walnuts
3 tablespoons butter, margarine, or shortening	

Mrs. Charles Galle
Hollandale, WI

These dainty rolls are an example of the goodies cooks often made when baked goods weren't so readily available.

1 In a large mixing bowl stir together 2 cups of the flour and the yeast; set aside. In a medium saucepan heat and stir milk; sugar; butter, margarine, or shortening; and salt just until warm (120° to 130°) and butter almost melts. Add milk mixture to flour mixture; add eggs. Beat with an electric mixer on low to medium speed for 30 seconds, scraping sides of bowl constantly. Beat on high speed for 3 minutes. Using a wooden spoon, stir in as much of the remaining flour as you can.

2 Turn dough out onto a lightly floured surface. Knead in enough of the remaining flour to make a moderately soft dough that is smooth and elastic (3 to 5 minutes total). Shape into a ball. Place in a lightly greased bowl; turn once to grease surface. Cover and let rise in a warm place until double (about 1 hour).

3 Punch dough down. Turn out onto a lightly floured surface. Divide dough in half. Cover; let rest for 10 minutes. Lightly grease baking sheets; set aside.

4 Roll each half of dough into a 12×8-inch rectangle. Cut each rectangle into twelve 1-inch-wide strips. Roll each strip into a snail shape, tucking end of strip under roll. Place 2 inches apart on prepared baking sheets. Cover and let rise in a warm place until double (about 30 minutes).

5 Bake in a 375° oven for 12 to 15 minutes or until golden brown. Remove from pans; cool on wire racks. Drizzle with Powdered Sugar Icing; sprinkle with chopped nuts. Makes 24 snails.

Powdered Sugar Icing: In a small bowl combine 1½ cups sifted powdered sugar, 2 tablespoons milk, and ½ teaspoon vanilla. Add enough additional milk, 1 teaspoon at a time, to make icing of drizzling consistency.

Nutrition Facts per snail: 136 calories, 4 g total fat (1 g saturated fat), 23 mg cholesterol, 76 mg sodium, 22 g carbohydrate, 1 g fiber, 3 g protein. Daily Values: 3% vit. A, 2% calcium, 5% iron.

Choco-Peanut Butter Ring

Prep: 25 minutes **Rise:** 1½ hours **Bake:** 20 minutes

1979

Arlene Wahl
Castalia, OH

A favorite combination of chocolate and peanut butter provide the flavor for this attractive bread ring.

2 to 2½ cups all-purpose flour
1 package active dry yeast
½ cup milk
½ cup sugar
¼ cup butter or margarine
¾ teaspoon salt
1 egg
¼ cup peanut butter
½ cup semisweet chocolate pieces, melted and cooled

1 In a medium mixing bowl combine 1 cup of the flour and the yeast; set aside. In a small saucepan heat and stir milk, ¼ cup of the sugar, 2 tablespoons of the butter or margarine, and the salt just until warm (120° to 130°) and butter or margarine almost melts. Add milk mixture to flour mixture; add egg. Beat with an electric mixer on low to medium speed for 30 seconds, scraping sides of bowl constantly. Beat on high speed for 3 minutes. Using a wooden spoon, stir in as much of the remaining flour as you can.

2 Turn dough out onto a lightly floured surface. Knead in enough of the remaining flour to make a moderately soft dough (3 to 5 minutes total). Shape dough into a ball. Place in a lightly greased bowl; turn once to grease surface. Cover; let rise in a warm place until double (1 to 1¼ hours).

3 Lightly grease a large baking sheet; set aside. Punch dough down; turn dough out onto a lightly floured surface. Cover and let rest for 10 minutes. Roll dough into an 18×8-inch rectangle.

4 For filling, in a small bowl combine peanut butter, remaining sugar, and remaining butter. Stir in melted chocolate; spread over dough. Starting from a long side, roll up dough; seal edge and ends. Place on prepared baking sheet, forming into a ring. Moisten ends with water and firmly attach together. Slice through dough at 1-inch intervals, cutting two-thirds of the way to the other edge. Lift and twist slices slightly to expose filling. Cover; let rise until nearly double (30 to 45 minutes).

5 Bake in a 350° oven for 20 to 25 minutes or until bread sounds hollow when tapped. If necessary to prevent overbrowning, cover with foil after 15 minutes of baking. Remove from baking sheet. Serve warm, or cool on a wire rack. Makes 16 to 18 servings.

Nutrition Facts per serving: 162 calories, 7 g total fat (3 g saturated fat), 22 mg cholesterol, 167 mg sodium, 20 g carbohydrate, 1 g fiber, 3 g protein. Daily Values: 4% vit. A, 2% calcium, 5% iron.

Double-Chocolate Scones

Prep: 20 minutes **Bake:** 18 minutes

2 cups all-purpose flour
⅓ cup unsweetened cocoa powder
⅓ cup packed brown sugar
2 teaspoons baking powder
¾ teaspoon baking soda
⅛ teaspoon salt
½ cup butter

1 beaten egg yolk
1 8-ounce carton plain yogurt
½ cup miniature semisweet chocolate
    pieces
1 recipe Powdered Sugar Glaze
    Powdered sugar (optional)

1997

Honee Aylmer
Lemoore, CA

Chocoholics take notice—
these scones contain both
cocoa powder and
semisweet chocolate pieces
for extra chocolate flavor.

1 In a large bowl combine flour, cocoa powder, brown sugar, baking powder, baking soda, and salt. Using a pastry blender or two knives, cut in butter until mixture resembles coarse crumbs. Make a well in the center of the flour mixture.

2 In another bowl combine egg yolk and yogurt; add to flour mixture. Add chocolate pieces. Stir just until moistened (batter should be lumpy).

3 Turn dough out onto a lightly floured surface. Quickly knead dough 10 to 12 strokes or until nearly smooth. Roll or pat dough into a 9-inch circle; cut into 10 wedges. Place wedges 1 inch apart on an ungreased baking sheet.

4 Bake in a 375° oven about 18 minutes or until bottoms are lightly browned. Remove from baking sheet; cool slightly. Drizzle with Powdered Sugar Glaze. If desired, dust tops of glazed scones with powdered sugar. Serve warm. Makes 10 scones.

Powdered Sugar Glaze: In a small bowl stir together ½ cup sifted powdered sugar, 1 tablespoon melted butter or margarine, 1 teaspoon milk, and 1 teaspoon vanilla. Stir in enough additional milk, ¼ teaspoon at a time, to make a glaze of drizzling consistency.

Nutrition Facts per scone: 289 calories, 14 g total fat (7 g saturated fat), 50 mg cholesterol, 317 mg sodium, 37 g carbohydrate, 1 g fiber, 5 g protein. Daily Values: 13% vit. A, 13% calcium, 13% iron.

Pear-Walnut Muffins

Prep: 20 minutes **Bake:** 20 minutes

Meri Villane
Colorado Springs, CO

Meri stirs together brown sugar and walnuts to make a crunchy topping for these moist pear-filled muffins.

1½ cups all-purpose flour
½ cup packed brown sugar
2 teaspoons baking powder
1 teaspoon ground cinnamon
½ teaspoon ground ginger
⅛ teaspoon salt
1 slightly beaten egg

½ cup cooking oil
½ cup plain low-fat yogurt
½ teaspoon vanilla
1 pear, cored, peeled, and finely chopped
3 tablespoons finely chopped walnuts
2 tablespoons brown sugar

1 Lightly grease twelve 2½-inch muffin cups or line with paper bake cups; set aside. In a medium bowl combine flour, the ½ cup brown sugar, baking powder, cinnamon, ginger, and salt. Make a well in the center of the flour mixture.

2 In another bowl combine egg, oil, yogurt, and vanilla; add to flour mixture. Stir just until moistened (batter should be lumpy). Fold in pear.

3 Spoon batter into prepared muffin cups, filling each two-thirds full. For topping, combine walnuts and the 2 tablespoons brown sugar. Sprinkle over batter.

4 Bake in a 400° oven about 20 minutes or until golden brown. Cool in muffin cups on a wire rack for 5 minutes. Remove from cups; serve warm. Makes 12 muffins.

Nutrition Facts per muffin: 206 calories, 11 g total fat (2 g saturated fat), 18 mg cholesterol, 77 mg sodium, 26 g carbohydrate, 1 g fiber, 3 g protein. Daily Values: 1% vit. A, 1% vit. C, 7% calcium, 7% iron.

Peanutty Pancakes, page 84

Breakfast & Brunch

French Onion Omelet

Prep: 25 minutes **Bake:** 10 minutes

Edwina Gadsby
Great Falls, MT

Technically, this omelet is more Italian in design than French because it is served open-faced and is baked. Doesn't matter. The combination of Swiss cheese and onions—a takeoff on the classic soup combo—makes it delicious!

1 tablespoon olive oil	6 eggs
2 cups coarsely chopped red onion	¼ cup water
¼ cup chopped shallots (optional)	¼ teaspoon salt
2 teaspoons sugar	¼ teaspoon ground white pepper
¼ cup sliced green onions	1 cup shredded Swiss cheese
2 teaspoons Dijon-style mustard	(4 ounces)
½ teaspoon dried thyme, crushed	

1 In a 10-inch ovenproof skillet heat oil over medium heat. Add red onion, shallots (if desired), and sugar. Cook for 12 to 15 minutes or until tender and golden brown, stirring often. Remove ¼ cup of the cooked onion mixture; set aside. Stir green onions, mustard, and thyme into skillet.

2 In a medium mixing bowl beat together eggs, water, salt, and white pepper. Stir in ¾ cup of the cheese. Pour egg mixture into skillet over green onion mixture. Bake in a 375° oven for 10 to 15 minutes or until set. Top with remaining cheese and reserved onion mixture. Cut into wedges to serve. Makes 6 servings.

Nutrition Facts per serving: 202 calories, 13 g total fat (5 g saturated fat), 230 mg cholesterol, 245 mg sodium, 9 g carbohydrate, 1 g fiber, 13 g protein. Daily Values: 15% vit. A, 6% vit. C, 18% calcium, 6% iron.

Camembert Soufflé

Prep: 35 minutes **Bake:** 40 minutes

5 egg yolks
7 egg whites
¼ cup chopped celery
2 tablespoons thinly sliced green onion
1 small clove garlic, minced
3 tablespoons butter or margarine
3 tablespoons all-purpose flour
1 teaspoon dry mustard

¼ teaspoon salt
Dash pepper
1 cup milk
5 ounces Camembert cheese, rind removed and cut up (½ cup)
½ cup grated Parmesan cheese or Romano cheese (2 ounces)

1979

*Marlene McCall
Overland Park, KS*

"Outstanding!" is the only way to describe this light-as-air, double-cheese dish.

1 Allow egg yolks and egg whites to stand at room temperature for 30 minutes. Meanwhile, in a medium saucepan cook celery, green onion, and garlic in butter or margarine about 5 minutes or until tender. Stir in flour, mustard, salt, and pepper. Stir in milk all at once. Cook and stir until thickened and bubbly. Reduce heat; add Camembert and Parmesan or Romano cheeses, a little at a time, stirring until melted. Remove from heat; set aside.

2 In a medium mixing bowl beat egg yolks with an electric mixer on high speed for 5 minutes or until thick and lemon colored. Gradually beat in cheese mixture. Wash beaters with warm, soapy water; dry beaters. In a large mixing bowl beat egg whites until stiff peaks form (tips stand straight). Gently fold 1 cup of the stiffly beaten egg whites into egg yolk-cheese mixture. Gradually pour over remaining egg whites, folding to combine. Turn into an ungreased 2- to 2½-quart soufflé dish. Bake in a 350° oven about 40 minutes or until a knife inserted near center comes out clean. Serve immediately. Makes 6 servings.

Nutrition Facts per serving: 269 calories, 20 g total fat (11 g saturated fat), 220 mg cholesterol, 608 mg sodium, 6 g carbohydrate, 0 g fiber, 17 g protein. Daily Values: 24% vit. A, 2% vit. C, 28% calcium, 5% iron.

c'est magnifique!

During the 1970s, interest in French cooking and French ingredients was flourishing. Creative cooks were attempting new "classical" combinations to meet American tastes. Camembert Soufflé, above, is a good example. This dish combines the traditional French soufflé technique with a smooth, creamy, full-flavored French cheese. The result is pure pleasure!

Hash Brown Omelet

Prep: 15 minutes **Cook:** 12 minutes

4 slices bacon
2 cups refrigerated shredded hash
    brown potatoes (about half of a
    20-ounce package)
¼ cup chopped onion
¼ cup chopped green sweet pepper
4 eggs

¼ cup milk
½ teaspoon salt
    Dash ground black pepper
1 cup shredded cheddar cheese
    (4 ounces)
    Bias-sliced green onions (optional)

1960

Mrs. W.F. Grossnickle
Greensboro, NC

Four traditional breakfast favorites—bacon, hash browns, eggs, and cheese—come together in this hearty breakfast skillet.

1 In a large skillet cook bacon until crisp. Drain bacon on paper towels, reserving 2 tablespoons drippings in skillet. Crumble bacon; set aside. Combine potatoes, chopped onion, and sweet pepper; pat into the skillet. Cook, uncovered, over low heat about 7 minutes or until crisp and brown, turning once.

2 Meanwhile, in a small mixing bowl beat together eggs, milk, salt, and black pepper; pour over potato mixture. Top with cheese and bacon. Cover; cook over low heat for 5 to 7 minutes or until egg mixture is set. Loosen omelet; fold in half. Turn out of skillet onto plate. Cut into wedges to serve. If desired, garnish with green onions. Makes 4 servings.

Nutrition Facts per serving: 325 calories, 18 g total fat (9 g saturated fat), 249 mg cholesterol, 661 mg sodium, 22 g carbohydrate, 2 g fiber, 18 g protein. Daily Values: 19% vit. A, 27% vit. C, 26% calcium, 12% iron.

family meals on the double

In the 1960s, the trend toward hurry-up family meals was just beginning. Women were leaving home to work full time or to volunteer in community projects. They no longer had time to prepare traditional meals. They preferred to put meals on the table fast, and cooking with convenience products ranging from condensed soup to cake mixes to refrigerated or frozen hash-brown potatoes—as in Hash Brown Omelet, above—was an easy solution to the never-ending what-are-we-having dilemma.

Herbed Ham and Vegetable Quiche

Prep: 35 minutes **Bake:** 25 minutes **Stand:** 10 minutes

Laurie Wethington
Farmington Hills, MI

Refrigerated biscuits make a tender, easy crust for this colorful brunch headliner.

2 cups thinly sliced zucchini and/or yellow summer squash
1 cup chopped onion
½ cup sliced fresh mushrooms
½ cup chopped red sweet pepper
1 tablespoon margarine or butter
¼ cup snipped fresh parsley or 1 tablespoon dried parsley
2 tablespoons snipped fresh basil or 1 teaspoon dried basil, crushed
1 teaspoon snipped fresh oregano or ¼ teaspoon dried oregano, crushed

¼ teaspoon garlic powder
⅛ teaspoon ground black pepper
2 beaten eggs
1 cup diced cooked ham
1 cup shredded mozzarella cheese (4 ounces)
½ cup shredded fontina cheese (2 ounces)
1 17.3-ounce package (8) refrigerated large southern-style biscuits
Fresh basil leaves (optional)

1 Grease a 10-inch quiche dish; set aside. For filling, in a large skillet cook the zucchini and/or summer squash, onion, mushrooms, and sweet pepper in hot margarine or butter about 6 minutes or just until tender, stirring occasionally. Remove from heat. Stir in parsley, basil, oregano, garlic powder, and black pepper. Stir in eggs, ham, mozzarella cheese, and fontina cheese; set aside.

2 For crust, in prepared quiche dish arrange 7 slightly flattened biscuits around edge, allowing dough to extend over side. Place the remaining biscuit in bottom of dish. Pinch edges to seal. Flatten slightly to form an even crust.

3 Spread filling evenly in crust. Bake in a 375° oven about 25 minutes or until a knife inserted near center comes out clean. To prevent overbrowning, cover edge with foil for the last 5 to 10 minutes of baking. Let stand 10 minutes. Cut into wedges to serve. If desired, garnish with fresh basil leaves. Makes 6 servings.

Nutrition Facts per serving: 438 calories, 23 g total fat (8 g saturated fat), 105 mg cholesterol, 1,290 mg sodium, 39 g carbohydrate, 2 g fiber, 20 g protein. Daily Values: 20% vit. A, 42% vit. C, 22% calcium, 18% iron.

Pork-Spinach Pie

Prep: 15 minutes **Bake:** 65 minutes **Stand:** 10 minutes

½ of a 10-ounce package frozen
  chopped spinach, thawed
1 9-inch frozen unbaked deep-dish
  pastry shell
1 cup shredded Monterey Jack or
  Swiss cheese (4 ounces)

½ pound bulk pork sausage
½ cup herb-seasoned stuffing mix
3 beaten eggs
1¼ cups milk

Barbara Stewart
Yuba City, CA

**Pork sausage adds an
extra zing of flavor to this
hearty, quichelike pie.**

1 Drain thawed spinach well, pressing out excess liquid; set aside. Place frozen pie shell in its pan on a baking sheet; do not prick. Bake in a 400° oven for 5 minutes. Remove from oven. Sprinkle cheese in bottom of partially baked pie shell; set aside. Reduce oven temperature to 325°.

2 Meanwhile, in a skillet cook sausage until browned; drain off fat. Stir stuffing mix and spinach into sausage; spoon over cheese. Combine eggs and milk; pour over sausage mixture. Bake, uncovered, in the 325° oven about 65 minutes or until knife inserted near center comes out clean. Let stand 10 minutes before serving. Makes 6 servings.

Nutrition Facts per serving: 434 calories, 30 g total fat (12 g saturated fat), 148 mg cholesterol, 628 mg sodium, 22 g carbohydrate, 1 g fiber, 16 g protein. Daily Values: 47% vit. A, 4% vit. C, 25% calcium, 10% iron.

real cooks do make quiche

Although quiche in the United States can be traced back to the early 1940s, it wasn't until notable cooks, such as Craig Claiborne and James Beard, began promoting the savory custard pie in the late 1940s and 1950s that it began to grow in popularity. When Julia Child featured it on her television show in the mid-60s, quiche became a household favorite. Julia encouraged her viewers to be creative with the seasonings and ingredients for the classic pie, and cooks have done just that ever since.

Brunch Scrambled Eggs

Start to finish: 20 minutes

Robin Cronin
Royal Oak, MI

Robin's easy recipe takes scrambled eggs to a new level. The chopped spinach and herb make the eggs colorful and fresh-tasting. The Colby and feta cheeses give them extra flavor.

1 10-ounce package frozen chopped spinach, thawed
12 eggs
½ cup milk
½ teaspoon dried oregano or thyme, crushed, or 1½ teaspoons snipped fresh oregano or thyme
¼ teaspoon salt
⅛ teaspoon pepper
2 tablespoons butter or margarine
1 cup shredded Colby or cheddar cheese (4 ounces)
1 cup crumbled feta cheese (4 ounces)

1 Drain thawed spinach well, pressing out excess liquid; set aside. In a large mixing bowl beat together eggs, milk, dried oregano or thyme (if using), salt, and pepper. In a large skillet melt butter or margarine over medium heat; pour in egg mixture. Cook, without stirring, until mixture begins to set on the bottom and around edge. Using a large spatula, lift and fold partially cooked eggs so uncooked portion flows underneath. Stir in spinach, Colby or cheddar cheese, and half of the feta cheese. Continue cooking and stirring for 2 to 3 minutes or until eggs are cooked through but are still glossy and moist. Transfer to serving bowl; sprinkle with remaining feta cheese and, if using, the fresh oregano or thyme. Makes 6 servings.

Nutrition Facts per serving: 330 calories, 25 g total fat (12 g saturated fat), 472 mg cholesterol, 631 mg sodium, 5 g carbohydrate, 1 g fiber, 22 g protein. Daily Values: 68% vit. A, 19% vit. C, 35% calcium, 15% iron.

bring on brunch

The word brunch was coined in the late 1800s in England as a combination of breakfast and lunch. Back then it was a meal eaten after returning from hunting. The hybrid meal became fashionable in America during the 1930s and had a revival in the 1970s. Today, going out or staying home for weekend brunch is as popular as ever. No matter where the brunch is served, it most likely will feature a hearty egg dish, such as Brunch Scrambled Eggs, above.

Baked Eggs with Cheese and Basil Sauce

Prep: 15 minutes **Bake:** 18 minutes

1993

*Angela Bumbalo
East Amherst, NY*

Angela's recipe dresses up baked eggs with a creamy basil sauce for a special breakfast or brunch.

3 tablespoons margarine or butter
2 tablespoons all-purpose flour
¼ teaspoon salt
⅛ teaspoon pepper
3 tablespoons snipped fresh basil or
    ½ teaspoon dried basil, crushed
1 cup milk

Nonstick cooking spray
4 eggs
Salt
Pepper
¼ cup shredded mozzarella cheese
    (1 ounce)
Snipped fresh basil (optional)

1 For basil sauce, in a small saucepan melt the margarine or butter over medium heat. Stir in the flour, the ¼ teaspoon salt, the ⅛ teaspoon pepper, and, if using, the dried basil. Add milk all at once. Cook and stir until thickened and bubbly. Cook and stir 1 minute more. Remove from heat. Stir in the 3 tablespoons fresh basil, if using.

2 Coat four 8- to 10-ounce round baking dishes or 6-ounce custard cups with cooking spray. To assemble, spoon about 2 tablespoons basil sauce into each dish. Gently break an egg into the center of each dish; season with salt and pepper. Spoon remaining sauce over eggs. Bake in a 350° oven for 18 to 20 minutes or until eggs are set. Sprinkle with cheese. Let stand until cheese melts. If desired, garnish with additional snipped basil. Makes 4 servings.

Nutrition Facts per serving: 213 calories, 16 g total fat (4 g saturated fat), 221 mg cholesterol, 406 mg sodium, 7 g carbohydrate, 0 g fiber, 11 g protein. Daily Values: 23% vit. A, 2% vit. C, 15% calcium, 6% iron.

Baked Italian Omelet

Prep: 20 minutes **Bake:** 30 minutes **Stand:** 10 minutes

- 1 10-ounce package frozen chopped spinach, thawed
- 8 beaten eggs
- 1 cup ricotta cheese
- ½ cup milk
- ½ teaspoon dried basil, crushed
- ¼ teaspoon salt
- ¼ teaspoon fennel seed, crushed
- ¼ teaspoon pepper
- 1 cup chopped tomatoes
- 1 cup shredded mozzarella cheese (4 ounces)
- ½ cup thinly sliced green onions
- ½ cup diced salami

Dawn K. Murphy
Hercules, CA

When you're having guests for breakfast or brunch, don't fret over fussy omelets. This fix-and-forget egg dish bakes while you mingle.

1 Grease a 3-quart rectangular baking dish; set aside. Drain thawed spinach well, pressing out excess liquid; set aside. In a large bowl combine eggs and ricotta cheese; beat just until combined. Stir in milk, basil, salt, fennel seed, and pepper. Fold in spinach, tomatoes, mozzarella, green onions, and salami.

2 Spread mixture evenly into the prepared dish. Bake in a 325° oven for 30 to 35 minutes or until a knife inserted near center comes out clean. Let stand for 10 minutes. Makes 6 to 8 servings.

Nutrition Facts per serving: 281 calories, 18 g total fat (8 g saturated fat), 318 mg cholesterol, 620 mg sodium, 8 g carbohydrate, 1 g fiber, 22 g protein. Daily Values: 51% vit. A, 21% vit. C, 28% calcium, 14% iron.

Basil-Tomato Tart

Prep: 40 minutes **Bake:** 25 minutes

½ of a 15-ounce package (1 crust) folded refrigerated unbaked piecrust

1½ cups shredded mozzarella cheese (6 ounces)

5 Roma tomatoes (about 12 ounces)

1 cup loosely packed fresh basil (leaves only)

4 cloves garlic

⅓ cup mayonnaise or salad dressing

¼ cup grated Parmesan cheese

⅛ teaspoon ground white pepper

Shredded fresh basil (optional)

Kathleen M. Bonerb
Glen, NH

Whether you serve it for breakfast or brunch or as an appetizer at an afternoon get-together, be prepared. Your guests will ask you to share your recipe for this garden-fresh breakfast dish.

1 Unfold piecrust according to package directions. Place in a 9-inch quiche dish or glass pie plate. Flute edge. Line the unpricked pastry with a double thickness of foil. Bake in a 450° oven for 8 minutes. Remove foil. Bake for 4 to 5 minutes more or until pastry is set and dry. Remove from oven. Sprinkle with ½ cup of the mozzarella cheese. Place on a wire rack to cool slightly. Reduce oven temperature to 375°.

2 Meanwhile, cut tomatoes into ½-inch slices; drain on paper towels. Arrange tomato slices on melted cheese in the pie shell. In a food processor bowl combine the 1 cup basil and the garlic; cover and process until coarsely chopped. Sprinkle mixture over tomatoes.

3 In a medium bowl combine remaining mozzarella cheese, mayonnaise or salad dressing, Parmesan cheese, and white pepper. Spoon cheese mixture over basil mixture and tomatoes.

4 Cover edge with foil. Bake in the 375° oven for 20 minutes. Uncover and bake 5 to 10 minutes more or until top is golden brown and bubbly. Serve warm. If desired, garnish with shredded basil. Makes 4 servings.

Nutrition Facts per serving: 532 calories, 38 g total fat (14 g saturated fat), 50 mg cholesterol, 625 mg sodium, 33 g carbohydrate, 2 g fiber, 15 g protein. Daily Values: 19% vit. A, 32% vit. C, 39% calcium, 6% iron.

Mediterranean **Strata**

Prep: 20 minutes **Bake:** 35 minutes **Stand:** 5 minutes

Marilou Robinson
Portland, OR

The flavors of roasted red peppers, green olives, and feta cheese give this dish a fresh, new taste.

Nonstick cooking spray
3 cups cubed Italian bread
2 large onions, thinly sliced
4 cloves garlic, minced
2 tablespoons olive oil
½ cup chopped roasted red sweet
   peppers

½ cup chopped pitted green olives
½ cup crumbled feta cheese (2 ounces)
6 eggs
1 14½-ounce can chicken broth
¼ cup dry white wine or chicken broth
¼ teaspoon ground black pepper

1 Coat a 10-inch quiche dish with cooking spray. Arrange the bread cubes in dish; set aside.

2 In a large skillet cook the onions and garlic in hot oil over medium heat about 10 minutes or until onions are golden brown, stirring frequently. Remove from heat. Stir in the roasted red sweet peppers and olives. Spoon mixture evenly over bread cubes in dish. Sprinkle with feta cheese.

3 In a large mixing bowl beat together eggs, the 14½ ounces chicken broth, the ¼ cup wine or chicken broth, and the black pepper. Pour egg mixture over bread mixture in dish.

4 Bake in a 350° oven for 35 to 45 minutes or until a knife inserted near the center comes out clean. Let stand for 5 to 10 minutes before serving. Makes 8 servings.

Nutrition Facts per serving: 173 calories, 11 g total fat (3 g saturated fat), 166 mg cholesterol, 515 mg sodium, 11 g carbohydrate, 1 g fiber, 8 g protein. Daily Values: 12% vit. A, 46% vit. C, 6% calcium, 9% iron.

Cheese, Bacon, and Bread Bake

Prep: 30 minutes **Bake:** 25 minutes

1½ cups all-purpose flour
1½ teaspoons baking powder
½ teaspoon baking soda
½ teaspoon dried dillweed or
    ½ teaspoon dried thyme, crushed
½ teaspoon finely shredded lemon peel
1 8-ounce carton dairy sour cream
8 slices bacon
½ cup ricotta cheese

½ cup shredded Swiss cheese
    (2 ounces)
1 3-ounce package cream cheese,
    cut into small cubes
3 tablespoons milk
2 teaspoons Dijon-style mustard
1 green onion, finely chopped
1 tablespoon snipped fresh parsley

Roxanne E. Chan
Albany, CA

The savory dill-accented bread shell holds a hearty mixture of ricotta cheese, Swiss cheese, cream cheese, and crispy bacon. A marinated fresh fruit compote would make a perfect companion.

1 In a medium bowl combine flour, baking powder, baking soda, dillweed or thyme, and lemon peel. Stir in sour cream. On a floured surface, knead dough just until smooth. Cover; set aside.

2 In a 10-inch ovenproof skillet cook bacon until crisp. Drain bacon on paper towels, reserving 1 tablespoon drippings in skillet. Crumble bacon; set aside. Cool skillet slightly. Press dough onto the bottom and ½ inch up the side of skillet; sprinkle with all but 2 tablespoons of the crumbled bacon.

3 In a medium bowl combine ricotta cheese, Swiss cheese, cream cheese, milk, mustard, green onion, and parsley; spread into skillet. Bake in a 400° oven about 25 minutes or until bread is golden brown. Cool slightly. Sprinkle with reserved bacon; cut into wedges to serve. Makes 8 servings.

Nutrition Facts per serving: 272 calories, 17 g total fat (10 g saturated fat), 44 mg cholesterol, 365 mg sodium, 19 g carbohydrate, 1 g fiber, 10 g protein. Daily Values: 14% vit. A, 2% vit. C, 17% calcium, 8% iron.

Brunch Turnovers

Prep: 20 minutes **Bake:** 25 minutes

1988

*Betsy Ziegler
Alexandria, VA*

Betsy created these hearty ham-and-Swiss-stuffed triangles by modifying a dessert recipe based on puff pastry.

1   17¼-ounce package (2 sheets)
     frozen puff pastry
2   tablespoons finely chopped onion
1   tablespoon margarine or butter
1   beaten egg
1   cup shredded Swiss cheese
     (4 ounces)

⅔   cup finely chopped cooked ham
     (3 ounces)
1   tablespoon snipped fresh parsley
½   teaspoon dried dillweed or
     1 teaspoon snipped fresh dill
Dash garlic powder
Dash pepper

1 Let frozen puff pastry stand at room temperature about 1 hour or until thawed. In a small saucepan cook onion in hot margarine or butter until tender. For filling, in a medium bowl combine egg, Swiss cheese, ham, parsley, dillweed, garlic powder, and pepper. Stir in onion mixture; set aside.

2 On a lightly floured surface, roll each pastry sheet into a 10½-inch square; cut into 3½-inch squares (18 total). Place 1 packed tablespoon of the filling just off center on each square. Moisten edges with water; fold in half diagonally. Seal edges by pressing with tines of a fork or fingers. Place turnovers on an ungreased baking sheet.

3 Bake turnovers in a 400° oven about 25 minutes or until golden brown. Serve hot. Makes 18 turnovers.

To Make Ahead: Bake turnovers; cool. Pack in an airtight freezer container; seal and freeze for up to 3 months. To serve, place frozen turnovers on baking sheet. Bake in a 375° oven about 15 minutes or until heated through.

Nutrition Facts per turnover: 162 calories, 12 g total fat (1 g saturated fat), 20 mg cholesterol, 195 mg sodium, 10 g carbohydrate, 0 g fiber, 4 g protein. Daily Values: 3% vit. A, 1% vit. C, 6% calcium, 1% iron.

Peanutty Pancakes

Prep: 10 minutes **Cook:** 3 minutes per pancake

1995

Guy Bickley
Bristol, VA

Choose creamy or chunky peanut butter for this family-pleasing pancake mix fix-up.
(Pictured on page 66.)

1 cup packaged pancake mix
2 tablespoons sugar
1 egg
⅓ cup peanut butter
1 5-ounce can (⅔ cup) evaporated milk

¼ cup water
¼ cup margarine or butter, softened
2 tablespoons honey

1 In a large bowl stir together the pancake mix and sugar. In a medium bowl beat the egg with a whisk or fork. Beat in the peanut butter. Stir in the evaporated milk and water. Add egg mixture to the pancake mix all at once. Stir just until combined (batter should be slightly lumpy).

2 Lightly grease a griddle or heavy skillet; preheat over medium heat. For standard-size pancakes, pour about ¼ cup of the batter onto the hot griddle. (Use 1 to 2 tablespoons for smaller pancakes.) Cook over medium heat until pancakes are golden brown, turning to cook second sides when pancakes have bubbly surfaces and edges are slightly dry. Remove from griddle; keep warm.

3 Meanwhile, combine margarine or butter and honey. If desired, heat until margarine or butter is melted. Serve with pancakes. Makes eight 3-inch pancakes.

Nutrition Facts per pancake: 230 calories, 14 g total fat (4 g saturated fat), 33 mg cholesterol, 331 mg sodium, 22 g carbohydrate, 1 g fiber, 7 g protein. Daily Values: 9% vit. A, 5% vit. C, 9% calcium, 5% iron.

Three-Grain Yeast Waffles

Prep: 15 minutes **Chill:** Overnight **Bake:** Per waffle baker directions

1 cup whole wheat flour
1 cup unprocessed wheat bran
1 cup yellow cornmeal
1 cup nonfat dry milk powder
1 package active dry yeast
¼ teaspoon salt
2½ cups water

2 eggs
3 tablespoons cooking oil
3 tablespoons honey
   Butter or margarine (optional)
   Maple syrup or maple-flavored
      syrup (optional)

1 In large mixing bowl combine flour, wheat bran, cornmeal, dry milk powder, yeast, and salt. Add water, eggs, oil, and honey; beat with an electric mixer on medium speed for 1 minute. Cover loosely; chill overnight.

2 Stir mixture. For each waffle, pour about 1 cup batter onto preheated, lightly greased waffle iron. Close lid quickly; do not open during baking. Bake according to manufacturer's directions. When done, use a fork to lift waffle off grid. Repeat with remaining batter. Serve warm. If desired, pass butter or margarine and/or syrup. Makes about sixteen 4-inch waffles.

Nutrition Facts per waffle: 125 calories, 4 g total fat (1 g saturated fat), 27 mg cholesterol, 70 mg sodium, 20 g carbohydrate, 3 g fiber, 5 g protein. Daily Values: 5% vit. A, 6% calcium, 7% iron.

Mary Love Chambers
Holly Hill, FL

Surprise your youngsters by serving these wholesome waffles with butter molded into whimsical shapes. To shape, press slightly softened butter into a small cookie cutter lined with plastic wrap; freeze until firm. When firm, lift the butter from the cookie cutter using the plastic wrap.

whole grains galore

In the early 1980s, Americans rediscovered whole grains. Cooks put everything from cracked wheat to buckwheat groats to triticale flour in breads, pastry, pizza crusts, pancakes, and even main dishes. The renewed interest in grains was just one part of a huge trend toward eating more wholesome, less-refined foods. The recipe for Three-Grain Yeast Waffles, above, uses a combination of whole wheat flour, unprocessed wheat bran, and yellow cornmeal, which gives it a healthy 3 grams of fiber.

Oatmeal Waffles

Prep: 10 minutes **Bake:** Per waffle baker directions

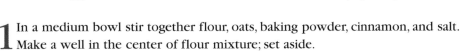

1½ cups all-purpose flour	1½ cups milk
1 cup quick-cooking rolled oats	⅓ cup butter or margarine, melted
1 tablespoon baking powder	2 tablespoons brown sugar
½ teaspoon ground cinnamon	Powdered sugar (optional)
¼ teaspoon salt	Fresh fruit (optional)
2 eggs	Vanilla yogurt (optional)

*Randy Hieronymus
Coral Springs, FL*

Enjoy these hearty waffles with lots of fresh fruit for Sunday brunch.

1 In a medium bowl stir together flour, oats, baking powder, cinnamon, and salt. Make a well in the center of flour mixture; set aside.

2 In another medium bowl beat eggs slightly. Stir in milk, butter or margarine, and brown sugar. Add egg mixture all at once to flour mixture; stir until combined.

3 Pour about 1¼ cups batter onto grids of a preheated, lightly greased waffle baker. Close lid quickly; do not open during baking. Bake according to manufacturer's directions. When done, use a fork to lift waffle off grid. Repeat with remaining batter. If desired, sprinkle with powdered sugar and top with fruit and yogurt. Makes about twelve 4-inch waffles.

Nutrition Facts per waffle: 168 calories, 8 g total fat (4 g saturated fat), 52 mg cholesterol, 231 mg sodium, 20 g carbohydrate, 1 g fiber, 5 g protein. Daily Values: 9% vit. A, 11% calcium, 7% iron.

whipping up waffles

Waffles have a long, rich history in American cooking. The Pilgrims learned about the crispy treat as they passed through Holland on their way to the colonies. Thomas Jefferson brought a long-handled waffle iron back with him from France. After World War I, electric waffle irons made the web-patterned cakes easier and quicker than ever. During this era, waffles were not only a breakfast dish, but also appeared as sandwiches for lunch and topped with creamed mixtures for Sunday-night supper. At the 1964 World's Fair, Belgian waffles, a thick, heavy waffle, became an instant hit. Today, cooks dress waffles up with the likes of fresh fruit and creamy yogurt, as in Oatmeal Waffles, above.

Scallops and Shrimp
with Linguine, page 134

Main Dishes

Italian Beef and Spinach Pie

Prep: 25 minutes **Bake:** 47 minutes **Stand:** 10 minutes

1998

Karen Smith, Winslow Columbia, SC

Savory and satisfying, Karen's cheese-and-meat-filled pie is also loaded with veggies, including spinach, sweet pepper, mushrooms, and tomato.

1 10-ounce package frozen chopped spinach, thawed
1 unbaked 9-inch pastry shell
½ pound lean ground beef
¼ pound mild bulk Italian turkey sausage
¾ cup chopped red and/or yellow sweet pepper
½ cup sliced fresh mushrooms
1 clove garlic, minced
1 cup water
½ cup tomato paste
1½ teaspoons dried Italian seasoning, crushed
½ teaspoon salt
⅔ cup light ricotta cheese
¾ cup shredded mozzarella cheese (3 ounces)
1 cup chopped tomato
Fresh oregano (optional)

1 Drain thawed spinach well, pressing out excess liquid; set aside. Line pastry shell with a double thickness of foil. Bake in a 450° oven for 8 minutes. Remove foil. Bake for 4 to 5 minutes more or until set and dry; remove from oven. Reduce oven temperature to 350°.

2 In a large skillet cook the beef, sausage, sweet pepper, mushrooms, and garlic until meat is no longer pink and vegetables are tender. Drain off fat. Stir in the water, tomato paste, Italian seasoning, and salt. Bring to boiling; reduce heat. Cover and simmer for 10 minutes.

3 Meanwhile, in a medium bowl stir together spinach, ricotta cheese, and ¼ cup of the mozzarella cheese. Spoon the spinach mixture into baked pastry shell. Top with the meat mixture. To prevent overbrowning, cover the edge of pastry with foil. Bake in the 350° oven for 45 minutes. Remove foil. Top pie with tomato and remaining mozzarella cheese. Bake for 2 minutes more or until heated through and cheese is melted. Let stand for 10 minutes. If desired, garnish with fresh oregano. Makes 8 servings.

Nutrition Facts per serving:
290 calories,
16 g total fat
(5 g saturated fat),
33 mg cholesterol,
417 mg sodium,
22 g carbohydrate,
2 g fiber,
16 g protein. Daily Values: 34% vit. A,
51% vit. C,
12% calcium,
19% iron.

Spicy Panbroiled Steak

Start to finish: 25 minutes

1 teaspoon garlic salt
1 teaspoon ground cumin
1 teaspoon dried oregano, crushed
2 tablespoons olive oil
1 medium red sweet pepper, cut into thin bite-size strips (1 cup)
1 medium onion, chopped (½ cup)
1 or 2 chipotle peppers in adobo sauce, drained and chopped
1 pound boneless beef top loin steak, cut ¾ inch thick
1 medium tomato, seeded and chopped (½ cup)
Flour tortillas, warmed
Purchased guacamole
Fresh cilantro (optional)

1999

Barbara J. Morgan
Concord, CA

If you like fajitas, you'll love Barbara's variation that spotlights the smoky-spicy flavor of chipotle peppers. Look for canned chipotle peppers in adobo sauce in the Mexican food section of your supermarket or at a Mexican grocery store.

1 In a small bowl combine garlic salt, cumin, and oregano. In a large skillet heat 1 tablespoon of the oil over medium-high heat. Add 2 teaspoons of the garlic salt mixture, the sweet pepper, onion, and chipotle peppers. Cook and stir for 2 to 3 minutes or just until vegetables are tender. Using a slotted spoon, remove vegetables from skillet; keep warm.

2 Add remaining oil, remaining garlic salt mixture, and the meat to same skillet. Cook meat over medium-high heat about 4 minutes on each side or until meat is slightly pink in the center. Transfer meat to a serving platter, reserving drippings in skillet. Thinly slice meat; keep warm.

3 Return vegetables to skillet. Stir in tomato; heat through. Spoon vegetables over meat. To serve, fill tortillas with meat-vegetable mixture; roll up. Serve with guacamole. If desired, garnish with fresh cilantro. Makes 4 servings.

Nutrition Facts per serving: 341 calories, 15 g total fat (3 g saturated fat), 65 mg cholesterol, 772 mg sodium, 25 g carbohydrate, 1 g fiber, 26 g protein. Daily Values: 20% vit. A, 62% vit. C, 6% calcium, 31% iron.

Beef Steaks with **Pepper-Onion Relish**

Start to finish: 30 minutes

Marie Rizzio
Traverse City, MI

Sweet peppers, onion, olive oil, red wine vinegar, and garlic make up the flavorful Italian-inspired relish.

¼ cup seasoned fine dry bread crumbs
¼ cup grated Parmesan cheese
1 tablespoon snipped fresh parsley
¼ teaspoon salt
 Dash ground black pepper
1 beaten egg
1 tablespoon water
3 cloves garlic, minced
6 beef tenderloin steaks, cut ½ inch thick (1 to 1¼ pounds)

2 tablespoons olive oil or cooking oil
3 red, green, and/or yellow sweet peppers, cut into bite-size strips
2 large onions, thinly sliced and separated into rings (3 cups)
1 sprig fresh rosemary or ½ teaspoon dried rosemary, crushed
3 tablespoons red wine vinegar
1 tablespoon butter or margarine
 Snipped fresh rosemary (optional)

1 In a shallow dish combine bread crumbs, Parmesan cheese, parsley, salt, and black pepper. In another dish stir together the egg and water. Rub about half of the garlic over steaks. Dip steaks in egg mixture; coat with crumb mixture. Set aside.

2 For the relish, in a large skillet heat 1 tablespoon of the oil over medium heat. Add the remaining garlic, the sweet peppers, onion, and rosemary sprig or dried rosemary; cover and cook for 10 to 15 minutes or until tender, stirring occasionally. Remove fresh rosemary, if used. Stir in vinegar. Remove from heat; keep warm.

3 Meanwhile, in a large skillet heat butter or margarine and remaining oil over medium-high heat. Add meat; reduce heat to medium. Cook, uncovered, to desired doneness, turning once. (Allow 6 to 8 minutes for rare or 10 to 12 minutes for medium doneness.) Serve with the relish. If desired, sprinkle with snipped rosemary. Makes 6 servings.

Nutrition Facts per serving: 273 calories, 15 g total fat (5 g saturated fat), 91 mg cholesterol, 377 mg sodium, 15 g carbohydrate, 3 g fiber, 21 g protein. Daily Values: 8% vit. A, 98% vit. C, 10% calcium, 16% iron.

Somerset **Sirloin**

Prep: 5 minutes **Marinate:** 2 hours **Broil:** 16 minutes

2 pounds beef sirloin steak, cut
    1½ inches thick
1 tablespoon olive oil
¼ teaspoon salt
¼ teaspoon pepper
2 tablespoons Worcestershire sauce
2 tablespoons butter

1 pound fresh mushrooms
    (such as button or shiitake)
¼ teaspoon salt
⅛ teaspoon pepper
½ cup half-and-half or light cream
    Cracked black pepper

1 Brush both sides of steak with olive oil. Sprinkle with ¼ teaspoon salt and the ¼ teaspoon pepper. Place steak in a shallow baking dish. Drizzle with Worcestershire sauce. Cover and marinate in the refrigerator for 2 hours.

2 Transfer meat to the unheated rack of a broiler pan. Broil meat 4 to 5 inches from the heat to desired doneness, turning once. (Allow 16 to 20 minutes for medium-rare or 20 to 25 minutes for medium doneness.)

3 Meanwhile, in a large skillet melt butter over medium heat. Add mushrooms, ¼ teaspoon salt, and the ⅛ teaspoon pepper. Cook mushrooms for 5 to 6 minutes or just until tender, stirring occasionally. Stir in half-and-half or light cream. Bring to boiling; reduce heat. Simmer, uncovered, for 8 to 10 minutes or until cream is slightly thickened. Place the steak on a serving platter; spoon mushroom sauce over. Garnish with cracked black pepper. Makes 6 to 8 servings.

Nutrition Facts per serving: 413 calories, 30 g total fat (12 g saturated fat), 116 mg cholesterol, 371 mg sodium, 4 g carbohydrate, 1 g fiber, 32 g protein. Daily Values: 6% vit. A, 2% vit. C, 4% calcium, 24% iron.

Southwestern Meat Loaf

Prep: 15 minutes **Bake:** 65 minutes **Stand:** 10 minutes

1 **slightly beaten egg**	½ **teaspoon salt**
¾ **cup soft bread crumbs (1 slice bread)**	¼ **teaspoon ground cinnamon**
¾ **cup salsa**	⅛ **teaspoon ground cloves**
⅓ **cup raisins**	1½ **pounds lean ground beef**
¼ **cup finely chopped almonds, toasted**	¼ **cup salsa**
¼ **cup finely chopped onion**	**Salsa (optional)**
½ **teaspoon sugar**	

Bernard Merino
San Francisco, CA

For a meat loaf that is decidedly different from your usual recipe, try this version. Salsa, raisins, spices, and almonds give it pizzazz.

1 In a large bowl stir together the egg, bread crumbs, the ¾ cup salsa, the raisins, almonds, onion, sugar, salt, cinnamon, and cloves. Add ground beef; mix well. In a shallow baking pan pat meat mixture into an 8×4×2-inch oval loaf. (Or, pat meat mixture into an 8×4×2-inch loaf pan.) Bake in a 350° oven for 1 hour.

2 Drain off fat. Insert a meat thermometer into center of loaf. Spoon the ¼ cup salsa over meat loaf. Bake for 5 to 10 minutes more or until thermometer registers 160°. Transfer meat loaf to a serving platter. Let stand 10 minutes before serving.

3 To serve, slice meat loaf with a thin-bladed serrated knife. If desired, serve meat loaf with additional salsa. Makes 6 servings.

Nutrition Facts per serving: 312 calories, 18 g total fat (6 g saturated fat), 107 mg cholesterol, 426 mg sodium, 14 g carbohydrate, 1 g fiber, 25 g protein. Daily Values: 6% vit. A, 21% vit. C, 3% calcium, 20% iron.

Beef Potpie with Cornmeal-Cheese Crust

Prep: 40 minutes **Cook:** 1 hour **Bake:** 20 minutes

1 pound boneless beef chuck, cut into
  ¼-inch pieces
1 tablespoon cooking oil
1 large green sweet pepper, chopped
  (1⅓ cups)
1 medium onion, chopped (½ cup)
1 14½-ounce can diced tomatoes,
  undrained
1 8¾-ounce can whole kernel corn,
  drained

⅔ cup water
¼ cup tomato paste
1 or 2 fresh jalapeño peppers,
  seeded and chopped*
1 tablespoon chili powder
1 teaspoon sugar
¼ teaspoon salt
1 recipe Cornmeal-Cheese Crust
½ cup shredded cheddar cheese
  (2 ounces) (optional)

1989

Chris Gibson
Fontana, WI

Chris created this robust
potpie to satisfy the
hearty appetites of her
two teenagers.

1 In a large saucepan brown the beef, half at a time, in hot oil. Remove beef with a slotted spoon. Cook sweet pepper and onion in drippings until tender. Add beef, undrained tomatoes, corn, water, tomato paste, jalapeño peppers, chili powder, sugar, and salt. Bring to boiling; reduce heat. Cover; simmer about 1 hour or until meat is tender, stirring twice.

2 Meanwhile, prepare Cornmeal-Cheese Crust. On a lightly floured surface, roll dough for crust into a 12×8-inch rectangle. Spoon beef mixture into a 2-quart rectangular baking dish. Carefully top with crust, fluting extra crust against sides of dish. Cut slits in top of crust for steam to escape. Bake, uncovered, in a 425° oven about 20 minutes or until crust is golden brown. If desired, sprinkle with cheddar cheese; let stand for 5 minutes. Makes 6 servings.

Cornmeal-Cheese Crust: In a medium bowl combine 1 cup all-purpose flour, ½ cup yellow cornmeal, and ½ teaspoon salt. Using a pastry blender or two knives, cut in ½ cup butter and ¼ cup finely shredded cheddar cheese until mixture resembles coarse crumbs. Sprinkle with ¼ cup cold water, 1 tablespoon at a time, tossing gently until all is moistened. Form into ball.

*Note: Because chile peppers, such as jalapeños, contain volatile oils that can burn your skin and eyes, avoid direct contact with them as much as possible. When working with chile peppers, wear plastic or rubber gloves. If your bare hands do touch the chile peppers, wash your hands well with soap and water.

Nutrition Facts per serving: 528 calories, 33 g total fat (16 g saturated fat), 98 mg cholesterol, 747 mg sodium, 39 g carbohydrate, 5 g fiber, 21 g protein. Daily Values: 31% vit. A, 80% vit. C, 7% calcium, 22% iron.

Shredded-Beef **Sandwiches**

Prep: 15 minutes   **Cook:** 5½ to 12 hours

Mrs. Jim Lanz
Sartell, MN

With the help of a crockery cooker, you can have tender beef for sandwiches waiting when you walk in the door. Just shred the meat and pile it on French rolls for a great meal in a bun.

1 3-pound beef chuck pot roast
1 large onion, cut up
3 bay leaves
½ teaspoon salt
¼ teaspoon garlic powder

⅛ teaspoon ground cloves
⅓ cup vinegar
8 French rolls, split
   Spinach or lettuce leaves (optional)

1 Trim fat from roast. If necessary, cut roast to fit into a 3½- or 4-quart electric slow crockery cooker; place roast and onion in cooker. Add bay leaves, salt, garlic powder, and cloves; pour vinegar over roast and onion. Cover and cook on low-heat setting for 11 to 12 hours or on high-heat setting for 5½ to 6 hours.

2 Remove meat; use two forks to shred meat. Discard any bones and fat. Strain meat juices; skim off fat.

3 If desired, toast rolls and line with spinach or lettuce leaves. Place shredded meat on rolls. Drizzle meat with some of the reserved juices; serve remaining juices with sandwiches for dipping. Makes 8 servings.

Nutrition Facts per serving: 314 calories, 9 g total fat (3 g saturated fat), 93 mg cholesterol, 438 mg sodium, 22 g carbohydrate, 2 g fiber, 34 g protein. Daily Values: 2% vit. C, 5% calcium, 26% iron.

between two slices of bread

From colonial citizens wrapping leftover meat in pastry to the latest knife-and-fork bistro creations, sandwiches have long been a favorite meal. Club sandwiches, heros, reubens, and Philadelphia cheese steaks as well as sloppy joes, coney islands, and tuna melts are all products of the American culinary imagination. Another classic that remains popular is the shredded beef sandwich. Some cooks make theirs from grilled beef while others prefer meat that's oven-roasted with seasonings. Shredded-Beef Sandwiches, above, rely on the convenience of a crockery cooker to achieve the long, slow cooking that gives the sandwich its unbeatable flavor and melt-in-your-mouth tenderness.

Chile Pepper Cheeseburgers

Prep: 20 minutes **Grill:** 20 minutes

⅓ cup finely chopped green onions
3 tablespoons fat-free plain yogurt
1 to 4 tablespoons finely chopped
   fresh jalapeño peppers*
½ teaspoon salt
½ teaspoon ground black pepper
2 pounds lean ground beef or
   uncooked ground turkey

6 ounces Monterey Jack cheese with
   jalapeño peppers, cut into 8 slices
8 Kaiser rolls, split and toasted
   Leaf lettuce
   Sliced tomato
1 recipe Lime Mayonnaise

Diane Halferty
Seattle, WA

Sprinkle hickory chips over the coals to impart a wonderful smoky flavor to these spicy burgers. The refreshing lime-flavored mayonnaise offsets the heat of the burgers.

1 In a medium bowl combine green onions, yogurt, jalapeño peppers, salt, and black pepper. Add beef or turkey; mix well. Shape mixture into 8 patties, each about ¾ inch thick.

2 In a grill with a cover arrange medium-hot coals around drip pan. Test for medium heat above pan. Place burgers on grill rack over drip pan. Cover and grill for 20 to 24 minutes or until no pink remains, turning once. Top each patty with a slice of cheese for the last 2 minutes of grilling time. Serve patties on Kaiser rolls with lettuce, tomato, and Lime Mayonnaise. Makes 8 servings.

Lime Mayonnaise: In a small bowl combine ⅓ cup mayonnaise or salad dressing or light mayonnaise dressing or salad dressing, 1 teaspoon Dijon-style mustard, ½ teaspoon finely shredded lime peel, and 1 teaspoon lime juice. Cover; chill until serving time.

*Note: Because chile peppers, such as jalapeños, contain volatile oils that can burn your skin and eyes, avoid direct contact with them as much as possible. When working with chile peppers, wear plastic or rubber gloves. If your bare hands do touch the chile peppers, wash your hands well with soap and water.

Nutrition Facts per serving: 543 calories, 30 g total fat (11 g saturated fat), 94 mg cholesterol, 688 mg sodium, 33 g carbohydrate, 2 g fiber, 33 g protein. Daily Values: 7% vit. A, 30% vit. C, 24% calcium, 24% iron.

Double-Crust Pizza Casserole

Prep: 25 minutes **Bake:** 35 minutes **Stand:** 5 minutes

3 cups all-purpose flour
3 cups packaged instant mashed potatoes
2 cups milk
½ cup butter or margarine, melted
1 pound lean ground beef
¾ pound bulk Italian sausage
1 large onion, coarsely chopped (1 cup)
1 8-ounce can tomato sauce

1 6-ounce can Italian-style tomato paste
½ of 1.3- to 1.5-ounce package sloppy joe seasoning mix (about 2 tablespoons)
1 2¼-ounce can sliced ripe olives, drained (optional)
1 cup shredded mozzarella cheese (4 ounces)
1 tablespoon cornmeal

1998

Lisa Kelly Thomson
Lexington, KY

Lisa adapted one of her mother's recipes to create this hearty main dish. A simple salad is all you need to add for a satisfying meal.

1 For crust, combine flour, potatoes, milk, and butter or margarine; set aside. (Mixture stiffens somewhat as it stands.)

2 For filling, in a 12-inch skillet or a Dutch oven cook beef, sausage, and onion until meat is no longer pink. Drain off fat. Stir in tomato sauce, tomato paste, seasoning mix, and, if desired, olives.

3 Using floured fingers, press half of the dough into the bottom and about 1½ inches up the sides of a 13×9×2-inch baking pan or a 3-quart rectangular baking dish. Spread filling over crust; sprinkle with mozzarella cheese. Between two large sheets of waxed paper, roll remaining crust into a 15×11-inch rectangle; remove top sheet and invert over filling. Remove paper. Trim edges as necessary. Turn edges of top crust under and seal to bottom crust. Sprinkle with cornmeal. Bake in a 425° oven about 35 minutes or until heated through and crust is golden brown. Let stand for 5 minutes before serving. Makes 12 servings.

Nutrition Facts per serving: 428 calories, 20 g total fat (10 g saturated fat), 69 mg cholesterol, 715 mg sodium, 41 g carbohydrate, 2 g fiber, 20 g protein. Daily Values: 15% vit. A, 27% vit. C, 13% calcium, 16% iron.

Chili-Corn Bread Pie

Prep: 35 minutes **Bake:** 30 minutes **Stand:** 10 minutes

Mary Beth Welter
St. Paul, MN

Mary Beth uses convenient refrigerated corn bread twists to make a quick crust for this hearty Tex-Mex pie, then fills the crust with a well-seasoned mixture of ground beef, vegetables, and chili beans.

¾ pound lean ground beef
1 medium onion, chopped (½ cup)
1 small green sweet pepper, coarsely chopped (½ cup)
1 15-ounce can chili beans with chili gravy or chili beans, undrained
1 8-ounce can tomato sauce
1 6-ounce can tomato paste
2 to 3 tablespoons chili powder
½ teaspoon ground cumin
½ teaspoon bottled hot pepper sauce
1 11½-ounce package (8) refrigerated corn bread twists
1 8-ounce carton dairy sour cream
2 tablespoons all-purpose flour
1 cup shredded cheddar cheese
2 cups corn chips, coarsely crushed (about 1 cup)
  Chopped green sweet pepper (optional)

1 In a large skillet cook the ground beef, onion, and sweet pepper until ground beef is no longer pink; drain off fat. Stir in undrained beans, tomato sauce, tomato paste, chili powder, cumin, and hot pepper sauce. Bring to boiling; reduce heat. Simmer, uncovered, for 5 minutes, stirring frequently.

2 Meanwhile, for crust, lightly grease a 9- or 10-inch pie plate. Unwrap and separate corn bread twists, but do not uncoil. Arrange corn bread coils in pie plate, pressing onto the bottom and up the sides, extending about ½ inch above edge of pie plate.

3 Spoon ground beef mixture into crust. Stir together sour cream and flour; spread evenly over ground beef mixture. Sprinkle with cheddar cheese and crushed corn chips. Place on a baking sheet. Bake, uncovered, in a 375° oven for 30 minutes. Let stand 10 minutes before serving. If desired, garnish with chopped sweet pepper. Makes 8 servings.

Nutrition Facts per serving: 492 calories, 26 g total fat (11 g saturated fat), 54 mg cholesterol, 753 mg sodium, 43 g carbohydrate, 5 g fiber, 21 g protein. Daily Values: 28% vit. A, 23% vit. C, 18% calcium, 20% iron.

Southwestern Ribs with a Rub

Prep: 20 minutes **Cook:** 25 minutes **Grill:** 1¼ hours

4 cups mesquite chips	½ teaspoon coarsely ground black pepper
1 cup catsup	½ teaspoon bottled hot pepper sauce
½ cup light-colored corn syrup	¼ teaspoon ground cumin or chili powder
¼ cup white vinegar	⅛ teaspoon ground red pepper
¼ cup packed brown sugar	4 pounds pork loin back ribs
¼ cup finely chopped onion	1 recipe Rib Rub
2 tablespoons prepared mustard	
1½ teaspoons Worcestershire sauce	
2 cloves garlic, minced	

Robert A. Kowalewski
Berwyn, IL

Robert pats pork ribs with a peppery rub, slathers them with a zippy barbecue sauce, then grills them over mesquite chips for a great smoke flavor.

1 At least 1 hour before grilling, cover mesquite chips with water and soak; drain before using. For sauce, in a 1½-quart saucepan combine catsup, corn syrup, white vinegar, brown sugar, onion, mustard, Worcestershire sauce, garlic, black pepper, hot pepper sauce, cumin or chili powder, and ground red pepper. Bring to boiling; reduce heat. Simmer, uncovered, for 25 to 30 minutes or until thickened, stirring occasionally.

2 Cut the ribs into serving-size pieces. Pat the Rib Rub evenly onto all sides of ribs. In a grill with a cover arrange medium-hot coals around a drip pan. Test for medium heat above pan. Put some of the drained mesquite chips onto coals. Place ribs on grill rack over the drip pan. Cover and grill for 1¼ to 1½ hours or until ribs are tender and no pink remains, adding charcoal and mesquite chips as needed. Brush ribs with some of the sauce during the last 10 minutes of grilling. Pass remaining sauce. Makes 6 servings.

Rib Rub: In a blender container or small food processor bowl combine 2 teaspoons dried rosemary, 2 teaspoons dried thyme, 2 teaspoons dried minced onion, 2 teaspoons dried minced garlic, 1 teaspoon coarse salt, and ¾ teaspoon ground black pepper. Blend or process until coarsely ground.

Nutrition Facts per serving: 497 calories, 17 g total fat (6 g saturated fat), 84 mg cholesterol, 1,057 mg sodium, 44 g carbohydrate, 1 g fiber, 42 g protein. Daily Values: 5% vit. A, 20% vit. C, 5% calcium, 26% iron.

Lemony **Italian Salad**

Prep: 35 minutes **Chill:** 1 to 2 hours

1999

Robin Whitmore
Scottsdale, AZ

For an eye-catching presentation, arrange the tomatoes, cheese, spinach, lentils, and prosciutto in rows on a large square or rectangular serving platter.

⅔ cup dry brown lentils
1⅓ cups water
5 plum tomatoes, chopped (about 1¾ cups)
¾ cup finely shredded Parmesan cheese (3 ounces)
¾ cup finely shredded Asiago cheese (3 ounces)
2 cups baby fresh spinach leaves or torn fresh spinach

½ pound thinly sliced prosciutto or ham (about 12 slices)
⅓ cup vinegar
⅓ cup olive oil
2 tablespoons lemon juice
1 tablespoon Dijon-style mustard
2 teaspoons snipped fresh rosemary
¼ teaspoon salt
⅛ teaspoon pepper

1 Rinse lentils; place in a small saucepan with the water. Bring to boiling; reduce heat. Cover and simmer for 20 to 25 minutes or just until tender. Drain and chill for 1 to 2 hours or until thoroughly chilled.

2 Arrange the tomatoes, cheeses, spinach, cooked lentils, and prosciutto or ham on a large serving platter or in a serving dish.

3 For dressing, in a screw-top jar combine vinegar, olive oil, lemon juice, mustard, rosemary, salt, and pepper. Cover and shake well. Drizzle over salad. Makes 8 to 10 servings.

Nutrition Facts per serving: 340 calories, 23 g total fat (4 g saturated fat), 19 mg cholesterol, 869 mg sodium, 15 g carbohydrate, 1 g fiber, 20 g protein. Daily Values: 14% vit. A, 26% vit. C, 17% calcium, 16% iron.

cooks' round table revisited

The first edition of the *Better Homes and Gardens® New Cook Book,* in 1930, proclaimed the durable loose-leaf binder as the perfect place to keep "choice recipes" from *Better Homes and Gardens®* magazine. Purchasing the book allowed readers to become members of the Cooks' Round Table (the forerunner of the Prize Tested Recipes Contest), which enabled them to submit their recipes for endorsement by the magazine. By 1937, the pages featuring the selected recipes included holes to make it convenient to place them in the ringbound cookbook.

Santa Fe **Pork Pie**

Prep: 30 minutes **Bake:** 15 minutes

1995

Ellen Burr
Truro, MA

Cilantro, spices, and chile peppers give a Southwestern kick to Ellen's biscuit-topped pie. Round out the meal with sliced fresh fruit or a mixed greens salad drizzled with your favorite dressing.

3   medium potatoes (1 pound), peeled and cut into ½-inch cubes (about 3 cups)
1⅓ cups chicken broth
1   medium stalk celery, sliced (½ cup)
4   cloves garlic, minced
1   teaspoon chili powder
1   teaspoon ground cumin
1   teaspoon ground coriander
1   teaspoon dried oregano, crushed
1   teaspoon dried thyme, crushed
½   teaspoon celery salt
1   pound boneless pork loin, cut into 1-inch cubes
2   tablespoons cooking oil
1   4½-ounce can diced green chile peppers, drained
¼   cup snipped fresh cilantro
1   4½-ounce package (6) refrigerated biscuits

1 In a medium saucepan combine the potatoes, chicken broth, celery, and garlic. Bring to boiling; reduce heat. Cover and simmer for 8 minutes.

2 Meanwhile, for filling, in a medium bowl combine the chili powder, cumin, coriander, oregano, thyme, and celery salt. Add pork cubes; toss to coat. In a large skillet cook pork, half at a time, in hot oil for 4 to 5 minutes or until no pink remains. Drain off fat. Return all meat to skillet. Add potato mixture. Stir in chile peppers and cilantro. Bring to boiling.

3 Transfer hot mixture to a 2-quart casserole. Snip each biscuit into four pieces; arrange on top of hot mixture. Bake, uncovered, in a 425° oven about 15 minutes or until biscuits are golden brown. If necessary to prevent overbrowning, cover loosely with foil for the last 5 minutes of baking. Makes 6 servings.

Nutrition Facts per serving: 286 calories, 12 g total fat (3 g saturated fat), 34 mg cholesterol, 731 mg sodium, 31 g carbohydrate, 1 g fiber, 16 g protein. Daily Values: 2% vit. A, 22% vit. C, 5% calcium, 16% iron.

Spicy Pecan Pork

Prep: 15 minutes **Cook:** 6 minutes

¾	pound boneless pork loin	½	cup fine dry bread crumbs
1	egg	½	cup ground toasted pecans
1	egg white	⅓	cup all-purpose flour
2	to 3 tablespoons Dijon-style mustard	2	tablespoons cooking oil
½	teaspoon ground red pepper		Sliced fresh chile peppers (optional)*

1994

Lori Connors
Opelika, AL

Satisfy a craving for breaded pork tenderloin with this distinctive version. Dijon-style mustard and ground red pepper provide a pleasant spiciness; ground pecans add crunch to the bread crumb coating.

1 Cut pork loin crosswise into 4 equal slices. Place a meat slice between two sheets of plastic wrap; pound with the flat side of a meat mallet to ¼-inch thickness. Repeat with remaining meat slices. In a shallow dish beat together egg, egg white, mustard, and ground red pepper just until combined. In another dish stir together bread crumbs and pecans; place flour in a third dish.

2 Coat each pork slice with flour, dip in egg mixture, and finally in crumb mixture. In a 12-inch skillet heat oil over medium-high heat. Add pork slices. Cook for 6 to 8 minutes or until tender and just slightly pink, turning once. (If necessary, reduce heat to medium to avoid burning.) If desired, top each serving with sliced chile peppers. Makes 4 servings.

*Note: Because chile peppers contain volatile oils that can burn your skin and eyes, avoid direct contact with them as much as possible. When working with chile peppers, wear plastic or rubber gloves. If your bare hands do touch the chile peppers, wash your hands well with soap and water.

Nutrition Facts per serving: 375 calories, 23 g total fat (4 g saturated fat), 103 mg cholesterol, 374 mg sodium, 18 g carbohydrate, 2 g fiber, 24 g protein. Daily Values: 4% vit. A, 2% vit. C, 6% calcium, 13% iron.

Pork and **Green Chiles Casserole**

Prep: 25 minutes **Bake:** 25 minutes **Stand:** 3 minutes

1993

Betty Cornelison
Portland, OR

Diced green chile peppers
and a little salsa add spunk
to this hearty rice, bean,
and pork dish. It will receive
a top rating from those who
love Mexican food.

1¼ pounds lean boneless pork
 1 tablespoon cooking oil
 1 15-ounce can black beans or pinto
   beans, rinsed and drained
 1 14½-ounce can diced tomatoes
 1 10¾-ounce can condensed cream of
   chicken soup
 2 4½-ounce cans diced green chile
   peppers, drained

 1 cup quick-cooking brown rice
 ¼ cup water
 2 tablespoons salsa
 1 teaspoon ground cumin
 ½ cup shredded cheddar cheese
   (2 ounces)

1 Cut pork into thin bite-size strips. In a large skillet stir-fry pork, half at a time, in hot oil until no pink remains; drain. Return all meat to skillet. Stir in beans, tomatoes, soup, chile peppers, brown rice, water, salsa, and cumin. Heat and stir just until bubbly; pour into a 2-quart casserole.

2 Bake, uncovered, in a 375° oven for 25 minutes. Remove from oven. Sprinkle with cheese; let stand for 3 to 4 minutes to melt cheese. Makes 6 servings.

Nutrition Facts per serving: 350 calories, 14 g total fat (5 g saturated fat), 69 mg cholesterol, 1,242 mg sodium, 28 g carbohydrate, 5 g fiber, 30 g protein. Daily Values: 9% vit. A, 58% vit. C, 15% calcium, 14% iron.

mexican food goes mainstream

At one time, Americans thought Mexican food was exotic and assumed anything with a chile pepper in it was a true south-of-the-border dish. Over the years, Mexican and Tex-Mex eateries have sprung up all over the country, educating American palates to more authentic fare. Today, Mexican and Tex-Mex specialties are served everywhere—even in schools. Cooks have been quick to adapt the foods they enjoy at Mexican restaurants to their own kitchens. Their efforts have resulted in such recipes as Pork and Green Chiles Casserole, above, which is a family-pleasing casserole with Mexican accents. It was a winner in the 1993 Best-Ever Casseroles category of Prize Tested Recipes.

Holiday **Pork Roast**

Prep: 15 minutes **Marinate:** 6 to 24 hours **Roast:** 2 hours **Stand:** 15 minutes

1964

Mrs. James P. Kelly
Royal Oak, MI

Lean pork loin keeps this festive entrée low in calories and fat—a healthful way to celebrate the holidays.

2 tablespoons dry mustard
2 teaspoons dried thyme, crushed
1 4- to 5-pound boneless pork top loin roast (double loin, tied)
¼ cup dry sherry
¼ cup soy sauce

2 cloves garlic, minced
1 tablespoon grated fresh ginger or
    1 teaspoon ground ginger
½ cup currant jelly
1 tablespoon dry sherry
2 teaspoons soy sauce

1 Combine dry mustard and thyme; rub on all sides of roast. Place meat in a plastic bag set in a deep bowl. Combine the ¼ cup sherry, the ¼ cup soy sauce, the garlic, and ginger; pour over meat. Seal bag and marinate in refrigerator for at least 6 hours or up to 24 hours, turning occasionally.

2 Remove meat from marinade; discard marinade. Place meat on rack in a shallow roasting pan. Insert a meat thermometer in center of roast. Roast, uncovered, in a 325° oven for 2 to 2½ hours or until meat thermometer registers 155°. Cover roast and let stand 15 minutes. Temperature of meat will rise 5° during standing.

3 Meanwhile, in a small saucepan melt the currant jelly; add the 1 tablespoon sherry and the 2 teaspoons soy sauce, stirring until smooth. Spoon a little of the jelly mixture over each serving of meat. Makes 10 to 12 servings.

Nutrition Facts per serving: 311 calories, 10 g total fat (3 g saturated fat), 106 mg cholesterol, 235 mg sodium, 11 g carbohydrate, 0 g fiber, 40 g protein. Daily Values: 1% vit. A, 2% vit. C, 4% calcium, 10% iron.

white house winners

An intriguing way to see how tastes have changed over the last century is to take a look at main-dish favorites of American presidents. Theodore Roosevelt pined for roast suckling pig. Warren Harding favored roast filet mignon. Franklin Roosevelt was partial to boiled salmon with egg sauce. Meat loaf and tuna noodle casserole were Harry Truman's top choices. Beef stroganoff was a favorite of John Kennedy. Lyndon Johnson opted for chili. Ronald Reagan requested broiled swordfish with lemon butter. Bill Clinton often asked for chicken enchiladas.

Feta-Stuffed Pita Burgers

Prep: 15 minutes **Grill:** 15 minutes

2 tablespoons milk
2 tablespoons cornmeal
1 tablespoon finely chopped onion
1 clove garlic, minced
¼ teaspoon salt
¼ teaspoon dried oregano, crushed
¼ teaspoon ground cumin

⅛ teaspoon ground red pepper
⅛ teaspoon lemon-pepper seasoning
½ pound lean ground lamb
½ pound lean ground beef
¼ cup finely crumbled feta cheese
2 large pita bread rounds, split
1½ cups shredded fresh spinach

1990

Ellen Burr
Truro, MA

For a tasty flavor combo,
Ellen uses both ground lamb
and ground beef in these
juicy grilled burgers.
Seasonings such as red
pepper, lemon-pepper,
cumin, and oregano add
a burst of flavor.

1 In a medium bowl combine the milk, cornmeal, onion, garlic, salt, oregano, cumin, red pepper, and lemon-pepper seasoning. Add meats; mix well. Shape into 8 oval patties, each about ¼ inch thick. Place 1 tablespoon feta in center of each of 4 of the ovals. Top with remaining ovals; press edges to seal. Reshape patties as necessary.

2 Grill patties on the rack of an uncovered grill directly over medium-hot coals for 7 minutes. Turn and grill for 8 to 10 minutes more or until no pink remains; serve in pitas with shredded spinach. Makes 4 servings.

Nutrition Facts per serving: 345 calories, 17 g total fat (7 g saturated fat), 80 mg cholesterol, 493 mg sodium, 22 g carbohydrate,1 g fiber, 25 g protein. Daily Values: 9% vit. A, 6% vit. C, 10% calcium, 17% iron.

Herb-Roasted Lamb with Black Beans

Prep: 20 minutes **Roast:** 2½ hours

Ellen Burr
Truro, MA

Garlic, lime, and a homemade herb rub flavor the lamb as it roasts. Then, it's served with a savory black bean sauce enticingly seasoned with green chile peppers, onion, fresh cilantro, and a touch of red wine vinegar.

1 5- to 6-pound bone-in leg of lamb
2 cloves garlic, peeled and sliced
1 medium lime
1 recipe Herb Rub
1 large onion, chopped (1 cup)
2 15-ounce cans black beans, rinsed and drained

1 4½-ounce can diced green chile peppers, rinsed and drained
1 4-ounce jar chopped pimiento, drained
¼ cup snipped fresh cilantro
1 tablespoon red wine vinegar

1 Remove fell (paper-thin, pinkish-red layer) from lamb; discard. Trim fat from lamb. Cut slits in meat; insert garlic slices in slits. Drizzle meat with lime juice; rub with Herb Rub. Place on a rack in a roasting pan. Insert a meat thermometer without touching bone. Roast in a 325° oven for 2½ to 3 hours or until thermometer registers 140° for medium-rare or 155° for medium. Transfer meat to a serving platter; keep warm while preparing black bean sauce.

2 For black bean sauce, skim fat from meat juices. In a large saucepan combine 2 tablespoons of the meat juices and the onion; cook until tender. Stir in beans, chile peppers, pimiento, cilantro, and vinegar. Bring to boiling; reduce heat. Cook for 5 minutes. Serve with lamb. Makes 10 to 12 servings.

Herb Rub: In a small bowl stir together 1 teaspoon dried oregano, crushed; 1 teaspoon ground coriander; ½ teaspoon dried thyme, crushed; ½ teaspoon ground cumin; ½ teaspoon chili powder; and ¼ teaspoon salt.

Nutrition Facts per serving: 242 calories, 8 g total fat (3 g saturated fat), 80 mg cholesterol, 362 mg sodium, 15 g carbohydrate, 4 g fiber, 32 g protein. Daily Values: 3% vit. A, 26% vit. C, 5% calcium, 22% iron.

Spicy **Grilled Lamb**

Prep: 15 minutes **Marinate:** Overnight **Grill:** 50 minutes **Stand:** 15 minutes

1983

Nina Bruner
Merritt Island, FL

Glazed carrots and baked potatoes are ideal accompaniments for this mustard-and-herb-marinated entrée.

- 1 3½- to 4-pound boneless leg of lamb, butterflied
- 1 8-ounce jar (1 cup) Dijon-style mustard
- ¼ cup olive oil
- 2 tablespoons dry red wine
- 2 cloves garlic, minced
- 1 teaspoon dried rosemary, crushed
- 1 teaspoon dried basil, crushed
- ½ teaspoon dried oregano, crushed
- ½ teaspoon dried thyme, crushed
- ¼ teaspoon pepper

1 Remove fell (paper-thin, pinkish-red layer) from lamb; discard. Trim fat from lamb. Using the flat side of a meat mallet, pound lamb to an even thickness (1½ to 2 inches thick).

2 In a small bowl combine mustard, olive oil, red wine, garlic, rosemary, basil, oregano, thyme, and pepper. Place lamb in a shallow dish. Spread ½ cup of the mustard mixture over both sides of lamb; cover and chill remaining mustard mixture. Cover; marinate lamb overnight in refrigerator.

3 Drain meat; discard the marinade. To keep the meat from curling during grilling, insert a long metal skewer through the meat at a diagonal; insert another long metal skewer through the meat at a diagonal, forming an "x" with the first skewer.

4 In a grill with a cover arrange medium coals around drip pan. Test for medium-low heat above the pan. Insert a meat thermometer into center of lamb. Place lamb, fat side up, on grill rack over the drip pan. Cover and grill for 50 to 60 minutes or until thermometer registers 140°. Let stand for 15 minutes before serving; remove skewers. To serve, in a small saucepan heat reserved mustard mixture; spoon mustard mixture evenly over meat. Makes 12 servings.

Nutrition Facts per serving: 229 calories, 11 g total fat (2 g saturated fat), 84 mg cholesterol, 175 mg sodium, 3 g carbohydrate, 0 g fiber, 29 g protein. Daily Values: 1% vit. C, 4% calcium, 17% iron.

Chicken Marinara with Mushrooms

Start to finish: 20 minutes

- 12 ounces dried linguine or spaghetti
- 4 cloves garlic, minced
- 2 tablespoons lower-fat margarine
- 1 pound skinless, boneless chicken breast halves, cut into thin bite-size strips
- ½ teaspoon dried chervil, crushed
- ½ teaspoon dried basil, crushed
- ¼ teaspoon dried thyme, crushed
- 6 ounces fresh mushrooms, sliced
- 1 27½-ounce jar light spaghetti sauce
- ½ cup dry white wine
- 2 teaspoons sugar (optional)

*Kim Harris
Columbus, OH*

For full-bodied mushroom flavor, make Kim's zesty marinara sauce with a mixture of wild mushrooms, such as shiitake, crimini, and porcini.

1 Cook pasta according to package directions; drain and keep warm. Meanwhile, in a large skillet cook garlic in hot margarine for 30 seconds. Add half of the chicken and half of each of the herbs. Cook and stir for 3 to 4 minutes or until chicken is no longer pink. Remove chicken, reserving drippings in skillet. Repeat with the remaining chicken and herbs.

2 Add mushrooms to drippings in skillet. Cook and stir about 3 minutes or until tender. Add spaghetti sauce, wine, and, if desired, sugar. Return chicken to skillet; heat through. Serve over the hot pasta. Makes 6 servings.

Nutrition Facts per serving: 426 calories, 7 g fat (1 g saturated fat), 40 mg cholesterol, 128 mg sodium, 64 g carbohydrate, 4 g fiber, 25 g protein. Daily Values: 14% vit. A, 23% vit. C, 3 % calcium, 26% iron.

Italian Chicken and Artichokes

Prep: 35 minutes **Cook:** 40 minutes

1 large onion, chopped (1 cup)
1 cup sliced fresh mushrooms
¼ cup chopped green sweet pepper
¼ cup chopped carrot
1 clove garlic, minced
3 tablespoons olive oil or cooking oil
¼ cup all-purpose flour
½ teaspoon salt
¼ teaspoon ground black pepper
2 pounds meaty chicken pieces
    (breasts, thighs, and drumsticks),
    skinned

1 14½- or 16-ounce can stewed
    tomatoes, undrained
1 9-ounce package frozen artichoke
    hearts, cut up, or one 14-ounce
    can artichoke hearts, drained and
    quartered
1 8-ounce can tomato sauce
½ cup dry white wine
1 teaspoon dried Italian seasoning,
    crushed
    Hot cooked fettuccine or rice

*Marianne Young
Rochester, NY*

The flavors of classic Italian ingredients—olive oil, garlic, tomatoes, and wine—blend well in this hearty chicken dish. Serve it over a mound of hot cooked pasta or rice.

1 In a 12-inch skillet cook onion, mushrooms, sweet pepper, carrot, and garlic in 1 tablespoon of the oil until tender. Remove vegetables from skillet; set aside.

2 In a plastic bag combine flour, salt, and black pepper. Add chicken pieces, a few at a time, shaking to coat. Brown chicken in remaining hot oil over medium heat for 10 minutes, turning occasionally (sprinkle any remaining flour mixture over chicken before browning). Drain off fat.

3 Return vegetables to skillet; add undrained tomatoes, artichoke hearts, tomato sauce, wine, and Italian seasoning. Bring to boiling; reduce heat. Cover and simmer for 35 to 40 minutes or until chicken is tender and no longer pink, stirring once or twice. Transfer chicken to platter; keep warm. Boil sauce gently, uncovered, about 5 minutes or until desired consistency. Serve chicken and sauce over hot cooked pasta or rice. Makes 6 servings.

Nutrition Facts per serving: 508 calories, 14 g total fat (2 g saturated fat), 61 mg cholesterol, 593 mg sodium, 62 g carbohydrate, 6 g fiber, 31 g protein. Daily Values: 21% vit. A, 21% vit. C, 27% calcium, 23% iron.

Plum Wonderful Chicken

Prep: 35 minutes **Bake:** 40 minutes

Norma J. Keleher
Pacific Grove, CA

Frozen lemonade concentrate and plum sauce are Norma's secrets to this glaze's tantalizing sweet-sour flavor.

2 tablespoons olive oil or cooking oil
2½ to 3 pounds meaty chicken pieces, skinned
¼ cup chopped onion
1 clove garlic, minced
1 teaspoon grated fresh ginger
⅓ cup bottled plum sauce (half of an 8½-ounce jar)

¼ cup frozen lemonade concentrate
¼ cup bottled chili sauce
2 tablespoons soy sauce
1 tablespoon lemon juice
1 teaspoon dry mustard
  Sesame seed (optional)
  Thinly sliced green onion (optional)

1 In a skillet heat oil over medium heat. Add chicken and cook about 10 minutes or until browned on all sides, turning often to brown evenly. Remove chicken; place in a 3-quart rectangular baking dish. Drain drippings from skillet, reserving 1 tablespoon drippings in skillet. Add the onion, garlic, and ginger. Cook until onion is tender.

2 For sauce, in a small bowl stir together the plum sauce, lemonade concentrate, chili sauce, soy sauce, lemon juice, and dry mustard; carefully stir into onion mixture. Bring to boiling; reduce heat. Cover and simmer for 5 minutes; spoon sauce over chicken in dish. Bake, uncovered, in a 350° oven for 40 to 45 minutes or until chicken is tender and no longer pink, spooning sauce over chicken occasionally. To serve, if desired, sprinkle with sesame seed and green onion. Makes 6 servings.

Nutrition Facts per serving: 239 calories, 9 g total fat (2 g saturated fat), 77 mg cholesterol, 556 mg sodium, 14 g carbohydrate, 0 g fiber, 26 g protein. Daily Values: 3% vit. A, 9% vit. C, 1% calcium, 8% iron.

Chicken à la Maria

Prep: 15 minutes **Bake:** 30 minutes

1 10-ounce package frozen chopped spinach, thawed	2 tablespoons all-purpose flour
8 medium skinless, boneless chicken breast halves (about 2 pounds)	¼ teaspoon salt
Salt	¼ teaspoon ground white pepper
Ground white pepper	1 cup milk
½ cup sliced green onions	¼ pound cooked ham, diced
2 tablespoons butter or margarine	3 tablespoons seasoned fine dry bread crumbs
	1 tablespoon grated Parmesan cheese

1 Drain thawed spinach well, pressing out excess liquid; set aside. Season chicken lightly with salt and white pepper. Arrange in a 3-quart rectangular baking dish. In a saucepan cook green onions in hot butter or margarine until tender. Stir in flour, the ¼ teaspoon salt, and the ¼ teaspoon white pepper; stir in milk all at once. Cook and stir until thickened and bubbly. Stir in spinach and ham.

2 Spoon spinach mixture over chicken. In a small bowl combine bread crumbs and Parmesan cheese; sprinkle over chicken and spinach mixture. Bake, uncovered, in a 350° oven for 30 to 35 minutes or until chicken is tender and no longer pink. Makes 8 servings.

Nutrition Facts per serving: 226 calories, 7 g total fat (3 g saturated fat), 85 mg cholesterol, 492 mg sodium, 7 g carbohydrate, 1 g fiber, 32 g protein. Daily Values: 33% vit. A, 19% vit. C, 11% calcium, 10% iron.

1981

Mrs. John Coder
Timonium, MD

Ham and spinach in a creamy sauce complement tender chicken breasts in this elegant entrée. It can be easily halved; just bake it in a 2-quart square baking dish.

kitchen-duty shortcuts

In Grandma's day, a recipe that called for skinless, boneless chicken breast halves, such as Chicken à la Maria, above, would have been frowned upon. It would have meant skinning and boning the breasts of four chickens by hand. Over the last 25 years, the appearance of work-saving ingredients, such as chicken pieces, shredded cheeses, cut-up vegetables, and torn salad greens, have greatly altered cooking methods. Now more elaborate dishes can be brought to the table in minutes rather than hours.

Chicken-Artichoke **Turnovers**

Prep: 30 minutes **Bake:** 25 minutes

Carmela M. Meely
Walnut Creek, CA

Next time you grill or broil chicken, make extra so you'll have enough leftover for these plump poultry turnovers filled with cheese, artichokes, and green chile peppers. Frozen patty shells make them easy to prepare.

1 10-ounce package (6) frozen patty shells
¼ cup light dairy sour cream
1 to 1½ teaspoons chili powder
2 cloves garlic, minced
1 teaspoon lemon juice
1½ cups chopped cooked chicken
¾ cup shredded Monterey Jack cheese (3 ounces)
¾ cup coarsely chopped, drained artichoke hearts (half of a 14-ounce can)
1 4½-ounce can diced green chile peppers, drained
2 green onions, thinly sliced
1 tablespoon snipped fresh parsley
Milk

1 Thaw patty shells; set aside. For filling, in a medium bowl stir together sour cream, chili powder, garlic, and lemon juice. Stir in chicken, Monterey Jack cheese, artichoke hearts, chile peppers, green onions, and parsley.

2 On a lightly floured surface roll each patty shell into a 7-inch circle. Place about ½ cup filling on half of each circle. For each turnover, moisten edge of circle with water; fold other half of circle over filling. Press with tines of a fork to seal.

3 Line a baking sheet with foil; place turnovers on baking sheet. Cut slits in the top of each turnover for steam to escape. Brush tops with milk. Bake in a 400° oven for 25 to 30 minutes or until golden brown. Makes 6 turnovers.

Nutrition Facts per turnover: 367 calories, 23 g total fat (4 g saturated fat), 48 mg cholesterol, 378 mg sodium, 22 g carbohydrate, 1 g fiber, 18 g protein. Daily Values: 8% vit. A, 17% vit. C, 13% calcium, 7% iron.

Funky **Chicken**

Prep: 10 minutes **Bake:** 35 minutes

1980

Karen G. Love
Wichita, KS

Minimal ingredients make this main dish a winner when you're in a hurry and need something fast. Serve it with rice pilaf and steamed broccoli or asparagus.

2 pounds frozen fried chicken
 Garlic powder
1 cup apricot preserves

1 medium onion, chopped (½ cup)
½ cup bottled barbecue sauce
2 tablespoons soy sauce

1 Arrange frozen chicken in a single layer in an ungreased 13×9×2-inch baking pan. Sprinkle chicken lightly with garlic powder. Bake, uncovered, in a 375° oven for 15 minutes.

2 Meanwhile, in a small bowl combine the apricot preserves, onion, barbecue sauce, and soy sauce. Spoon over chicken. Bake, uncovered, for 20 to 25 minutes more or until chicken is heated through. Makes 6 servings.

Nutrition Facts per serving: 408 calories, 20 g total fat (5 g saturated fat), 117 mg cholesterol, 1,240 mg sodium, 38 g carbohydrate, 2 g fiber, 23 g protein. Daily Values: 3% vit. A, 10% vit. C, 4% calcium, 7% iron.

beat-the-clock recipes

In the late 1970s, everyone was in a time crunch. They were so busy they no longer had time to prepare meals in traditional ways and wanted great-tasting recipes that took only minutes. Responding to this need, *Better Homes and Gardens*® magazine sponsored the Busy People's Recipe Contest, asking readers for the recipes they cooked when they were caught in a race against time. After combing thousands of entries and conducting intensive tast-testing, the judges selected 28 prizewinners. Funky Chicken, above, which won 8th place, was published along with the other winners in the April 1980 issue.

Basil Chicken in Coconut Sauce

Start to finish: 50 minutes

4 medium skinless, boneless chicken
    breast halves (about 1 pound), cut
    into 1-inch pieces
½ teaspoon salt
½ teaspoon ground cardamom
½ teaspoon ground cinnamon
½ teaspoon ground cloves
½ teaspoon ground coriander
½ teaspoon ground cumin
½ teaspoon cracked black pepper
¼ teaspoon ground turmeric
¼ teaspoon chili powder
1 large red onion, chopped (1 cup)

5 cloves garlic, minced
2 fresh jalapeño peppers, seeded and
    finely chopped*
1 tablespoon olive oil
1 13½- or 14-ounce can unsweetened
    coconut milk
2 teaspoons cornstarch
3 tablespoons snipped fresh basil
1 tablespoon finely chopped fresh
    ginger
  Hot cooked rice
  Fresh basil leaves (optional)

1997

Neeraja Narayanan
New York City, NY

Neeraja has no trouble producing big flavors in her tiny Manhattan kitchen. Her spectacular curry sauce fuses tastes from India, where she grew up, with those from Thailand. It was declared the 1997 grand prize winner of the year.

1 Place chicken in a medium bowl. In a small bowl stir together the salt, cardamom, cinnamon, cloves, coriander, cumin, cracked pepper, turmeric, and chili powder. Sprinkle spice mixture over chicken, tossing to coat. Cover and let stand at room temperature for 30 minutes. (Or, cover and chill for 1 to 2 hours.)

2 In a large nonstick wok or skillet cook and stir the onion, garlic, and jalapeño peppers in hot oil over medium-high heat for 2 minutes. Remove onion mixture from wok or skillet. Add half of the chicken to wok or skillet. Cook and stir for 2 to 3 minutes or until chicken is tender and no longer pink. Remove chicken from the wok. (If necessary, add additional oil.) Cook and remove the remaining chicken as above.

3 In a small bowl stir together coconut milk and cornstarch. Carefully add to wok or skillet. Cook and stir until bubbly. Return the chicken and onion mixture to wok. Stir in snipped basil and ginger. Cook and stir about 2 minutes more or until heated through. Serve over rice. If desired, garnish with basil leaves. Makes 4 servings.

*Note: Because chile peppers, such as jalapeños, contain volatile oils that can burn your skin and eyes, avoid direct contact with them as much as possible. When working with chile peppers, wear plastic or rubber gloves. If your bare hands do touch the chile peppers, wash your hands well with soap and water.

Nutrition Facts per serving: 361 calories, 25 g total fat (17 g saturated fat), 59 mg cholesterol, 350 mg sodium, 11 g carbohydrate, 1 g fiber, 24 g protein. Daily Values: 1% vit. A, 24% vit. C, 3% calcium, 17% iron.

Grecian-Style Chicken

Start to finish: 30 minutes

¼ cup toasted wheat germ or fine dry bread crumbs

4 medium skinless, boneless chicken breast halves (about 1 pound)

2 tablespoons olive oil or cooking oil

1 small zucchini, halved lengthwise and sliced (1 cup)

½ of a medium green sweet pepper, chopped

½ of a medium onion, sliced and separated into rings

2 cloves garlic, minced

⅛ teaspoon salt
Dash ground black pepper

2 medium tomatoes, cut into wedges

2 tablespoons water

4 teaspoons lime juice or lemon juice

3 cups hot cooked orzo, couscous, or rice

½ cup crumbled feta cheese (2 ounces)

Georgia L. Olin
Columbia, MO

Accented with olive oil, garlic, tomatoes, and feta cheese, this Mediterranean-style main dish takes only 30 minutes to make.

1 Place wheat germ or bread crumbs in a shallow bowl; coat chicken with the wheat germ or bread crumbs. In a large skillet heat 1 tablespoon of the oil over medium heat; add chicken and cook for 10 to 12 minutes or until tender and no longer pink, turning once. Remove chicken from skillet; keep warm.

2 In same skillet heat remaining oil; add zucchini, sweet pepper, onion, garlic, salt, and black pepper and cook for 3 minutes. Add tomato wedges, water, and lime or lemon juice; cook for 1 minute more. Remove from heat.

3 To serve, divide orzo, couscous, or rice among four dinner plates. Spoon vegetable mixture over; place chicken on top of vegetables. Sprinkle feta cheese over chicken. Makes 4 servings.

Nutrition Facts per serving: 418 calories, 13 g total fat (4 g saturated fat), 78 mg cholesterol, 299 mg sodium, 38 g carbohydrate, 4 g fiber, 36 g protein. Daily Values: 8% vit. A, 46% vit. C, 11% calcium, 19% iron.

Thai Chicken and Nectarine Salad

Start to finish: 40 minutes

1989

Patricia Burgess
Ocean Isle Beach, NC

A peppery-sweet dressing provides the crowning touch to this pasta salad entrée. Warmed crusty French rolls are all you need to add.

¼ cup reduced-sodium chicken broth
3 tablespoons reduced-sodium soy sauce
2 tablespoons bottled hoisin sauce
1 tablespoon sugar
1 tablespoon salad oil or olive oil
2 teaspoons toasted sesame oil
3 cloves garlic, minced
1½ teaspoons grated fresh ginger

1 teaspoon crushed red pepper
⅛ teaspoon ground black pepper
¾ pound skinless, boneless chicken breast halves
4 ounces dried angel hair pasta
3 medium nectarines, plums, or peeled peaches, pitted and sliced
2 cups shredded bok choy
2 green onions, thinly sliced

1 For dressing, in a screw-top jar combine broth, soy sauce, hoisin sauce, sugar, salad or olive oil, sesame oil, garlic, ginger, crushed red pepper, and black pepper. Cover; shake well. Set aside.

2 In a large skillet cook chicken, covered, in a small amount of boiling water for 12 to 15 minutes or until tender and no longer pink; drain. Cool slightly; cut into cubes. Cook pasta according to package directions; drain.

3 In a large bowl toss pasta with 3 tablespoons of the dressing. Divide pasta mixture among four dinner plates. Top with the chicken, fruit, bok choy, and green onions. Drizzle with remaining dressing. Makes 4 servings.

Nutrition Facts per serving: 359 calories, 9 g total fat (2 g saturated fat), 45 mg cholesterol, 644 mg sodium, 46 g carbohydrate, 2 g fiber, 23 g protein. Daily Values: 17% vit. A, 29% vit. C, 4% calcium, 15% iron.

Peanut-Ginger Chicken with California Salsa

Prep: 30 minutes **Marinate:** 12 to 24 hours **Grill:** 35 minutes

½ cup boiling water
½ cup creamy peanut butter
¼ cup bottled chili sauce
3 tablespoons soy sauce
2 tablespoons cooking oil
2 tablespoons vinegar
4 cloves garlic, minced
1 tablespoon grated fresh ginger or
⠀⠀¾ teaspoon ground ginger
¼ teaspoon ground red pepper
12 chicken thighs (about 3 pounds),
⠀⠀skinned

1 cup chopped, peeled fresh fruit
⠀⠀(such as peaches, nectarines,
⠀⠀pears, or plums)
1 cup chopped, seeded cucumber
2 tablespoons thinly sliced green onion
2 tablespoons snipped fresh parsley or
⠀⠀fresh cilantro
1 tablespoon sugar
1 tablespoon cooking oil
1 tablespoon vinegar
⠀⠀Ti leaves (optional)*
⠀⠀Fresh peach, nectarine, pear, or plum
⠀⠀wedges (optional)

1992

Leisla Sansom
Alexandria, VA

"The fruity cucumber salsa and gingery chicken remind me of the delicious spice combinations used on faraway tropical islands," says Leisla. Her extra-special grilled chicken won top prize in the June 1992 Barbecue Contest.

1 For marinade, in a small bowl gradually stir the boiling water into peanut butter. (The mixture will stiffen at first.) Stir in chili sauce, soy sauce, the 2 tablespoons oil, the 2 tablespoons vinegar, the garlic, ginger, and ground red pepper; cool.

2 Place the chicken in a plastic bag set in a shallow bowl. Pour marinade over chicken. Seal the bag; turn to coat chicken thighs with marinade. Marinate in refrigerator for at least 12 hours or up to 24 hours, turning the bag occasionally.

3 For California salsa, in a medium bowl combine chopped fruit, cucumber, green onion, parsley or cilantro, sugar, the 1 tablespoon oil, and the 1 tablespoon vinegar. Cover and chill for 1 to 2 hours.

4 In a grill with a cover arrange medium-hot coals around drip pan. Test for medium heat above the pan. Remove chicken from marinade; discard marinade. Place chicken on the grill rack over drip pan. Cover and grill for 35 to 45 minutes or until tender and no longer pink.

5 If desired, serve chicken on ti leaves. If desired, garnish with fruit wedges. Spoon some of the California salsa over chicken; pass remaining salsa. Makes 6 servings.

*Note: If using ti leaves, be sure they have not been sprayed or treated in a way that would make them unsafe for contact with food. Wash them well first, as you would any other produce.

Nutrition Facts per serving: 290 calories, 15 g total fat (3 g saturated fat), 91 mg cholesterol, 426 mg sodium, 13 g carbohydrate, 2 g fiber, 27 g protein. Daily Values: 7% vit. A, 18% vit. C, 3% calcium, 9% iron.

Creamy Turkey Pie

Prep: 25 minutes **Bake:** 30 minutes **Stand:** 5 minutes

1993

David L. Huston
Waukegan, IL

This toothsome turkey-and-mushroom pie sports a tender biscuit crust and a rich cottage cheese topper. If you can't find bulk turkey sausage at your local supermarket, buy uncooked ground turkey and add your own seasonings.

1 pound bulk turkey sausage or uncooked ground turkey*
1 medium onion, chopped (½ cup)
1 3-ounce package cream cheese, cubed
1 4½-ounce jar sliced mushrooms, drained
1 7½-ounce package (10) refrigerated biscuits
1 egg
1 cup cream-style cottage cheese
1 tablespoon all-purpose flour
  Chopped tomato (optional)
  Snipped fresh chives (optional)

1 In a large skillet cook turkey sausage or ground turkey and onion until meat is browned. Drain off fat. Stir in cream cheese until melted; stir in mushrooms. Cover and keep warm.

2 For crust, lightly grease a 9-inch deep-dish pie plate. Arrange biscuits in pie plate, pressing together onto the bottom and up sides to form an even crust. Spoon turkey mixture into crust, spreading evenly.

3 In a blender container or food processor bowl combine egg, cottage cheese, and flour. Cover and blend or process until smooth. Spread evenly over turkey mixture. Bake, uncovered, in a 350° oven about 30 minutes or until edge is browned and top is set. Let stand for 5 to 10 minutes before serving. If desired, garnish with chopped tomato and snipped chives. Makes 6 servings.

*Note: If using ground turkey, add ¼ teaspoon salt; ¼ teaspoon dried sage, crushed; and ¼ teaspoon pepper to meat mixture.

Nutrition Facts per serving: 420 calories, 24 g total fat (10 g saturated fat), 85 mg cholesterol, 1,406 mg sodium, 26 g carbohydrate, 2 g fiber, 26 g protein. Daily Values: 9% vit. A, 1% vit. C, 6% calcium, 17% iron.

Roasted Potato and Turkey Salad

Prep: 30 minutes **Bake:** 45 minutes

Amy Loucks
Cambridge, MA

This stick-to-the-ribs salad can easily be made ahead. Roast the potatoes, cook the bacon, and whisk the dressing in advance; refrigerate, then arrange the salad just before serving.

12 whole tiny new potatoes
(about 1 pound)
2 tablespoons olive oil
½ teaspoon salt
½ teaspoon pepper
⅓ cup olive oil
2 tablespoons Dijon-style mustard
4 cloves garlic, minced
½ teaspoon pepper

1 pound cooked turkey, cut into bite-size strips (3 cups)
4 slices bacon or turkey bacon, crisp-cooked, drained, and crumbled
1 small red onion, sliced and separated into rings
¼ cup snipped fresh Italian parsley
6 cups torn mixed greens (such as romaine, spinach, and leaf lettuce)

1 Scrub potatoes; prick each potato 2 or 3 times with a fork. Place potatoes in a shallow baking pan; drizzle with the 2 tablespoons olive oil. Sprinkle with the salt and ½ teaspoon pepper. Bake in a 400° oven about 45 minutes or until potatoes are tender, stirring twice. Cool completely. Cut cooled potatoes into quarters.

2 For dressing, in a small bowl whisk together the ⅓ cup olive oil, the mustard, garlic, and ½ teaspoon pepper.

3 In a large bowl combine the potatoes, turkey, bacon, red onion, and Italian parsley. Add the dressing, tossing gently to coat. Arrange the mixed greens on six dinner plates; spoon turkey mixture over greens. Makes 6 servings.

Nutrition Facts per serving: 359 calories, 20 g total fat (3 g saturated fat), 63 mg cholesterol, 422 mg sodium, 20 g carbohydrate, 2 g fiber, 26 g protein. Daily Values: 10% vit. A, 39% vit. C, 4% calcium, 20% iron.

Turkey Tamale Casserole

Prep: 20 minutes **Bake:** 27 minutes **Stand:** 5 minutes

1 pound uncooked ground turkey	1 cup chicken broth or water
2 cloves garlic, minced	1 2¼-ounce can sliced pitted ripe
1 15- to 17-ounce can cream-style corn	olives, drained
1 10½-ounce can chili without beans	1 cup shredded cheddar cheese
2 teaspoons dried oregano, crushed	(4 ounces)
½ teaspoon ground cumin	Dairy sour cream (optional)
¼ teaspoon salt	Thinly sliced green onion (optional)
8 6-inch corn tortillas	

Rose Tirey
Auburn, CA

Classic tamales, generally very time-consuming to make, get revised for busy cooks. This one-dish casserole only takes 20 minutes to make and about 25 minutes to bake.

1 In a large skillet cook turkey and garlic over medium heat until turkey is no longer pink. Drain off fat. Stir in corn, chili, oregano, cumin, and salt. Bring to boiling; reduce heat. Cover and simmer for 5 minutes. Remove from heat. Set aside.

2 Stack the tortillas; cut into 6 wedges. Place the wedges in a medium bowl; add broth or water. Let stand for 1 minute. Drain, reserving ¼ cup liquid. Stir the reserved liquid and the olives into turkey mixture. In a 2-quart rectangular baking dish layer 2 cups of the turkey mixture and half of the tortilla wedges; repeat layers. Top with remaining turkey mixture, spreading to cover tortilla wedges.

3 Bake, uncovered, in a 350° oven about 25 minutes or until heated through. Top with cheese; bake for 2 minutes more. Let stand for 5 minutes before serving. If desired, top each serving with sour cream and green onion. Makes 6 to 8 servings.

Nutrition Facts per serving: 416 calories, 21 g total fat (7 g saturated fat), 64 mg cholesterol, 988 mg sodium, 37 g carbohydrate, 2 g fiber, 24 g protein. Daily Values: 17% vit. A, 9% vit. C, 21% calcium, 23% iron.

Pecan Salmon with Sweet Pepper Mayo

Prep: 25 minutes **Chill:** 30 minutes **Cook:** 6 minutes

Devon Delaney
Princeton, NJ

Devon stirs mango chutney and roasted sweet peppers into mayonnaise to create a delectable topping for salmon that's cooked to moist, tender perfection.

1½ pounds fresh or frozen skinless salmon fillet
¾ cup finely chopped pecans
½ cup fine dry bread crumbs
½ to 1 teaspoon ground black pepper
½ teaspoon salt
1 egg
2 tablespoons water
⅓ cup all-purpose flour

½ of a 7-ounce jar roasted red sweet peppers (about ½ cup), drained
¼ cup mayonnaise or salad dressing
1 tablespoon mango chutney, finely chopped
1 tablespoon lemon juice
¼ teaspoon garlic salt
⅛ teaspoon ground red pepper
2 tablespoons cooking oil

1 Thaw fish, if frozen. Rinse fish; pat dry with paper towels. Slice fish in half horizontally so that it is of nearly an even thickness (about ½ inch thick). Cut fish into 6 equal portions.

2 In a shallow dish combine pecans, bread crumbs, black pepper, and salt. In another dish beat together egg and water; place flour in a third dish. Coat each fish portion with flour, dip in egg mixture, and finally in pecan mixture. Place portions on a large plate; cover and chill for up to 30 minutes while preparing mayonnaise mixture.

3 For mayonnaise mixture, pat the drained, roasted red sweet peppers dry on paper towels; coarsely chop. In a small serving bowl stir together chopped peppers, mayonnaise or salad dressing, chutney, lemon juice, garlic salt, and ground red pepper. Set aside.

4 In a 12-inch nonstick skillet heat oil over medium-high heat. Add fish; cook for 3 minutes. Turn fish; cook for 3 to 4 minutes more or until fish flakes easily when tested with a fork. (Reduce heat as necessary during cooking to prevent overbrowning.) Serve with mayonnaise mixture. Makes 6 servings.

Nutrition Facts per serving: 379 calories, 26 g total fat (4 g saturated fat), 61 mg cholesterol, 457 mg sodium, 17 g carbohydrate, 2 g fiber, 20 g protein. Daily Values: 11% vit. A, 59% vit. C, 2% calcium, 13% iron.

Scallops and Shrimp with Linguine

Start to finish: 35 minutes

Theresa Smith
Tinley Park, IL

Elegant, yet simple to make, this deftly seasoned dish combines seafood with vegetables and pasta. (Pictured on page 88.)

1 pound fresh or frozen sea scallops
½ pound fresh or frozen medium shrimp in shells
¼ teaspoon crushed red pepper
2 cups fresh pea pods or one 6-ounce package frozen pea pods
10 ounces dried linguine
2 tablespoons olive oil or cooking oil
2 tablespoons butter or margarine
½ cup sliced green onions
3 cloves garlic, minced

2 tablespoons snipped fresh parsley or 2 teaspoons dried parsley
1 tablespoon snipped fresh basil or 1 teaspoon dried basil, crushed
¼ cup oil-pack dried tomatoes, drained and chopped, or 1 small tomato, seeded and chopped
3 tablespoons shaved Parmesan cheese or Romano cheese (optional)
Fresh basil (optional)

1 Thaw scallops and shrimp, if frozen. Cut scallops in half. Peel and devein shrimp. In a medium bowl combine scallops, shrimp, and crushed red pepper; set aside.

2 Thaw pea pods, if frozen. Cut pea pods in half; set aside. Cook pasta according to package directions; drain and return hot pasta to saucepan.

3 Meanwhile, in a large skillet heat oil and butter or margarine over medium-high heat. Add green onions and garlic; cook for 30 seconds. Add half of the seafood mixture. Stir in dried parsley, if using, and dried basil, if using. Cook and stir for 3 to 4 minutes or until scallops and shrimp turn opaque. Remove seafood mixture with a slotted spoon; set aside. Repeat with remaining seafood mixture.

4 Return all of the seafood mixture to skillet. Add pea pods and tomatoes. Cook and stir for 2 minutes more. Add seafood mixture to pasta. Add fresh parsley, if using, and snipped fresh basil, if using. Toss to combine. If desired, top with Parmesan or Romano cheese and garnish with fresh basil. Makes 6 servings.

Nutrition Facts per serving: 366 calories, 12 g total fat (3 g saturated fat), 84 mg cholesterol, 367 mg sodium, 41 g carbohydrate, 3 g fiber, 22 g protein. Daily Values: 11% vit. A, 41% vit. C, 6% calcium, 17% iron.

Seafood Tacos with Cilantro Salsa

Start to finish: 30 minutes

- 1 14½-ounce can chunky salsa-style tomatoes or diced tomatoes
- ¼ cup snipped fresh cilantro
- 2 shallots or green onions, chopped
- 1 clove garlic, minced
- 1 tablespoon vinegar
- 1 tablespoon lime juice
- ½ to 1 fresh serrano pepper, seeded and diced*
- 1 tablespoon cooking oil
- 1 small jicama, peeled and cut into thin bite-size strips (about 2 cups)

- 2 medium red and/or yellow sweet peppers, cut into thin bite-size strips
- 1 medium zucchini, cut into thin bite-size strips (1¼ cups)
- ¾ pound chunk-style shrimp-, lobster-, or crab-flavored fish
- 3 tablespoons lime juice
- ¼ to ½ teaspoon ground red pepper
- 6 8-inch flour tortillas
- 1 cup shredded Monterey Jack cheese (4 ounces)
   Torn mixed greens (optional)

Lynn Moretti
Oconomowoc, WI

Suit your fancy by taking your choice of a variety of convenient chunk-style fish (or surimi) for these seafood and vegetable tacos. For a special meal, serve the salsa on the side spooned into a quartered sweet pepper.

1 For the salsa, combine the tomatoes, cilantro, shallots or green onions, garlic, vinegar, the 1 tablespoon lime juice, and serrano pepper. Cover and chill.

2 Pour oil into wok or 12-inch skillet. (Add more oil as necessary during cooking.) Preheat over medium-high heat. Stir-fry jicama and sweet peppers in hot oil about 2 minutes or until crisp-tender. Add the zucchini; stir-fry for 1 minute more. Add the chunk-style fish; cover and heat through. Stir in the 3 tablespoons lime juice and the ground red pepper. Serve fish mixture in the tortillas with the salsa, Monterey Jack cheese, and, if desired, torn mixed greens. Makes 6 servings.

*Note: Because chile peppers contain volatile oils that can burn your skin and eyes, avoid direct contact with them as much as possible. When working with chile peppers, wear plastic or rubber gloves. If your bare hands do touch the chile peppers, wash your hands well with soap and water.

Nutrition Facts per serving: 299 calories, 12 g total fat (4 g saturated fat), 37 g cholesterol, 1,442 mg sodium, 41 g carbohydrate, 0 g fiber, 17 g protein. Daily Values: 51% vit. A, 186% vit. C, 21% calcium, 19% iron.

Deep-Dish Seafood Pizza

Prep: 35 minutes **Bake:** 30 minutes

1½ cups frozen, peeled, cooked shrimp
1 cup frozen crab-flavored fish pieces
½ of a 10-ounce package frozen chopped spinach, thawed
2½ to 3 cups all-purpose flour
1 package active dry yeast
¼ teaspoon salt
1 cup warm water (120° to 130°)
2 tablespoons cooking oil

1½ cups shredded mozzarella cheese (6 ounces)
2 slightly beaten eggs
¾ cup shredded extra-sharp cheddar cheese
½ cup ricotta cheese
¼ cup grated Parmesan cheese or Romano cheese (1 ounce)
⅛ teaspoon ground nutmeg
Cornmeal

1995

*Julie Brady
Stoneham, MA*

Attention pizza lovers! Here's the ultimate splurge—Julie's homemade crust topped with shrimp, spinach, and four cheeses.

1 Thaw shrimp and fish; pat dry with paper towels. Drain thawed spinach well, pressing out excess liquid; set aside.

2 For crust, in a large mixing bowl combine 1¼ cups of the flour, the yeast, and salt. Add water and oil. Beat with electric mixer on medium speed for 30 seconds, scraping bowl constantly. Beat for 3 minutes more. Using a wooden spoon, stir in as much of the remaining flour as you can.

3 Turn dough out onto a lightly floured surface. Knead in enough of the remaining flour to make a moderately stiff dough that is smooth and elastic (6 to 8 minutes total). Cover; let rest for 10 minutes.

4 Meanwhile, set aside ½ cup of the shrimp and ½ cup of the mozzarella cheese. Coarsely chop fish. In a medium bowl combine remaining shrimp, remaining mozzarella cheese, the fish, spinach, eggs, cheddar cheese, ricotta cheese, Parmesan or Romano cheese, and nutmeg.

5 Grease a 12-inch pizza pan. Sprinkle with cornmeal. On a lightly floured surface, roll dough into a 13-inch circle. Transfer to prepared pan. Build up edge slightly. Bake in a 450° oven for 10 to 12 minutes or until lightly browned. Spread seafood mixture over crust. Sprinkle with reserved shrimp and reserved mozzarella cheese. Bake for 20 to 25 minutes more or until cheese is melted. Makes 8 servings.

Nutrition Facts per serving: 368 calories, 15 g total fat (7 g saturated fat), 143 mg cholesterol, 549 mg sodium, 33 g carbohydrate, 1 g fiber, 25 g protein. Daily Values: 23% vit. A, 3% vit. C, 28% calcium, 22% iron.

Vegetable **Pastitsio**

Prep: 35 minutes **Bake:** 35 minutes **Stand:** 5 minutes

Westy Gabany
Olney, MD

Westy made this great-tasting, meatless version of the popular Greek dish low in fat by using just a little margarine or butter and fat-free milk.

Nonstick cooking spray
8 ounces dried penne or elbow macaroni
½ cup refrigerated or frozen egg product, thawed
¼ teaspoon salt
¼ teaspoon ground nutmeg
2 cups fresh spinach leaves
1 medium onion, chopped (½ cup)
1 clove garlic, minced
1 tablespoon chicken broth or water
4 teaspoons margarine or butter
1 8-ounce can tomato sauce

1 cup loose-pack frozen whole kernel corn
1 cup cubed, cooked potatoes
¾ teaspoon dried mint, crushed
½ teaspoon dried oregano, crushed
¼ teaspoon salt
¼ teaspoon ground cinnamon
¼ teaspoon pepper
3 tablespoons all-purpose flour
1½ cups fat-free milk
¼ cup grated Parmesan cheese (1 ounce)
¼ teaspoon ground nutmeg

1 Coat a 2-quart square baking dish with cooking spray; set aside. Cook pasta according to package directions; drain, reserving hot water. Rinse pasta with cold water; drain.

2 In a large bowl combine cooked pasta, egg product, ¼ teaspoon salt, and ¼ teaspoon nutmeg. Spread mixture evenly into prepared dish. Add spinach to reserved cooking water; let stand for 2 minutes or until wilted. Drain; arrange over pasta mixture.

3 In a large nonstick skillet cook onion and garlic in the broth or water and 1 teaspoon of the margarine or butter over medium heat about 3 minutes or until onion is tender. Add tomato sauce, corn, potatoes, mint, oregano, ¼ teaspoon salt, the cinnamon, and pepper; cook and stir until heated through. Spread mixture over spinach.

4 In a saucepan melt remaining margarine or butter. Stir in flour. Add milk all at once. Cook and stir until thickened and bubbly. Cook and stir for 1 minute more. Stir in Parmesan cheese and ¼ teaspoon nutmeg. Spread over vegetable mixture.

5 Bake, uncovered, in a 350° oven about 35 minutes or until top is firm. Let stand 5 minutes before serving. Makes 6 servings.

Nutrition Facts per serving: 321 calories, 6 g total fat (2 g saturated fat), 5 mg cholesterol, 602 mg sodium, 54 g carbohydrate, 3 g fiber, 14 g protein. Daily Values: 28% vit. A, 26% vit. C, 187% calcium, 22% iron.

Artichoke and **Basil Hero**

Start to finish: 30 minutes

1 cup fresh basil (leaves only)
¼ cup olive oil or salad oil
2 tablespoons grated Parmesan cheese
1 tablespoon capers, drained
1 tablespoon white wine vinegar
2 teaspoons Dijon-style mustard
1 clove garlic, quartered

1 16-ounce loaf unsliced French bread
1 14-ounce can artichoke hearts,
   drained and sliced
4 ounces sliced provolone cheese
1 medium tomato, thinly sliced
2 cups torn fresh spinach

Ellen Nishimura
Fair Oaks, CA

Basil, spinach, tomato, and artichoke hearts combine with cheese for a hearty sandwich. But the caper vinaigrette takes it out of the realm of ordinary.

1 In a blender container or food processor bowl combine the basil, oil, Parmesan cheese, capers, vinegar, mustard, and garlic. Cover; blend or process until nearly smooth. Set aside.

2 Cut bread in half lengthwise. Hollow out each half, leaving a ½- to 1-inch shell. (Save bread crumbs for another use.) Spread the basil mixture over cut side of each bread half. On the bottom half, layer artichoke hearts, provolone cheese, tomato, and spinach. Cover with bread top. Cut sandwich crosswise into 6 pieces. Makes 6 servings.

Nutrition Facts per serving: 396 calories, 17 g total fat (5 g saturated fat), 14 mg cholesterol, 887 mg sodium, 46 g carbohydrate, 4 g fiber, 15 g protein. Daily Values: 16% vit. A, 18% vit. C, 24% calcium, 23% iron.

Tortilla and Black Bean **Casserole**

Prep: 25 minutes **Bake:** 30 minutes **Stand:** 10 minutes

1992

Merry Hoover
Long Beach, CA

Although it won the side-dish category in 1992, this layered Southwestern-style casserole is hearty enough to be served as a main dish.

2   large onions, chopped (2 cups)
1½ cups chopped green sweet pepper
1   14½-ounce can diced tomatoes or whole tomatoes, cut up (undrained)
¾   cup picante sauce
2   cloves garlic, minced
2   teaspoons ground cumin
2   15-ounce cans black beans or red kidney beans, rinsed and drained
10 or 12 6-inch corn tortillas

2   cups shredded Monterey Jack or cheddar cheese (8 ounces)
2   cups shredded lettuce (optional)
2   medium tomatoes, chopped (optional)
    Sliced green onion (optional)
    Sliced pitted ripe olives (optional)
    Picante sauce
½   cup dairy sour cream or plain yogurt (optional)

1 In a large skillet combine onions, sweet pepper, undrained canned tomatoes, the ¾ cup picante sauce, the garlic, and cumin. Bring to boiling; reduce heat. Simmer, uncovered, for 10 minutes. Stir in beans.

2 Spread one-third of the bean mixture over bottom of a 3-quart rectangular baking dish. Top with half of the tortillas, overlapping as necessary; sprinkle with half of the cheese. Add another one-third of the bean mixture, remaining tortillas, and remaining bean mixture. Cover and bake in a 350° oven for 30 to 35 minutes or until heated through. Sprinkle with remaining cheese. Let stand for 10 minutes before serving.

3 If desired, top with lettuce, tomatoes, green onion, and ripe olives. Cut into squares to serve. Serve with additional picante sauce and, if desired, sour cream or yogurt. Makes 6 to 8 servings.

Nutrition Facts per serving: 406 calories, 13 g total fat (7 g saturated fat), 33 mg cholesterol, 816 mg sodium, 56 g carbohydrate, 11 g fiber, 23 g protein. Daily Values: 17% vit. A, 63% vit. C, 42% calcium, 33% iron.

saluting barbecue

In 1991, with enthusiasm for grilling at an all-time high, *Better Homes and Gardens*® magazine launched the Great American Barbecue Contest, a search for the best grilled recipes and grilled side dishes in the country. In June 1992, the magazine showcased the results. There were eight top winners, including Tortilla and Black Bean Casserole, above, which won Merry Hoover $1,000 in the "go-alongs" category.

Potato Crust Vegetable Pizza

Prep: 20 minutes **Bake:** 30 minutes

3 medium baking potatoes, peeled (1 pound)
1 small onion
1 beaten egg yolk
2 teaspoons all-purpose flour
  Dash salt
6 teaspoons olive oil
1 cup thinly sliced zucchini
1 cup thinly sliced yellow summer squash
1 small yellow sweet pepper, chopped

1 small red onion, halved and thinly sliced
1 clove garlic, minced
½ of a 5.3-ounce package soft goat cheese (chèvre)
8 cherry tomatoes, quartered
¾ cup shredded mozzarella cheese (3 ounces)
1 tablespoon shredded fresh basil
  Fresh basil sprigs (optional)

1998

Karen Bowers
Flagstaff, AZ

Karen transforms shredded potatoes into a tasty crust that is topped with goat cheese and a mixture of squash, sweet pepper, and onion for an innovative pizza.

1 Shred potatoes and onion into a bowl of cold water; drain well, squeezing out excess moisture. In a medium bowl combine the potato mixture, egg yolk, flour, and salt; mix well.

2 In an 11×7×1½-inch baking pan heat 2 teaspoons of the oil in a 500° oven for 1 to 2 minutes. Remove from oven; carefully press potato mixture into bottom and up sides of pan. Brush the top of potato mixture with 2 teaspoons of the oil. Bake in the 500° oven about 30 minutes or until golden brown and crisp.

3 Meanwhile, in a medium bowl toss together zucchini, summer squash, sweet pepper, red onion, and garlic. In a large skillet heat remaining oil. Add zucchini mixture and cook until vegetables are crisp-tender, stirring often.

4 Carefully spread goat cheese over the potato crust. Top cheese with the hot vegetables and cherry tomatoes. Sprinkle with mozzarella cheese. Bake for 1 minute more to melt cheese. Sprinkle with fresh basil. If desired, garnish with fresh basil sprigs. Makes 6 to 8 servings.

Nutrition Facts per serving: 216 calories, 11 g total fat (4 g saturated fat), 55 mg cholesterol, 169 mg sodium, 21 g carbohydrate, 2 g fiber, 8 g protein. Daily Values: 11% vit. A, 91% vit. C, 10% calcium, 4% iron.

Tex-Mex Tortilla Soup, page 161

Soups & Stews

Vegetable-Sauerkraut Soup

Prep: 25 minutes **Cook:** 4½ to 12 hours

1987

Gene Orlowski
North Chicago, IL

According to Gene, potatoes, sauerkraut, smoked sausage, and vinegar are essentials for making this Polish-style soup. The rest of the ingredients depend on what you might have on hand.

- 4 cups chicken broth
- 1 10¾-ounce can condensed cream of mushroom soup
- 1 14- to 16-ounce can sauerkraut, rinsed and drained
- ¾ pound fully cooked Polish sausage, cubed
- 8 ounces fresh mushrooms, sliced (3 cups)
- 2 medium carrots, chopped (1 cup)
- 2 medium stalks celery, chopped (1 cup)
- 1 medium potato, cut into small cubes (about ⅔ cup)
- 1 medium onion, chopped (½ cup)
- ½ cup chopped cooked chicken
- 2 tablespoons vinegar
- 2 teaspoons dried dillweed
- ½ teaspoon pepper
- 2 slices bacon, crisp-cooked, drained, and crumbled (optional)
- 2 hard-cooked eggs, chopped (optional)

1 In a 3½- or 4-quart electric slow crockery cooker stir together all ingredients except bacon and hard-cooked eggs. Cover and cook on low-heat setting for 10 to 12 hours or on high-heat setting for 4½ to 6 hours. If necessary, skim off fat before serving. If desired, sprinkle each serving with bacon and chopped eggs. Makes 8 servings.

Stovetop Method: In a Dutch oven combine all ingredients except bacon and hard-cooked eggs. Bring to boiling; reduce heat. Cover and simmer about 40 minutes or until vegetables are tender. Serve as above.

Nutrition Facts per serving: 250 calories, 17 g total fat (6 g saturated fat), 39 mg cholesterol, 1,364 mg sodium, 13 g carbohydrate, 3 g fiber, 14 g protein. Daily Values: 39% vit. A, 13% vit. C, 4% calcium, 10% iron.

cooked chicken on call

When it came to making soup, cooks of yesteryear often would use the chicken left over from Sunday dinner. Today, that's only one option. Purchasing roasted chicken from the deli is a no-fuss alternative. A cooked bird will yield about 2½ to 3 cups chopped cooked meat. Or, you could use poached chicken breasts. To poach chicken, in a large skillet combine 12 ounces skinless, boneless chicken breasts and 1½ cups water. Bring to boiling; reduce heat. Cover; simmer for 12 to 14 minutes or until chicken is tender and no longer pink. Drain well and cut up. Twelve ounces yields about 2 cups cubed cooked chicken.

Tomato-Mushroom Soup

Prep: 20 minutes **Cook:** 20 minutes

1 medium onion, halved and thinly sliced	1¼ cups water
1 clove garlic, minced	¼ cup sweet vermouth or dry sherry
1 tablespoon margarine or butter	¼ cup tomato paste
1 tablespoon olive oil or cooking oil	¼ teaspoon pepper
4 cups sliced fresh mushrooms	¼ cup finely shredded or grated Parmesan cheese
1 10½-ounce can condensed chicken broth	2 tablespoons snipped fresh parsley or fresh basil

1991

Jane B. Adams
Fort Collins, CO

Jane often ladles this mushroom-packed soup over toasted slices of French bread in large, shallow bowls.

1 In a large saucepan cook onion and garlic in hot margarine or butter and oil about 5 minutes or until onion is tender. Add the mushrooms. Cover and cook about 5 minutes or until mushrooms are tender.

2 Stir in the broth, water, vermouth or sherry, tomato paste, and pepper. Bring to boiling; reduce heat. Cover and simmer for 20 minutes. Sprinkle each serving with some of the Parmesan cheese and fresh parsley or basil. Makes 4 servings.

Nutrition Facts per serving: 168 calories, 11 g total fat (3 g saturated fat), 8 mg cholesterol, 605 mg sodium, 10 g carbohydrate, 2 g fiber, 8 g protein. Daily Values: 10% vit. A, 11% vit. C, 8% calcium, 6% iron.

Beef-Vegetable Soup

Prep: 35 minutes **Cook:** 2½ hours

1954

Mrs. Robert D. Owen
York, PA

This rich and satisfying chili-flavored dish is filled with chunks of beef and a basketful of vegetables. Serve it with slices of crusty bread.

3 pounds meaty beef shank crosscuts
2 tablespoons cooking oil
6 cups water
2 cups tomato juice
4 teaspoons instant beef bouillon granules
1 tablespoon Worcestershire sauce
1 teaspoon chili powder
2 bay leaves

2 medium carrots, diagonally sliced (1 cup)
2 medium stalks celery, sliced (1 cup)
1 large potato, peeled and cubed (1 cup)
1 cup coarsely chopped cabbage
1 small onion, coarsely chopped (⅓ cup)

1 In a 4-quart Dutch oven brown meat, half at a time, in the hot oil; drain off fat. Return all meat to pan. Stir in the water, tomato juice, beef bouillon granules, Worcestershire sauce, chili powder, and bay leaves. Bring to boiling; reduce heat. Cover and simmer for 2 hours. Remove beef crosscuts. Skim fat from broth.

2 When cool enough to handle, remove meat from bones; discard bones. Coarsely chop meat.

3 Stir chopped meat, carrots, celery, potato, cabbage, and onion into broth. Bring to boiling; reduce heat. Cover and simmer 30 to 45 minutes or until vegetables and beef are tender. Discard bay leaves. Makes 8 servings.

Nutrition Facts per serving: 185 calories, 5 g total fat (2 g saturated fat), 55 mg cholesterol, 743 mg sodium, 9 g carbohydrate, 2 g fiber, 26 g protein. Daily Values: 43% vit. A, 31% vit. C, 5% calcium, 21% iron.

slow-simmering success

Vegetable soup flavored with beef or some other meat has been a standby for centuries. The Colonists kept a big pot of soup simmering on the back burner day in and day out, adding bits of leftovers whenever they had them. The long, slow simmering extracted wonderful flavor from the meat. So how did an old-fashioned dish, like Hearty Beef-Vegetable Soup, above, become a prizewinner? Undoubtedly it was the imaginative combination of seasonings.

Polenta **Beef Stew**

Prep: 25 minutes **Cook:** 2 hours

2000

Ted Badasci
Firebaugh, CA

Ted won second place in the *Better Homes and Gardens*® Century Standouts Contest with this stick-to-the-ribs sensation. He inherited this recipe from his grandmother who came from a part of Switzerland near the border with Italy. There, using polenta in a variety of ways, including as a topper for soups and stews, was traditional.

¼ cup all-purpose flour
1 teaspoon garlic powder
1 teaspoon dried thyme, crushed
1 teaspoon dried basil, crushed
½ teaspoon salt
½ teaspoon pepper
2 pounds boneless beef chuck steak, cut into 1-inch pieces
2 tablespoons olive oil
1 medium onion, chopped (½ cup)
6 cloves garlic, minced

1 teaspoon snipped fresh rosemary or ¼ teaspoon dried rosemary, crushed
1 14½-ounce can beef broth
1½ cups dry red wine
8 ounces boiling onions
5 medium carrots, cut into 1-inch chunks
1 recipe Polenta
½ cup snipped fresh Italian parsley
¼ cup tomato paste
   Fresh Italian parsley sprigs (optional)

1 In a medium bowl stir together the flour, garlic powder, thyme, basil, salt, and pepper. Coat meat with flour mixture. In a Dutch oven heat oil over medium-high heat; brown meat, half at a time, in hot oil. Return all meat to Dutch oven. Add chopped onion, garlic, and rosemary. Cook and stir until onion is tender. Add broth and wine. Bring to boiling; reduce heat. Cover and simmer for 1½ hours.

2 Add boiling onions and carrots. Bring to boiling; reduce heat. Cover and simmer about 30 minutes or until vegetables are tender.

3 Meanwhile, prepare Polenta. Just before serving, stir snipped parsley and tomato paste into stew. Serve stew in bowls with Polenta. If desired, garnish with parsley sprigs. Makes 8 servings.

Polenta: In a large saucepan bring 3 cups milk just to a simmer. In a medium bowl combine 1 cup cornmeal, 1 cup water, and 1 teaspoon salt. Stir cornmeal mixture slowly into hot milk. Cook and stir until mixture comes to a boil. Reduce heat to low. Cook for 10 to 15 minutes or until mixture is thick, stirring occasionally. If too thick, stir in additional milk. Stir in 2 tablespoons margarine or butter until melted.

Nutrition Facts per serving: 629 calories, 20 g total fat (9 g saturated fat), 112 mg cholesterol, 1,194 mg sodium, 64 g carbohydrate, 7 g fiber, 41 g protein. Daily Values: 128% vit. A, 22% vit. C, 26% calcium, 37% iron.

Italian Eggplant Beef Stew

Prep: 30 minutes **Cook:** 1 hour 5 minutes

1½ pounds beef stew meat, cut into 1-inch cubes
2 tablespoons cooking oil
3 medium tomatoes, peeled and cut into wedges, or one 14½-ounce can tomato wedges, undrained
1 cup beef broth
1 large onion, chopped (1 cup)
1 teaspoon chili powder
1 clove garlic, minced
½ teaspoon salt
¼ teaspoon dried oregano, crushed
¼ teaspoon ground black pepper
2 cups coarsely chopped peeled eggplant
1 cup dry white wine
1 large potato, peeled and cubed (1 cup)
1 large green sweet pepper, chopped (1 cup)
¾ cup sliced fresh mushrooms
2 fresh jalapeño peppers, seeded and coarsely chopped*
¼ cup grated Parmesan cheese

1982

Arthur Signorella
Du Bois, PA

Tomatoes, garlic, and oregano put Italian in this robust beef stew's name; jalapeño peppers and chili powder give it a Mexican-style flavor.

1 In a Dutch oven brown beef, half at a time, in the hot oil; drain off fat. Return all meat to Dutch oven. Add the fresh or undrained canned tomatoes, beef broth, onion, chili powder, garlic, salt, oregano, and black pepper. Bring to boiling; reduce heat. Cover and simmer for 45 minutes. Stir in the eggplant, wine, potato, sweet pepper, mushrooms, and jalapeño peppers. Return to boiling; reduce heat. Cover and simmer for 20 to 25 minutes more or until meat and vegetables are tender. Stir in the cheese; heat through. Makes 6 to 8 servings.

*Note: Because chile peppers, such as jalapeños, contain volatile oils that can burn your skin and eyes, avoid direct contact with them as much as possible. When working with chile peppers, wear plastic or rubber gloves or slip your hands into plastic bags. If your bare hands do touch the chile peppers, wash your hands well with soap and water.

Nutrition Facts per serving: 307 calories, 12 g total fat (4 g saturated fat), 63 mg cholesterol, 476 mg sodium, 15 g carbohydrate, 3 g fiber, 29 g protein. Daily Values: 9% vit. A, 121% vit. C, 8% calcium, 19% iron.

Green Chili **Stew**

Prep: 15 minutes **Cook:** 1¾ hours

1998

*Linda Boisseau
Fairbanks, AK*

Linda adds Southwestern flavor to her hearty stew with Mexican beer, salsa, hominy, green chile peppers, and cilantro. For extra kick, use medium-hot green salsa instead of mild.

2 pounds beef stew meat
¼ cup all-purpose flour
¼ cup margarine or butter
6 cloves garlic, minced
3 cups beef broth
1 12-ounce bottle dark (Mexican) beer
1 cup mild or medium-hot green salsa
2 tablespoons snipped fresh oregano
  or 2 teaspoons dried oregano,
  crushed

1 teaspoon ground cumin
3 medium potatoes, cubed (about
  2 cups)
1 14½-ounce can hominy, drained
2 4½-ounce cans diced green chile
  peppers, drained
12 green onions, bias-sliced into
  1-inch pieces
½ cup snipped fresh cilantro

1 Toss beef cubes with flour. In a 4½-quart Dutch oven brown the beef cubes, half at a time, in hot margarine or butter. Using a slotted spoon, remove meat from Dutch oven. Add garlic to Dutch oven; cook for 1 minute. Stir in broth, beer, salsa, oregano, and cumin. Return meat to Dutch oven. Bring to boiling; reduce heat.

2 Cover and simmer about 1¼ hours or until meat is nearly tender. Add potatoes; simmer about 30 minutes more or until meat and potatoes are tender. Stir in hominy, chile peppers, green onions, and cilantro; heat through. Makes 8 servings.

Nutrition Facts per serving: 392 calories, 16 g total fat (4 g saturated fat), 82 mg cholesterol, 720 mg sodium, 28 g carbohydrate, 1 g fiber, 32 g protein. Daily Values: 15% vit. A, 49% vit. C, 7% calcium, 38% iron.

Sausage Stew Pot

Prep: 25 minutes **Cook:** 15 minutes

1 pound fully cooked Polish sausage, halved lengthwise and sliced
8 ounces fresh mushrooms, sliced (3 cups)
1 large onion, halved and sliced
1 medium yellow, red, or green sweet pepper, cut into strips
1 clove garlic, minced
1 tablespoon cooking oil
4 cups water
2 cups shredded cabbage
1 cup dry brown lentils, rinsed and drained
2 tablespoons rice vinegar
1 tablespoon brown sugar
2 teaspoons instant chicken bouillon granules
⅛ teaspoon black pepper

1997

Beverly A. Gietzen
Pismo Beach, CA

Let a serving of this hearty Polish sausage, lentil, and vegetable stew chase away the chill on a cold day.

1 In a 4-quart Dutch oven cook the sausage, mushrooms, onion, sweet pepper, and garlic in hot oil about 5 minutes or until vegetables are just tender. Add the water, cabbage, lentils, vinegar, brown sugar, bouillon granules, and black pepper. Bring to boiling; reduce heat. Cover and simmer for 15 to 20 minutes or until vegetables and lentils are tender. Makes 5 servings.

Nutrition Facts per serving: 399 calories, 32 g total fat (9 g saturated fat), 61 mg cholesterol, 1,281 mg sodium, 17 g carbohydrate, 3 g fiber, 16 g protein. Daily Values: 13% vit. A, 92% vit. C, 6% calcium, 19% iron.

Black Bean and Sausage Posole

Prep: 15 minutes **Cook:** 30 minutes

Millie Hawkins
Colorado Springs, CO

What a lifesaver this recipe will be on those nights when you're in a hurry to create a tasty dinner. Taking only 15 minutes to prepare, it can then simmer unattended while you relax.

- 1 12-ounce package light bulk turkey-and-pork sausage
- 2 14½-ounce cans reduced-sodium chicken broth
- 1 15-ounce can black beans, rinsed and drained
- 1 14½-ounce can golden hominy, rinsed and drained
- 1 14½-ounce can Mexican-style stewed tomatoes, undrained
- 1 cup frozen loose-pack diced hash brown potatoes
- 1 small green sweet pepper, chopped (½ cup)
- 1 small onion, chopped (⅓ cup)
- 1 clove garlic, minced
- 1 teaspoon dried oregano, crushed
- ½ teaspoon chili powder

1 In a large saucepan brown the sausage; drain off fat. Stir in the chicken broth, black beans, hominy, undrained tomatoes, hash brown potatoes, sweet pepper, onion, garlic, oregano, and chili powder. Bring to boiling; reduce heat. Cover and simmer for 30 minutes. Makes 6 servings.

Nutrition Facts per serving: 292 calories, 14 g total fat (1 g saturated fat), 45 mg cholesterol, 1,295 mg sodium, 26 g carbohydrate, 4 g fiber, 17 g protein. Daily Values: 7% vit. A, 30% vit. C, 3% calcium, 15% iron.

help yourself to hominy

Over the years, posole, a traditional Christmas dish from Mexico's Pacific Coast region, has become popular in the Southwest. Taking its name from the type of hominy used to make it, this stick-to-the-ribs soup features pork in addition to golden hominy. The combination is simmered in broth or tomatoes along with onion, garlic, and seasonings, such as cumin, chili powder, dried chile peppers, or cilantro. Black Bean and Sausage Posole, above, is a quick-to-fix '90s variation that starts with turkey-and-pork sausage, rather than chunks of pork, and includes black beans and potatoes in addition to hominy.

Cassoulet-Style Stew

Prep: 50 minutes **Stand:** 1 hour **Cook:** 1¾ hours

1979

Maral Mahdasian
Newton, MA

On the next blustery day, stir together a potful of this tummy-warming, herb-seasoned lamb, bean, and vegetable combination. It makes enough for 12 hearty servings, so plan on leftovers to tuck in your freezer for another meal or two.

6   cups water
1   pound dry navy beans, rinsed and drained
1   meaty lamb shank (1 to 1½ pounds)
1   tablespoon olive oil or cooking oil
2   cups chopped celery (including leaves)
2   medium potatoes, coarsely chopped
¾   cup coarsely chopped carrot
¾   cup coarsely chopped parsnip
3   cloves garlic, minced
7   cups water

8   ounces fresh mushrooms, sliced (3 cups)
1¼ cups dry black-eyed peas, rinsed and drained
½   cup dry red wine or beef broth
2   teaspoons salt
½   teaspoon pepper
1   28-ounce can diced tomatoes, undrained
2   tablespoons snipped fresh thyme
1   tablespoon snipped fresh rosemary
Fresh rosemary sprigs (optional)

1 In a large saucepan combine the 6 cups water and the beans. Bring to boiling; reduce heat. Simmer, uncovered, for 2 minutes. Remove from heat. Cover and let stand for 1 hour. Drain and rinse beans.

2 In an 8- to 10-quart Dutch oven or kettle brown lamb shank in hot oil. Add celery, potatoes, carrot, parsnip, and garlic. Cook over medium-high heat for 5 minutes, stirring frequently. Add the 7 cups water, the mushrooms, black-eyed peas, wine or broth, salt, pepper, and drained beans. Bring to boiling; reduce heat. Cover and simmer about 1½ hours or until the beans and peas are tender. Remove lamb shank.

3 Add the undrained tomatoes, thyme, and snipped rosemary to bean mixture. When cool enough to handle, remove meat from bone; discard bone. Chop meat; add to bean mixture. Bring to boiling; reduce heat. Cover and simmer for 15 minutes more. If desired, garnish stew with fresh rosemary sprigs. Makes 12 servings.

To make ahead: Prepare stew as directed. Let cool for 30 minutes. Place stew in freezer containers; seal and freeze for up to 3 months. To serve, place frozen stew in a saucepan. Heat, covered, over medium-low heat about 45 minutes or until heated through, stirring occasionally and breaking apart.

Nutrition Facts per serving: 287 calories, 4 g total fat (1 g saturated fat), 14 mg cholesterol, 553 mg sodium, 46 g carbohydrate, 5 g fiber, 18 g protein. Daily Values: 24% vit. A, 29% vit. C, 10% calcium, 36% iron.

Curried Split Pea Soup

Prep: 10 minutes **Cook:** 5 hours

1 pound dry green split peas, rinsed and drained	2 medium carrots, chopped (1 cup)
1 pound ham hocks	2 bay leaves
½ pound cooked ham, cubed (1½ cups)	⅓ cup dried cranberries
3 medium stalks celery, chopped (1½ cups)	4 teaspoons curry powder
1 large onion, chopped (1 cup)	1 tablespoon dried marjoram, crushed
	¼ teaspoon pepper
	6 cups water

*Denise and Kirk Allen
Wilmington, NC*

Denise and Kirk say a Christmas ham glazed with curried cranberries inspired their exceptional curry-accented split pea soup.

1 In a 3½- or 4-quart electric slow crockery cooker combine split peas, ham hocks, ham, celery, onion, carrots, bay leaves, cranberries, curry powder, marjoram, and pepper. Add water. Cover and cook on low-heat setting for 10 to 12 hours or on high-heat setting for 5 to 6 hours. Discard bay leaves. Remove ham hocks. When cool enough to handle, remove meat from bones; discard bones. Coarsely chop meat. Return meat to soup. Makes 6 servings.

Nutrition Facts per serving: 376 calories, 4 g total fat (1 g saturated fat), 25 mg cholesterol, 626 mg sodium, 58 g carbohydrate, 6 g fiber, 29 g protein. Daily Values: 55% vit. A, 25% vit. C, 7% calcium, 34% iron.

can't miss crockery cooking

Cooking in crockery took on a whole new meaning in the 1970s with the introduction of the first crockery cooker. Within a few years, the appliance went from a trendy gadget to a kitchen basic. And why not? It allows cooks who are away from home for all or part of the day to start cooking a meal before they leave home. A number of manufacturers have developed larger models of the cookers, ideal for potluck dinners and tailgating, as well as smaller-size ones, perfect for keeping dips and other appetizers warm.

Spicy Szechwan **Pork Stew**

Prep: 20 minutes **Cook:** 55 minutes

*Don Gibson
Kaneohe, HI*

Even in sunny Hawaii, Don's family enjoys the robust flavor of this warming Oriental stew flavored with soy sauce, sherry, and four distinctive seasonings.

6 green onions	½ teaspoon crushed red pepper
2 pounds boneless pork shoulder	½ teaspoon fennel seed, crushed
6 cloves garlic, minced	½ teaspoon five-spice powder
1 tablespoon cooking oil	6 medium carrots, cut into thin
3 cups water	bite-size strips
⅓ cup reduced-sodium soy sauce	¼ cup cold water
⅓ cup dry sherry	3 tablespoons all-purpose flour
1½ teaspoons grated fresh ginger	Hot cooked rice or noodles (optional)

1 Cut green onions into 1-inch pieces. Separate white pieces from green onion tops; set both aside.

2 Trim fat from meat. Cut meat into 1-inch cubes. In a 4-quart Dutch oven brown meat and garlic, half at a time, in hot oil. Drain off fat. Return all of the pork mixture to Dutch oven. Add the white onion pieces, the 3 cups water, the soy sauce, sherry, ginger, red pepper, fennel, and five-spice powder. Bring to boiling; reduce heat. Cover and simmer for 30 minutes. Add carrots. Return to boiling; reduce heat. Cover and simmer about 25 minutes more or until meat and carrots are tender. Skim off fat.

3 In a small bowl stir together the ¼ cup cold water and the flour. Stir into meat mixture. Add green onion tops. Cook and stir until thickened and bubbly. Cook and stir for 1 minute more. If desired, serve with hot cooked rice or noodles. Makes 6 servings.

Nutrition Facts per serving: 264 calories, 9 g total fat (3 g saturated fat), 76 mg cholesterol, 616 mg sodium, 16 g carbohydrate, 3 g fiber, 25 g protein. Daily Values: 192% vit. A, 16% vit. C, 6% calcium, 13% iron.

Potato-Onion **Soup**

Start to finish: 25 minutes

1943

Mrs. Rex Davies
Milwaukee, WI

Mrs. Davies loaded her easy, yet tasty concoction with bacon, potatoes, and onion. Serve it with a turkey sandwich for lunch or a light supper.

6 slices bacon
5 cups sliced red potatoes
3 cups water
1 tablespoon instant chicken bouillon
   granules

3 medium onions, cut into very thin
   wedges (1½ cups)
2 cups milk
¼ teaspoon pepper

1 In a large skillet cook bacon over medium heat until bacon is crisp. Drain bacon on paper towels, reserving 1 tablespoon drippings in skillet. Crumble bacon; set aside.

2 In a large saucepan combine the potatoes, water, and chicken bouillon granules. Bring to boiling; reduce heat. Cover and simmer about 15 minutes or until potatoes are very tender.

3 Meanwhile, cook onions in the reserved bacon drippings over medium-low heat for 8 to 10 minutes or until tender and golden brown. Remove from skillet; set aside. Mash potatoes slightly with a potato masher. Stir in milk, pepper, onions, and bacon; heat through. If desired, season to taste with additional pepper. Makes 6 servings.

Nutrition Facts per serving: 201 calories, 6 g total fat (3 g saturated fat), 14 mg cholesterol, 600 mg sodium, 27 g carbohydrate, 3 g fiber, 8 g protein. Daily Values: 5% vit. A, 34% vit. C, 12% calcium, 7% iron.

Cream of Chicken and Cheese Soup

Start to finish: 40 minutes

2 cups water
1 small whole chicken breast (about ¾ pound)
1 small onion, chopped (⅓ cup)
1 small carrot, chopped (⅓ cup)
1 small stalk celery, chopped (⅓ cup)

1 10¾-ounce can condensed cream of chicken soup
½ cup milk
2 ounces American cheese, cubed (about ½ cup)
Shredded American cheese (optional)

1969

Mrs. Jay Palmer
Kansas City, MO

Although this recipe includes a can of condensed soup, tender chicken and sharp American cheese give Mrs. Palmer's creation a delightful homemade flavor.

1 In a large saucepan bring the water to boiling. Add chicken breast. Return to boiling; reduce heat. Cover and simmer for 20 to 25 minutes or until chicken is tender and no longer pink. Remove chicken.

2 Add onion, carrot, and celery to cooking liquid. Return to boiling; reduce heat. Simmer, uncovered, for 10 minutes.

3 When cool enough to handle, remove chicken from bones; discard bones. Chop the chicken. Stir soup and milk into vegetable mixture until smooth. Add chicken and cubed cheese; heat and stir until cheese melts. If desired, garnish with shredded cheese. Makes 4 servings.

Nutrition Facts per serving: 209 calories, 11 g total fat (5 g saturated fat), 47 mg cholesterol, 820 mg sodium, 11 g carbohydrate, 1 g fiber, 16 g protein. Daily Values: 38% vit. A, 4% vit. C, 15% calcium, 4% iron.

timesaving, work-saving soups

Canned condensed soups have provided the ultimate in convenience since the late 1890s. Not only did these heat-and-stir sensations take the drudgery out of soupmaking, they also served as the base for a plethora of sauces, casseroles, and other dishes. In the '50s and '60s cooking with soups was especially fashionable, and dressing up a condensed soup with fresh ingredients, as in Cream of Chicken and Cheese Soup, above, was an easy way to get "from-scratch" flavor in just minutes.

Catalan **Chicken Chowder**

Start to finish: 30 minutes

Janice Elder
Charlotte, NC

This hearty chicken-rice soup brings hungry folks flocking to the table whether you serve it for a weeknight family supper or a weekend get-together with friends.

1 5-ounce package saffron-flavored yellow rice mix
2 teaspoons olive oil
½ pound skinless, boneless chicken breast halves, cut into bite-size pieces
1 medium onion, chopped (½ cup)
1 clove garlic, minced
1 14½-ounce can diced tomatoes, undrained

1 14½-ounce can reduced-sodium chicken broth
½ of a 14-ounce can (about ¾ cup) artichoke hearts, drained and quartered
½ cup frozen loose-pack baby peas
½ of a 7-ounce jar roasted red sweet peppers, drained and cut into strips
2 tablespoons slivered almonds, toasted

1 Prepare rice according to package directions; keep warm. Meanwhile, in a large saucepan heat oil over medium-high heat. Add chicken, onion, and garlic; cook and stir about 5 minutes or until chicken is no longer pink.

2 Add undrained tomatoes, chicken broth, and artichoke hearts to chicken mixture. Bring to boiling; reduce heat. Simmer, uncovered, for 10 minutes, stirring occasionally. Add peas and roasted sweet pepper strips. Cook for 3 to 4 minutes more or until soup is heated through.

3 To serve, ladle soup into soup bowls. Spoon a mound of the cooked yellow rice in center of each bowl. Sprinkle with almonds. Makes 4 servings.

Nutrition Facts per serving: 321 calories, 10 g total fat (2 g saturated fat), 30 mg cholesterol, 1,099 mg sodium, 42 g carbohydrate, 4 g fiber, 19 g protein. Daily Values: 20% vit. A, 133% vit. C, 5% calcium, 23% iron.

Tex-Mex Tortilla Soup

Prep: 25 minutes **Cook:** 20 minutes

4 medium skinless, boneless chicken breast halves (about 1 pound total)
2 14½-ounce cans reduced-sodium chicken broth
1 14½-ounce can beef broth
1 14½-ounce can tomatoes, undrained and cut up
1 medium onion, chopped (½ cup)
¼ cup chopped green sweet pepper
1 cup frozen loose-pack whole kernel corn

1 to 2 teaspoons chili powder
½ teaspoon ground cumin
⅛ teaspoon ground black pepper
3 cups tortilla chips, coarsely crushed
1 cup shredded Monterey Jack cheese (4 ounces)
1 avocado, peeled, seeded, and cut into chunks (optional)
   Snipped fresh cilantro (optional)
   Sliced fresh jalapeño peppers (optional)*
   Lime wedges (optional)

1991

Nancy Savoie
Houston, TX

Nancy loved the tortilla soup served in a favorite Houston restaurant so much, she experimented in her own kitchen and came up with this version. (Pictured on page 142.)

1 Cut chicken into bite-size pieces; set aside. In a 4-quart Dutch oven combine chicken broth, beef broth, undrained tomatoes, onion, and sweet pepper. Bring to boiling. Add chicken. Return to boiling; reduce heat. Cover and simmer for 10 minutes. Add corn, chili powder, cumin, and black pepper. Return to boiling; reduce heat. Cover and simmer for 10 minutes more.

2 To serve, divide crushed tortilla chips among six soup bowls. Ladle soup over tortilla chips. Sprinkle with cheese. If desired, top with avocado, cilantro, and sliced jalapeño peppers. If desired, serve with lime wedges. Makes 6 servings.

*Note: Because chile peppers, such as jalapeños, contain volatile oils that can burn your skin and eyes, avoid direct contact with them as much as possible. When working with chile peppers, wear plastic or rubber gloves. If your bare hands do touch the chile peppers, wash your hands well with soap and water.

Nutrition Facts per serving: 259 calories, 10 g total fat (4 g saturated fat), 60 mg cholesterol, 896 mg sodium, 17 g carbohydrate, 2 g fiber, 27 g protein. Daily Values:12% vit. A, 23% vit. C, 19% calcium, 8% iron.

Spicy Shrimp **and Noodle Soup**

Start to finish: 35 minutes

Roxanne E. Chan
Albany, CA

Roxanne simmers succulent shrimp with ramen noodles, black beans, and zesty spices to make this crowd-pleasing soup.

1 pound fresh or frozen medium shrimp in shells
1 tablespoon lemon juice
¼ teaspoon chili powder
¼ teaspoon ground cumin
⅛ teaspoon pepper
5 cups water
2 3-ounce packages shrimp- or oriental-flavored ramen noodles

1 16-ounce jar salsa (about 1¾ cups)
1 15-ounce can black beans, rinsed and drained
1 8¾-ounce can no-salt-added whole kernel corn, drained
¼ cup snipped fresh cilantro
1 green onion, thinly sliced
   Shredded cheddar cheese (optional)
   Fresh cilantro sprigs (optional)

1 Thaw shrimp, if frozen. Peel and devein shrimp, leaving tails on if desired. In a medium bowl combine lemon juice, chili powder, cumin, and pepper; add shrimp. Toss to coat. Let shrimp stand for 20 minutes at room temperature, stirring occasionally.

2 Meanwhile, in a large saucepan bring the water to boiling. Stir in one of the noodle flavor packets (reserve remaining flavor packet for another use). Break ramen noodles into pieces; add to saucepan. Return to boiling; cook for 1 minute. Add the shrimp; cook for 1 to 2 minutes more or until shrimp turn pink. Stir in salsa, beans, corn, snipped cilantro, and green onion. Heat through.

3 To serve, ladle into soup bowls. If desired, top each serving with shredded cheese and garnish with cilantro sprigs. Makes 6 servings.

Nutrition Facts per serving: 251 calories, 6 g total fat (0 g saturated fat), 92 mg cholesterol, 976 mg sodium, 33 g carbohydrate, 6 g fiber, 20 g protein. Daily Values: 13% vit. A, 27% vit. C, 9% calcium, 19% iron.

Red Pepper and Snapper Soup

Start to finish: 50 minutes

1999

Patrick Murray
Chicago, IL

When you need a no-fail main dish, rely on this rich-tasting, easy-to-assemble fish soup. If red snapper or orange roughy isn't available, try it with cod or sole.

1¼ pounds fresh or frozen skinless red snapper, orange roughy, or other firm-fleshed fish fillets
2 tablespoons olive oil
3 medium red sweet peppers, coarsely chopped (2¼ cups)
1 cup chopped shallots or onions
3 14½-ounce cans reduced-sodium chicken broth (5¼ cups total)
¼ teaspoon salt
¼ teaspoon ground black pepper
⅛ teaspoon ground red pepper
½ cup snipped fresh Italian parsley
Fresh Italian parsley sprigs (optional)

1 Thaw fish, if frozen. Rinse fish; pat dry. Cut fish into 1-inch pieces; set aside. In a large saucepan or Dutch oven heat oil over medium heat. Add sweet peppers and shallots or onions; cook for 5 minutes. Carefully add 1 can of the broth. Bring to boiling; reduce heat. Cover and simmer about 20 minutes or until peppers are very tender. Remove from heat; cool slightly.

2 Pour half of the sweet pepper mixture into a blender container. Cover and blend until nearly smooth. Pour into a medium bowl. Repeat with remaining pepper mixture. Return all to saucepan or Dutch oven. Add remaining chicken broth, the salt, black pepper, and ground red pepper. Bring to boiling; reduce heat. Add fish to broth mixture. Cover and simmer about 5 minutes or until fish flakes easily when tested with a fork, stirring once or twice. Stir in snipped parsley. If desired, garnish soup with parsley sprigs. Makes 5 servings.

Nutrition Facts per serving: 223 calories, 8 g total fat (1 g saturated fat), 42 mg cholesterol, 859 mg sodium, 10 g carbohydrate, 0 g fiber, 27 g protein. Daily Values: 76% vit. A, 142% vit. C, 5% calcium, 8% iron.

Vegetable Chili with Cheese Topping

Prep: 20 minutes **Cook:** 45 minutes

Nonstick cooking spray
1¼ cups finely chopped zucchini
¾ cup finely chopped carrot
1 green onion, chopped
2 cloves garlic, minced
2 15-ounce cans hot-style chili beans
   in chili sauce
2 14½-ounce cans diced tomatoes,
   undrained
¼ cup catsup
1 tablespoon unsweetened cocoa
   powder

1 teaspoon chili powder
1 teaspoon ground cumin
1 teaspoon bottled hot pepper sauce
¼ teaspoon dried oregano, crushed
   Salt
   Black pepper
½ of an 8-ounce tub cream cheese with
   chive and onion
2 tablespoons milk
½ cup shredded cheddar cheese
   (2 ounces)
   Green onion strips (optional)

1997

*Jan Curry
Raleigh, NC*

A cheddar and cream
cheese topping provides a
soothing counterpoint
to this spunky cocoa-
accented chili.

1 Coat a large saucepan with cooking spray; heat over medium heat. Add zucchini, carrot, chopped green onion, and garlic; cook for 2 minutes. Add undrained chili beans, undrained tomatoes, catsup, cocoa powder, chili powder, cumin, hot pepper sauce, and oregano. Bring to boiling; reduce heat. Simmer, uncovered, about 45 minutes or until desired consistency, stirring occasionally. Season to taste with salt and black pepper.

2 Meanwhile, in a small bowl stir together cream cheese and milk until smooth. Stir in cheddar cheese. To serve, ladle chili into bowls. Spoon some of the cream cheese mixture onto each serving. If desired, garnish with green onion strips. Makes 6 servings.

Nutrition Facts per serving: 281 calories, 13 g total fat (5 g saturated fat), 30 mg cholesterol, 1,183 mg sodium, 39 g carbohydrate, 5 g fiber, 13 g protein. Daily Values: 69% vit. A, 48% vit. C, 17% calcium, 26% iron.

Tamale-Topped Lentil Soup

Prep: 20 minutes **Cook:** 35 minutes

Anne Glenn
Eugene, OR

The cheesy cornmeal topping is a hearty addition to this fiber-rich, meatless, lentil-and-vegetable soup.

3½ cups water
2 medium stalks celery, sliced (1 cup)
1 medium onion, chopped (½ cup)
½ cup dry brown lentils, rinsed and drained
1 14½-ounce can stewed tomatoes, undrained
2 medium carrots, sliced (1 cup)
1 cup frozen loose-pack whole kernel corn
1 cup frozen loose-pack cut green beans
1 cup sliced zucchini and/or yellow summer squash
1 small green sweet pepper, chopped (½ cup)
1 clove garlic, minced
¾ teaspoon salt
¾ teaspoon chili powder
¼ teaspoon ground cumin
⅛ teaspoon ground black pepper
1 recipe Tamale Topper
¼ cup shredded cheddar cheese (1 ounce)

1 In a 4-quart Dutch oven combine 1½ cups of the water, the celery, onion, and lentils. Bring to boiling; reduce heat. Cover and simmer about 20 minutes or until lentils are tender; drain. Add the remaining water, the undrained tomatoes, carrots, corn, green beans, zucchini and/or yellow squash, sweet pepper, garlic, salt, chili powder, cumin, and black pepper. Return to boiling; reduce heat.

2 Meanwhile, prepare Tamale Topper. Drop Tamale Topper in six portions onto hot stew. Cover (do not lift cover while cooking) and simmer about 15 minutes more or until a toothpick inserted in topper comes out clean. Sprinkle with the cheddar cheese just before serving. Makes 6 servings.

Tamale Topper: In a medium saucepan combine ⅔ cup cornmeal and ¼ teaspoon salt. Gradually stir in 1 cup milk. Cook and stir until thickened and bubbly. Gradually stir cornmeal mixture into 1 beaten egg. Stir in ½ cup shredded cheddar cheese (2 ounces).

Nutrition Facts per serving: 286 calories, 8 g total fat (4 g saturated fat), 53 mg cholesterol, 666 mg sodium, 43 g carbohydrate, 6 g fiber, 13 g protein. Daily Values: 68% vit. A, 30% vit. C, 23% calcium, 19% iron.

Root Veggie Soup with Curry Croutons

Prep: 25 minutes **Cook:** 25 minutes **Bake:** 15 minutes

1999

*Julie DeMatteo
Clementon, NJ*

For a golden crowning touch, sprinkle the optional croutons onto Julie's first-rate meal-in-a-bowl soup.

1 medium fennel bulb (4 to 5 ounces)
¼ cup chopped onion
1 clove garlic, minced
2 teaspoons cooking oil
3 cups chicken broth
1 medium turnip, peeled and cubed (about ¾ cup)
1 medium potato, peeled and cubed (about ⅔ cup)
1 medium carrot, sliced (½ cup)
¼ teaspoon ground white or black pepper

1 tablespoon olive oil
½ teaspoon curry powder
3 ¾-inch slices Italian bread, torn into bite-size pieces
1 15- or 19-ounce can white kidney (cannellini) beans, rinsed and drained
¼ cup half-and-half or light cream
Salt
Curry croutons (optional)

1 Cut off and discard upper stalks of fennel, snipping and reserving feathery leaves for garnish. Remove any wilted outer layers of fennel and discard; remove core. Finely chop remaining fennel; set aside.

2 In a large saucepan cook onion and garlic in hot cooking oil about 5 minutes or until onion is tender. Carefully add chopped fennel, broth, turnip, potato, carrot, and white or black pepper. Bring to boiling; reduce heat. Cover and simmer for 25 to 30 minutes or until vegetables are very tender. Cool slightly.

3 Meanwhile, if using, for curry croutons, in a medium bowl combine olive oil and curry powder. Add the torn bread pieces; toss until coated. Spread bread pieces in a single layer in a 15×10×1-inch baking pan. Bake in a 350° oven for 15 to 20 minutes or until croutons begin to brown, stirring once.

4 Place one-third of the vegetable mixture in a blender container or food processor bowl. Cover and blend or process until smooth; pour into a medium bowl. Repeat twice with remaining mixture. Return all to saucepan. Stir in beans and half-and-half or light cream; heat through. Season to taste with salt.

5 To serve, ladle soup into four soup bowls. If desired, float a few of the curry croutons on each serving. Garnish with snipped fennel leaves. Makes 4 servings.

Nutrition Facts per serving: 282 calories, 10 g total fat (2 g saturated fat), 6 mg cholesterol, 935 mg sodium, 42 g carbohydrate, 16 g fiber, 14 g protein. Daily Values: 42% vit. A, 20% vit. C, 8% calcium, 17% iron.

Gingered Pumpkin-Pear Soup

Start to finish: 25 minutes

½ cup chopped sweet onion
2 teaspoons grated fresh ginger
1 tablespoon margarine or butter
3 pears, peeled, cored, and sliced
1 15-ounce can pumpkin
1½ cups vegetable broth
1 cup milk

Salt
Pepper
¼ cup light dairy sour cream
½ teaspoon finely shredded lime peel
1 tablespoon lime juice
Lime peel (optional)

N. Coult and K. Moerke
Boulder, CO

A swirl of lime-laced sour cream adds a burst of citrus flavor to this smooth, golden, pumpkin soup. When hosting a dinner party, serve it as a first course for a touch of sophistication.

1 In a large saucepan cook onion and ginger in hot margarine or butter until onion is tender. Stir in pears; cook for 1 minute. Stir in pumpkin and vegetable broth. Bring mixture to boiling; reduce heat. Cover and simmer about 5 minutes more or until pears are tender. Cool slightly. Transfer half of the pumpkin mixture to a food processor bowl or blender container; cover and process or blend about 1 minute or until smooth. Repeat with remaining pumpkin mixture. Return pureed mixture to saucepan; stir in milk. Heat through. Season to taste with salt and pepper.

2 Meanwhile, stir together sour cream, the ½ teaspoon lime peel, and the lime juice. Drizzle some of the sour cream mixture over each serving of soup. If desired, garnish with additional lime peel. Makes 6 side-dish servings.

Nutrition Facts per serving: 129 calories, 4 g total fat (1 g saturated fat), 4 mg cholesterol, 310 mg sodium, 24 g carbohydrate, 5 g fiber, 3 g protein. Daily Values: 162% vit. A, 13% vit. C, 7% calcium, 8% iron.

Asparagus **and Leek Chowder**

Start to finish: 45 minutes

1973

Lynne Michelle Scott Ladd
Falls Church, VA

Serve this vegetable medley of mushrooms, leeks, asparagus, and corn as a first course to a light meal.

8 ounces fresh mushrooms, sliced
    (3 cups)
3 large leeks, sliced (1¼ cups)
1 10-ounce package frozen cut
    asparagus, thawed
3 tablespoons butter or margarine
3 tablespoons all-purpose flour
¼ teaspoon salt

Dash pepper
2 cups half-and-half, light cream, or
    milk
1 14½-ounce can chicken broth
1 cup frozen white whole kernel corn
    (shoe peg)
2 tablespoons chopped pimiento
    Dash crushed saffron (optional)

1 In a large saucepan cook mushrooms, leeks, and asparagus in hot butter or margarine about 10 minutes or until tender, stirring occasionally. Stir in flour, salt, and pepper. Add half-and-half, light cream, or milk and chicken broth; cook and stir until mixture is thickened and bubbly. Stir in the corn, pimiento, and if using, crushed saffron. Heat through but do not boil. Makes 8 side-dish servings.

Nutrition Facts per serving: 180 calories, 13 g total fat (7 g saturated fat), 34 mg cholesterol, 315 mg sodium, 13 g carbohydrate, 2 g fiber, 6 g protein. Daily Values: 15% vit. A, 25% vit. C, 9% calcium, 6% iron.

ladling up soup '70s-style

In the 1970s, many people took a breather from the complicated and fussy dishes they'd been eating and started getting back to basics. Simple foods, such as homemade breads and made-from-scratch soups, became the order of the day. Before long, restaurants specializing in soups became the "in" places to go. Cooks also tinkered with soups at home. Asparagus and Leek Chowder, above, is a twist on traditional chowder. It won in the chowders category in a 1973 Prize Tested Recipes contest. Lynne started with a chowder base made from light cream and broth, then added her favorite vegetables plus a pinch of saffron.

Springtime Soup

Start to finish: 25 minutes

1 pound fresh asparagus spears
1 medium onion, chopped (½ cup)
3 cloves garlic, minced
1 tablespoon olive oil
1 49½-ounce can chicken broth
½ cup dried orzo or other tiny pasta

3 cups snow pea pods, ends and strings removed
6 cups torn fresh spinach
¼ teaspoon pepper
¼ cup purchased pesto (optional)
¼ cup finely shredded Parmesan cheese

1998

Diane Barnette
Reno, NV

Garden-fresh asparagus, snow peas, and spinach make Diane's quick-to-fix tempter a vegetarian treat. If you enjoy the fragrant flavor of basil, don't forget the pesto. Use vegetable broth in place of the chicken broth, if you prefer.

1 Snap off and discard woody bases from asparagus. If desired, scrape off scales. Bias-slice the asparagus into 1-inch pieces; set aside.

2 Meanwhile, in a 4-quart Dutch oven cook the onion and garlic in hot oil until tender. Carefully add chicken broth; bring to boiling. Stir in pasta; reduce heat and boil gently for 5 minutes. Stir in asparagus and snow pea pods. Return soup to boiling; cook for 3 minutes more. Stir in spinach and pepper; cook for 1 minute more.

3 To serve, ladle soup into bowls. If desired, swirl some of the pesto into each bowl of soup. Sprinkle some of the Parmesan cheese on top of each. Makes 8 side-dish servings.

Nutrition Facts per serving: 133 calories, 4 g total fat (1 g saturated fat), 3 mg cholesterol, 634 mg sodium, 15 g carbohydrate, 3 g fiber, 10 g protein. Daily Values: 31% vit. A, 59% vit. C, 8% calcium, 18% iron.

Goldilocks Potatoes page 182

Side Dishes

Honey-Glazed Carrots

Start to finish: 18 minutes

Leona Laabs
Plymouth, WI

Whether you team it with meat, poultry, or fish, this simple, yet elegant, side dish is sure to be a favorite. If you can't find small carrots, use prepackaged peeled baby carrots or regular-size carrots cut into 2-inch pieces.

10 to 12 young, small carrots (about 1¼ pounds)
3 tablespoons butter or margarine
2 tablespoons honey
1 tablespoon brown sugar

1 If desired, remove tops from carrots or trim tops to ½ inch. In a large skillet cook carrots, covered, in a small amount of boiling, salted water for 8 to 10 minutes or just until tender. Drain carrots; remove from skillet.

2 For glaze, in the same skillet melt butter or margarine. Stir in honey and brown sugar. Cook and stir over medium heat about 2 minutes or until slightly thickened and bubbly. Add carrots, tossing gently until coated with glaze and heated through. Makes 4 to 6 servings.

Nutrition Facts per serving: 182 calories, 9 g total fat (6 g saturated fat), 25 mg cholesterol, 144 mg sodium, 25 g carbohydrate, 4 g fiber, 2 g protein. Daily Values: 407% vit. A, 22% vit. C, 4% calcium, 5% iron.

cream-of-the-crop carrots

The orange carrots we know today were developed by French growers in the mid-19th century, but they took a while to catch on. Toward the end of the 1800s and during the first 20 years of the 20th century, carrots still were considered a second-class vegetable. Cooks of that era preferred parsnips as a vegetable side dish and used carrots mostly to flavor soups and stews and for garnish. During the 1930s, cooks began to candy and glaze carrots like sweet potatoes. That is when recipes such as Honey-Glazed Carrots, above, became favorites.

Autumn Medley

Start to finish: 20 minutes

8 ounces parsnips, peeled and cut into thin bite-size strips (2¼ cups)

8 ounces carrots, peeled and cut into thin bite-size strips (2¼ cups)

¾ cup orange juice

⅓ cup dried cranberries

½ teaspoon ground ginger

2 firm ripe pears, peeled and cut into ½-inch slices

⅓ cup pecan halves

3 tablespoons brown sugar

2 tablespoons margarine or butter

1999

*Lorraine G. Carr
Rochester, MA*

Fresh pears, dried cranberries, and orange juice add a pleasant fruity flavor to this winning combo of parsnips and carrots.

1 In a large nonstick skillet combine parsnips, carrots, orange juice, dried cranberries, and ginger. Bring to boiling; reduce heat to medium. Cook, uncovered, for 7 to 8 minutes or until vegetables are crisp-tender and most of the liquid has evaporated, stirring occasionally.

2 Add pears, pecans, brown sugar, and margarine or butter to mixture in skillet; stir. Cook, uncovered, for 2 to 3 minutes more or until vegetables are glazed. Makes 6 servings.

Nutrition Facts per serving: 230 calories, 8 g total fat (1 g saturated fat), 0 mg cholesterol, 77 mg sodium, 40 g carbohydrate, 7 g fiber, 2 g protein. Daily Values: 90% vit. A, 43% vit. C, 4% calcium, 7% iron.

Stuffed Zucchini

Prep: 30 minutes **Bake:** 25 minutes

6 medium zucchini	¼ teaspoon salt
1½ cups soft bread crumbs	⅛ teaspoon pepper
¼ cup finely shredded cheddar cheese or Parmesan cheese (1 ounce)	1 slightly beaten egg
¼ cup finely chopped onion	¼ cup finely shredded cheddar cheese or Parmesan cheese (1 ounce)
1 tablespoon snipped fresh parsley	

1 Wash zucchini and trim ends; do not peel. In a covered Dutch oven cook whole zucchini in lightly salted boiling water for 5 minutes; drain and cool slightly. Cut a lengthwise slice off top of each zucchini. Remove pulp with spoon, leaving about a ¼-inch shell.

2 Chop enough of the pulp to measure 2 cups; place chopped pulp in a medium bowl. (Save remaining pulp for another use.) Stir the bread crumbs, ¼ cup cheddar or Parmesan cheese, the onion, parsley, salt, pepper, and egg into chopped pulp until well mixed. Fill zucchini shells with pulp mixture. Place in a shallow baking pan.

3 Bake in a 350° oven for 20 minutes. Sprinkle with ¼ cup cheddar or Parmesan cheese; bake for 5 to 10 minutes more or until golden brown and heated through. Makes 6 servings.

Nutrition Facts per serving: 93 calories, 4 g total fat (2 g saturated fat), 45 mg cholesterol, 229 mg sodium, 8 g carbohydrate, 1 g fiber, 5 g protein. Daily Values: 7% vit. A, 13% vit. C, 10% calcium, 5% iron.

1937

Mrs. John Aragni, Jr.
San Francisco, CA

In 1937, when this fresh-from-the-garden side dish first appeared, zucchini wasn't available in all supermarkets. The recipe helpfully pointed out that zucchini was Italian squash.

versatile italian import

Along with broccoli and artichokes, zucchini was introduced in the U.S. during the 1930s. A favorite of Italian immigrants in California, the slender green summer squash was used in recipes such as Stuffed Zucchini, above, during that period. But zucchini remained a specialty vegetable for most of the next 30 years. It wasn't until the late 1960s and early 1970s that home gardeners discovered the prolific vegetable and began filling their gardens to overflowing with it.

Tomato Melts

Prep: 15 minutes **Bake:** 15 minutes

1999

Kara Frank
Baton Rouge, LA

Topped with zesty cheese, colorful sweet pepper, and toasted almonds, these tasty tomatoes are so enticing seconds are hard to refuse.

3   large tomatoes (about 8 ounces each) or assorted small tomatoes (about 1½ pounds total)
1   cup shredded Monterey Jack cheese with jalapeño peppers or Monterey Jack cheese (4 ounces)

1   small green, yellow, purple, or red sweet pepper, finely chopped (½ cup)
¼   cup sliced almonds, toasted

1 Line a 15×10×1-inch baking pan with foil; set aside. Cut each large tomato into four slices or halve each small tomato. For each serving, arrange three large tomato slices, overlapping slightly, in the prepared baking pan. (Or, if using small tomatoes, arrange in a single layer in the prepared baking pan.) Sprinkle tomatoes with cheese, sweet pepper, and almonds. Bake in a 350° oven about 15 minutes or until cheese is bubbly. Using a large metal spatula, carefully lift tomatoes to serving plates, allowing excess juices to drain off. Makes 4 servings.

To grill tomatoes: Arrange ingredients as directed in a shallow disposable foil pan. In a grill with a cover arrange medium-hot coals around the edge of the grill; test for medium heat above the center of the grill. Place the pan with the tomatoes in the center of the grill rack. Cover and grill for 12 to 15 minutes or until cheese is bubbly.

Nutrition Facts per serving: 203 calories, 14 g total fat (6 g saturated fat), 25 mg cholesterol, 172 mg sodium, 13 g carbohydrate, 2 g fiber, 10 g protein. Daily Values: 21% vit. A, 79% vit. C, 20% calcium, 10% iron.

Green Beans Supreme

Prep: 15 minutes **Bake:** 30 minutes

3 14½-ounce cans cut green beans, drained, or 6 cups loose-pack frozen cut green beans
1 medium onion, sliced
1 tablespoon butter or margarine
1 8-ounce carton dairy sour cream
2 tablespoons all-purpose flour

½ teaspoon grated lemon peel
¼ teaspoon pepper
½ cup shredded American cheese (2 ounces)
⅓ cup fine dry bread crumbs
1 tablespoon butter or margarine, melted

1953

Ilo M. Creamer
Orient, OH

Ilo combined a lemony sour cream sauce and a cheesy crumb topping to make a delectable dress-up for green beans.

1 If using frozen beans, place beans in a large saucepan with ½ inch water. Bring to a boil; reduce heat. Cover; cook for 4 minutes or until just tender, stirring occasionally. Drain and set aside.

2 Meanwhile, in a small saucepan cook onion in 1 tablespoon butter or margarine until tender. In a large bowl stir together sour cream, flour, lemon peel, and pepper. Stir in beans and cooked onion. Spoon bean mixture into a 2-quart square or rectangular baking dish. Top with shredded cheese. In a small bowl combine bread crumbs and 1 tablespoon melted butter or margarine; sprinkle over beans.

3 Bake in a 350° oven about 30 minutes or until crumbs are browned and mixture is heated through. Makes 8 servings.

Nutrition Facts per serving: 151 calories, 11 g total fat (11 g saturated fat), 54 mg cholesterol, 424 mg sodium, 9 g carbohydrate, 2 g fiber, 4 g protein. Daily Values: 13% vit. A, 7% vit. C, 11% calcium, 6% iron.

spunky sour cream

While farm cooks had been using fresh soured cream to add a pleasant tang to all types of dishes for generations, it wasn't until the 1950s that dairy sour cream became widely available. Cooks across the country began commonly adding it to dishes such as Green Beans Supreme, above.

Spiced Vegetable-Stuffed Squash

Prep: 20 minutes **Bake:** 1 hour 5 minutes

2 medium acorn squash (about 1 pound each)	1 tablespoon brown sugar
2 small turnips, chopped (1½ cups)	½ teaspoon ground cinnamon
2 medium carrots, chopped (1 cup)	¼ teaspoon salt
1 tablespoon butter or margarine	¼ teaspoon ground nutmeg
	1 cup coarsely shredded, peeled apple

1982

*Mary Jeanne Brooks
Chelsea, OK*

For her entry in the Winter Vegetable Ideas category, Mary Jeanne teamed carrots, turnips, apples, and spices with acorn squash for a tasty side dish.

1 Quarter squash; remove seeds and strings. Place squash, cut sides down, in a 13×9×2-inch baking pan. Cover lightly with foil. Bake in a 350° oven for 30 minutes. Turn cut sides up; bake, covered, for 20 to 30 minutes more or until tender. Carefully scoop pulp out of each squash quarter, keeping shells intact and leaving a thin layer of squash in shells. Set shells aside. Place cooked pulp in a large bowl.

2 Meanwhile, in a covered saucepan cook turnips and carrots in boiling, lightly salted water about 20 minutes or until tender. Drain well. Add turnips and carrots to the squash pulp in bowl. Coarsely mash vegetables with a potato masher.

3 Add butter or margarine, brown sugar, cinnamon, salt, and nutmeg to mashed vegetables; stir to combine. Fold in apple. Spoon vegetable-apple mixture evenly into squash shells. Return to baking pan. Bake in the 350° oven for 15 to 20 minutes more or until heated through. Makes 8 servings.

Nutrition Facts per serving: 86 calories, 2 g total fat (1 g saturated fat), 4 mg cholesterol, 114 mg sodium, 17 g carbohydrate, 3 g fiber, 2 g protein. Daily Values: 84% vit. A, 29% vit. C, 5% calcium, 5% iron.

Goldilocks **Potatoes**

Prep: 15 minutes **Bake:** 15 minutes

1939

Mrs. Harvey M. Fry
Binghamton, NY

Yukon gold potatoes and cheese give these luscious potatoes their appealing color. (Pictured on page 172.)

2 pounds Yukon gold or other
     potatoes, peeled and cut up
¼ teaspoon salt
⅛ teaspoon pepper

Milk (optional)
½ cup whipping cream
⅓ cup shredded American or
     cheddar cheese

1 In a large saucepan cook potatoes, covered, in a large amount of boiling water for 15 to 20 minutes or until tender. Drain. Mash with a potato masher or beat with an electric mixer on low speed. Season with the salt and pepper. If necessary, add a small amount of milk to make of desired consistency.

2 Grease four 10-ounce individual casseroles or custard cups or a 1-quart casserole. Spoon potato mixture into prepared casseroles. In a chilled medium bowl beat whipping cream with chilled beaters of an electric mixer on medium speed until soft peaks form; fold in cheese. Spoon cheese mixture over potatoes. Bake in a 350° oven for 15 to 20 minutes or until lightly browned. Makes 4 servings.

Nutrition Facts per serving: 366 calories, 15 g total fat (9 g saturated fat), 52 mg cholesterol, 340 mg sodium, 51 g carbohydrate, 2 g fiber, 8 g protein. Daily Values: 16% vit. A, 49% vit. C, 12% calcium, 21% iron.

French Mashed Potatoes: Peel and cut up 2 pounds potatoes. In a large saucepan cook potatoes, covered, in a large amount of boiling water for 15 to 20 minutes or until tender. Drain. Mash with a potato masher or beat with an electric mixer on low speed. Add ½ cup warmed milk, 2 tablespoons butter or margarine, ½ teaspoon baking powder, ¼ teaspoon salt, and ⅛ teaspoon pepper to potatoes; beat until fluffy. Stir in 1 tablespoon finely chopped onion. Serve immediately. Makes 4 servings.

Nutrition Facts per serving: 288 calories, 7 g total fat (4 g saturated fat), 19 mg cholesterol, 289 mg sodium, 51 g carbohydrate, 2 g fiber, 6 g protein. Daily Values: 7% vit. A, 49% vit. C, 10% calcium, 21% iron.

Berlin Scalloped Potatoes

Prep: 20 minutes **Bake:** 32 minutes **Stand:** 5 minutes

1 10-ounce package frozen chopped
    spinach, thawed
4 slices bacon
1 medium onion, thinly sliced
1 5-ounce package dry scalloped
    potato mix

   Milk
1 to 2 teaspoons caraway seed
1 cup shredded provolone or
    mozzarella cheese (4 ounces)

1990

Antoinette M. Montgomery
Kirkwood, MO

To simplify an old German recipe, Antoinette substituted a scalloped potato mix for fresh potatoes. The result was this tasty side dish.

1 Drain thawed spinach well, pressing out excess liquid; set aside. In a large skillet cook bacon until crisp. Drain, reserving 1 tablespoon drippings in skillet. Crumble bacon; set aside.

2 In the same skillet cook the onion in reserved drippings over medium heat for 4 to 5 minutes or until tender. Add spinach; heat through.

3 In a 2-quart rectangular baking dish or oval au gratin dish combine potatoes and dry sauce mix from package. Stir in boiling water and milk as directed on package, omitting margarine or butter. Stir in the crumbled bacon, spinach-onion mixture, and caraway seed.

4 Bake, uncovered, in a 400° oven for 30 to 35 minutes or until potatoes are tender. Sprinkle with cheese; bake for 2 to 3 minutes more or until cheese is melted. Let stand for 5 minutes before serving. Makes 6 servings.

Nutrition Facts per serving: 216 calories, 12 g total fat (7 g saturated fat), 29 mg cholesterol, 661 mg sodium, 19 g carbohydrate, 3 g fiber, 10 g protein. Daily Values: 44% vit. A, 17% vit. C, 26% calcium, 8% iron.

Scalloped New Potatoes

Prep: 25 minutes **Bake:** 20 minutes

Jeanne Gedeon
Huntington, NY

Jeanne adds spinach, sweet pepper, and rosemary to give her version of scalloped potatoes a flavorful twist.

Nonstick cooking spray
2 pounds whole tiny new potatoes, sliced
3 tablespoons margarine or butter
1 large onion, chopped (1 cup)
3 cloves garlic, minced
3 tablespoons all-purpose flour
1¼ teaspoons dried rosemary, crushed
1 teaspoon dried parsley

½ teaspoon salt
¼ teaspoon ground black pepper
1¾ cups milk
6 cups torn spinach or 4 cups broccoli rabe, cut into 1½-inch pieces
1 small red sweet pepper, cut into thin bite-size strips
¾ cup shredded white cheddar cheese
¼ cup fine dry bread crumbs

1 Coat a 2-quart oval or rectangular baking dish with cooking spray; set aside. In a large saucepan cook potatoes, covered, in a moderate amount of boiling salted water about 5 minutes or just until tender. Drain and transfer to an extra-large bowl.

2 For sauce, in same saucepan melt 2 tablespoons of the margarine or butter over medium heat; add onion and garlic and cook about 5 minutes or just until tender. Stir in flour, rosemary, parsley, salt, and black pepper. Stir in milk all at once. Cook and stir over medium heat until thickened and bubbly.

3 Add spinach or broccoli rabe and sweet pepper to potatoes. Toss gently to combine. Pour sauce over potato mixture. Stir gently until coated. Spoon potato mixture into prepared baking dish (dish will be very full). Set baking dish on a baking sheet.

4 Sprinkle with cheese. Melt the remaining margarine or butter. Add bread crumbs, tossing to coat. Sprinkle over cheese. Bake in a 375° oven about 20 minutes or until edges are bubbly and crumbs are golden brown. Makes 10 to 12 servings.

Nutrition Facts per serving: 214 calories, 8 g total fat (3 g saturated fat), 12 mg cholesterol, 274 mg sodium, 30 g carbohydrate, 2 g fiber, 8 g protein. Daily Values: 35% vit. A, 54% vit. C, 14% calcium, 16% iron.

Lemon-Parsley Stuffing

Prep: 35 minutes **Bake:** 40 minutes

1985

Elise Roberts
Henderson, TX

To add a fresh, lemony accent to roast turkey or chicken, serve the bird with Elsie's sophisticated stuffing.

10 cups dry bread cubes (about 15 slices)*
 1 cup finely chopped onion
 ¾ cup snipped fresh parsley
 2 slightly beaten eggs
 ½ cup butter or margarine, melted
 4 teaspoons finely shredded lemon peel
 3 tablespoons lemon juice
 2 teaspoons dried marjoram, crushed
 1 teaspoon dried thyme, crushed
 ½ teaspoon pepper
 ¼ teaspoon salt
 2 cloves garlic, minced
 ½ to ¾ cup chicken broth

1 In a very large bowl combine dry bread cubes, onion, and parsley. In a small bowl combine eggs, melted butter or margarine, lemon peel, lemon juice, marjoram, thyme, pepper, salt, and garlic. Add to bread mixture. Add enough of the chicken broth to moisten, tossing gently.

2 Spoon stuffing into a 2-quart casserole. Bake, covered, in a 325° oven for 30 minutes. Uncover and bake until an instant-read thermometer inserted in center of stuffing registers 165° (10 to 15 minutes more). Makes about 8 cups stuffing.

*Note: To dry bread cubes, cut bread into cubes and place in a large shallow roasting pan. Bake, uncovered, in a 325° oven about 20 minutes or until dried, stirring once or twice. Set aside.

Nutrition Facts per ½-cup serving: 134 calories, 8 g total fat (4 g saturated fat), 43 mg cholesterol, 254 mg sodium, 13 g carbohydrate, 1 g fiber, 3 g protein. Daily Values: 9% vit. A, 11% vit. C, 4% calcium, 6% iron.

lip-smackin' lemon

Grated lemon peel adds a refreshing hint of citrus to a variety of recipes, including Lemon-Parsley Stuffing, above. To get the maximum lemon flavor, look for well-shaped fruit with smooth, evenly colored skin. Avoid bruised or wrinkled fruit. To avoid any bitterness, grate only the colored part of the peel. A medium lemon should yield about 2 teaspoons finely shredded peel.

Mediterranean Fig Dressing

Prep: 40 minutes **Bake:** 40 minutes

1 cup coarsely chopped dried figs
2 tablespoons brandy or desired wine
3 cups pita bread rounds, cut into
    thin strips
3 cups Italian bread cubes
2 cloves garlic, minced
⅓ cup margarine or butter
1 tablespoon snipped fresh thyme or
    1 teaspoon dried thyme, crushed

1 tablespoon snipped fresh rosemary
    or ½ teaspoon dried rosemary,
    crushed
1 large onion, chopped (1 cup)
½ cup chopped walnuts
1 to 1¼ cups chicken broth
    Fresh thyme sprigs (optional)

*Susan Scarborough
Jackonsville, FL*

Brandy- or wine-soaked
figs, and pita bread,
and a wonderful herb
combination send your taste
buds on an exotic trip.

1 In a small bowl combine figs and brandy or wine; set aside. Place pita bread strips and Italian bread cubes in a shallow baking pan; set aside.

2 In a large skillet cook garlic in hot margarine or butter for 1 minute; reserve 3 tablespoons of the margarine or butter mixture in skillet. Drizzle the remaining margarine mixture over bread strips and cubes; sprinkle with the snipped or dried thyme and the rosemary. Bake in a 350° oven for 15 to 20 minutes or until bread is toasted, stirring once.

3 Meanwhile, cook onion in the reserved margarine or butter mixture until tender; set aside. In a large bowl combine bread mixture, fig mixture, cooked onion mixture, and the walnuts. Add enough of the chicken broth to moisten, tossing gently. Spoon dressing into a 1½-quart casserole. Bake, covered, in the 350° oven for 40 to 45 minutes or until heated through. If desired, garnish with thyme sprigs. Makes 8 servings.

Nutrition Facts per serving: 254 calories, 13 g total fat (2 g saturated fat), 0 mg cholesterol, 357 mg sodium, 28 g carbohydrate, 2 g fiber, 5 g protein. Daily Values: 10% vit. A, 4% vit. C, 5% calcium, 10% iron.

Company **Cabbage**

Prep: 10 minutes **Cook:** 5 minutes

1979

Mrs. Loren D. Martin
Knoxville, TN

The peppy flavor of mustard and the crunch of pecans make this simple, yet special, vegetable dish good enough for company.

¼ cup water
1 teaspoon instant beef bouillon granules
5 cups coarsely shredded cabbage*
1 cup coarsely shredded carrots*
½ cup sliced green onions
¼ teaspoon salt

¼ teaspoon pepper
⅓ cup chopped pecans
2 tablespoons butter or margarine, melted
1 teaspoon prepared mustard
Paprika

1 In a large saucepan combine the water and beef bouillon granules; heat until dissolved. Add cabbage, carrots, green onions, salt, and pepper. Toss to mix. Cover and cook over medium-low heat about 5 minutes or until crisp-tender, stirring once or twice during cooking. Drain, if necessary. Combine pecans, butter or margarine, and mustard. Pour over vegetables; toss to mix. Spoon into serving dish. Sprinkle with paprika. Makes 6 servings.

*Note: If desired, substitute 6 cups packaged shredded cabbage with carrot (coleslaw mix) for the shredded cabbage and carrots.

Nutrition Facts per serving: 103 calories, 8 g total fat (3 g saturated fat), 11 mg cholesterol, 311 mg sodium, 7 g carbohydrate, 3 g fiber, 2 g protein. Daily Values: 51% vit. A, 31% vit. C, 4% calcium, 4% iron.

cabbage convenience

At harvest time, cooks of yesterday eased the tedious task of shredding head after head of cabbage for sauerkraut with what was known as a kraut cutter. They typically used a butcher knife to hand-shred cabbage for family-size portions of coleslaw or cooked cabbage. The introduction of the food processor in the '70s offered a quick way to shred or chop vegetables, including cabbage. Today prepackaged coleslaw mix, which became popular in the '90s, means recipes calling for shredded cabbage can be tossed together in no time at all.

Rice and Feta Salad

Prep: 45 minutes **Chill:** 4 to 24 hours

1 cup brown rice
½ teaspoon salt
4 ounces feta cheese, crumbled
1 large green and/or yellow sweet
  pepper, chopped (1 cup)
1 small onion, finely chopped (⅓ cup)

⅓ cup pine nuts or chopped pecans,
  toasted
1 2-ounce jar diced pimiento, drained
3 tablespoons olive oil or salad oil
2 tablespoons tarragon white wine
  vinegar*
⅛ teaspoon ground black pepper

*Stacey L. Swiantek
Snyder, NY*

Stacey's original salad called for wild pecan long-grain rice, which is often hard to find because it grows only in Louisiana. Brown rice and pine nuts or pecans are fine substitutes.

1 Cook brown rice and salt according to package directions; cool slightly. In a large bowl combine cheese, sweet pepper, onion, nuts, and pimiento; stir in cooled rice.

2 For dressing, stir together oil, vinegar, and black pepper; add to rice mixture. Toss gently to coat. Cover; chill for at least 4 hours or up to 24 hours. Makes 8 servings.

*Note: You can substitute 2 tablespoons white wine vinegar plus ⅛ teaspoon dried tarragon, crushed, for the tarragon white wine vinegar.

Nutrition Facts per serving: 212 calories, 12 g total fat (3 g saturated fat), 12 mg cholesterol, 160 mg sodium, 22 g carbohydrate, 1 g fiber, 6 g protein. Daily Values: 5% vit. A, 39% vit. C, 8% calcium, 7% iron.

Layered Cranberry-**Apple Mold**

Prep: 1 hour 30 minutes **Chill:** 6 hours

**Mrs. Henry Harris
Wilkes Barre, PA**

Shimmering with cranberries, this lemon-gelatin salad makes a welcome addition to a buffet table, especially at holiday time.

1 6-ounce package lemon-flavored
   gelatin
½ cup sugar
1 cup boiling water
1½ cups cranberry-apple drink
1 16-ounce can whole cranberry sauce

1 1.3-ounce envelope dessert topping
   mix
1 large unpeeled apple, cored and
   finely chopped (1¼ cups)
¼ cup mayonnaise or salad dressing
   Sugared cranberries (optional)*
   Fresh mint (optional)

1 In a medium bowl dissolve gelatin and sugar in the boiling water. Stir in cranberry-apple drink. Transfer 1¾ cups of the mixture to another bowl; cover and chill about 30 minutes or until partially set (the consistency of egg whites). Set remaining gelatin-drink mixture aside.

2 Fold cranberry sauce into partially set gelatin-drink mixture; pour into an 8-cup ring mold or a 2-quart square dish. Cover and chill about 30 minutes or until almost firm. Chill remaining gelatin-drink mixture about 30 minutes or until partially set (the consistency of egg whites).

3 Meanwhile, prepare topping mix according to package directions; fold into partially set gelatin-drink mixture along with apple and mayonnaise or salad dressing. Spoon over chilled cranberry sauce-gelatin layer in mold or dish.

4 Cover and chill about 6 hours or until firm. Unmold gelatin onto platter. (For easier unmolding, set mold into a sink filled with warm water for a several seconds or until gelatin separates from the mold.) If desired, garnish with sugared cranberries and fresh mint. Makes 12 servings.

*Note: For sugared cranberries, freeze cranberries; roll in sugar until coated.

Nutrition Facts per serving: 222 calories, 5 g total fat (2 g saturated fat), 2 mg cholesterol, 95 mg sodium, 44 g carbohydrate, 1 g fiber, 2 g protein. Daily Values: 1% vit. A, 18% vit. C, 2% calcium.

Cranberry **Fluff**

Prep: 20 minutes **Stand:** 1 hour

1961

Mrs. Donald Thompson
Marshalltown, IA

Although Mrs. Thompson won a Fall Fruit Salad category with this people-pleasing fruit-and-nut medley, it can also be served as a dessert.

1½ cups fresh cranberries, ground
2¼ cups tiny marshmallows
⅔ cup sugar
1½ cups chopped tart apples

½ cup seedless green grapes, halved
⅓ cup broken walnuts
¾ cup whipping cream
Lettuce cups (optional)

1 In a large bowl combine cranberries, marshmallows, and sugar. Cover and let stand at room temperature for 1 hour. Stir in apples, grapes, and walnuts; set aside.

2 In a chilled medium mixing bowl beat whipping cream with chilled beaters of an electric mixer on medium speed until soft peaks form. Fold into cranberry mixture. Serve immediately. (Or if desired, cover and chill for up to 24 hours.) If desired, spoon into lettuce cups to serve. Makes 6 to 8 servings.

Nutrition Facts per serving: 354 calories, 16 g total fat (7 g saturated fat), 41 mg cholesterol, 35 mg sodium, 55 g carbohydrate, 3 g fiber, 2 g protein. Daily Values: 13% vit. A, 14% vit. C, 3% calcium, 2% iron.

cranberries–an american standard

Native Americans were experts at using cranberries, a native North American fruit, long before the Pilgrims arrived. They crushed cranberries with dried deer meat and melted fat and pressed the mixture into cakes for emergency food. It was the Colonists, however, that gave the berries their English name. They thought the pink cranberry blossoms looked like the heads of cranes, so they called them craneberries, which was later shortened to cranberries. It didn't take cooks long to figure out how to use the tart, red fruit. Cookbooks, old and new alike, are brimming with cranberry sauces, pies, breads, cobblers, desserts, and salads, such as Cranberry Fluff, above.

Five-Fruit Salad with Peanut Butter Dressing

Start to finish: 25 minutes

1   6-ounce can frozen pineapple juice
       concentrate, thawed
¼   cup creamy peanut butter
½   cup salad oil
8   cups torn lettuce
1   cup fresh pineapple chunks or one
       8-ounce can pineapple chunks
       (juice pack), drained

1   cup fresh or thawed, frozen
       unsweetened peach slices* or one
       8½-ounce can peach slices
       (juice pack), drained
¼   of a medium cantaloupe, peeled and
       cut in wedges
½   cup seedless green grapes, halved
½   cup fresh strawberries, halved

*Jolie Steckart
De Pere, WI*

This interesting peanut butter-pineapple dressing can't miss when you drizzle it over summer-fresh fruit. In the winter, it's equally delicious over sliced apples or pears.

1 For dressing, in a blender container or food processor bowl combine the pineapple juice concentrate and peanut butter. Cover and blend or process until smooth. With blender or food processor running, slowly add the oil in a thin, steady stream until well blended. Transfer dressing to a storage container. Cover and chill until serving time. Stir before using.

2 To serve, line a large platter with the torn lettuce; arrange pineapple, peaches, cantaloupe, grapes, and strawberries on lettuce. Serve salad with dressing. Makes 8 servings.

*Note: Dip fresh or frozen peaches into lemon juice to prevent darkening.

Nutrition Facts per serving: 256 calories, 18 g total fat (3 g saturated fat), 0 mg cholesterol, 45 mg sodium, 23 g carbohydrate, 3 g fiber, 4 g protein. Daily Values: 10% vit. A, 51% vit. C, 3% calcium, 5% iron.

Cookies & Candies

Exquisite Almond Truffles, page 209

Oatmeal Jam Bars

Prep: 15 minutes **Bake:** 35 minutes

Ilene Smith
West Lebanon, IN

The down-home flavor of these blackberry jam bars brings back memories of the great home-style cooking of yesteryear. If you can't find blackberry jam, substitute red or black raspberry jam.

1⅓ cups all-purpose flour
¼ teaspoon baking soda
¼ teaspoon salt
¾ cup quick-cooking rolled oats
⅓ cup packed brown sugar
1 teaspoon finely shredded lemon peel

2 3-ounce packages cream cheese, softened
¼ cup butter, softened
¾ cup blackberry jam
1 teaspoon lemon juice

1 Grease a 9×9×2-inch baking pan; set aside. In a medium bowl combine the flour, baking soda, and salt. Add oats, brown sugar, and lemon peel; set aside.

2 In a large mixing bowl beat cream cheese and butter with an electric mixer on medium to high speed for 30 seconds. Add the flour mixture and beat on low speed until mixture is crumbly. Set aside 1 cup of the crumb mixture; pat remaining mixture into the bottom of prepared pan. Bake in a 350° oven for 20 minutes.

3 Meanwhile, in a small bowl stir together jam and lemon juice. Spread over prebaked crust. Sprinkle with the reserved crumbs. Bake for 15 minutes more or until brown. Cool in pan on wire rack; cut into bars. Makes 36 bars.

Nutrition Facts per bar: 76 calories, 3 g total fat (2 g saturated fat), 9 mg cholesterol, 56 mg sodium, 11 g carbohydrate, 0 g fiber, 1 g protein. Daily Values: 3% vit. A, 1% vit. C, 1% calcium, 2% iron.

Carrot and Zucchini Bars

Prep: 30 minutes **Bake:** 25 minutes

1½ cups all-purpose flour
¾ cup packed brown sugar
1 teaspoon baking powder
½ teaspoon ground ginger
¼ teaspoon baking soda
2 slightly beaten eggs
1½ cups shredded carrot

1 medium zucchini, shredded (1 cup)
½ cup raisins
½ cup chopped walnuts
½ cup cooking oil
¼ cup honey
1 teaspoon vanilla
1 recipe Citrus-Cream Cheese Frosting

1991

Deborah Covert
Exeter, NH

Deborah combined the flavors of carrot cake and zucchini bars to come up with these moist bar cookies.

1 In a large bowl combine flour, brown sugar, baking powder, ginger, and baking soda. In another large bowl stir together eggs, carrot, zucchini, raisins, walnuts, oil, honey, and vanilla. Add carrot mixture to flour mixture, stirring just until combined. Spread batter into an ungreased 13×9×2-inch baking pan.

2 Bake in a 350° oven about 25 minutes or until a toothpick inserted in the center comes out clean. Cool in pan on a wire rack. Frost with Citrus-Cream Cheese Frosting. Store, covered, in the refrigerator. Cut into bars. Makes 36 bars.

Citrus-Cream Cheese Frosting: In a medium mixing bowl beat one 8-ounce package cream cheese, softened, and 1 cup sifted powdered sugar with an electric mixer on medium speed until fluffy. Stir in 1 teaspoon finely shredded lemon peel or orange peel.

Nutrition Facts per bar: 125 calories, 7 g total fat (2 g saturated fat), 19 mg cholesterol, 46 mg sodium, 16 g carbohydrate, 0 g fiber, 2 g protein. Daily Values: 17% vit. A, 2% vit. C, 2% calcium, 3% iron.

bountiful baking

Zucchini was the trendy garden crop of the late 1960s and early 1970s. Many backyard gardeners planted the petite green squash without knowing that at harvesttime they would face basketloads of the vegetable. They searched for ways to use up their abundant supplies. Putting zucchini in baked goods was one creative solution. Zucchini makes the perfect secret ingredient for breads and cookies, such as Carrot and Zucchini Bars, above, because it adds moistness but very little flavor or calories.

Triple-Chocolate **Coffee Brownies**

Prep: 15 minutes **Bake:** 30 minutes

*Nancy Cersonsky
Oxford, CT*

Nancy turned a basic brownie mix into bars rich and fudgy enough to brag about. Better yet, these treats take just 15 minutes to stir together.

¼ cup water
2 teaspoons instant espresso coffee powder or 1 tablespoon instant coffee crystals
1 beaten egg
1 19- to 21½-ounce package fudge brownie mix

¼ cup cooking oil
¼ cup coffee liqueur or water
¾ cup milk chocolate pieces
¾ cup white baking pieces
½ cup semisweet chocolate pieces
½ cup chopped walnuts or pecans

1 Grease a 13×9×2-inch baking pan; set aside. In a large bowl combine water and espresso powder or coffee crystals; stir until dissolved. Stir in egg, brownie mix, oil, coffee liqueur or water, milk chocolate pieces, white baking pieces, semisweet chocolate pieces, and nuts. Stir just until combined. Spread batter into prepared pan.

2 Bake in a 350° oven for 30 minutes. Cool brownies completely in pan on a wire rack. Cut into bars. Makes 36 brownies.

Nutrition Facts per brownie: 125 calories, 6 g total fat (2 g saturated fat), 6 mg cholesterol, 48 mg sodium, 17 g carbohydrate, 1 g fiber, 1 g protein. Daily Values: 1% calcium, 4% iron.

brownie bonanza

The exact origin of brownies is hard to determine. Some say the bars are named after their rich brown color. Others claim they were invented by a frugal housewife who cut her fallen chocolate cake into bars. And still others claim they were first baked by a woman named Brownie. How ever brownies began, there are almost as many recipes for them as there are cooks. Brownies can be chocolate or blonde, chewy or cakelike, frosted or plain. You can make them from scratch, straight from a packaged mix, or by fixing up a mix, as in Triple-Chocolate Coffee Brownies, above.

Glistening Chocolate Melt-Aways

Prep: 40 minutes **Chill:** 1 hour **Bake:** 7 minutes

¾ cup butter, softened	2⅓ cups all-purpose flour
1 cup granulated sugar	1 cup semisweet chocolate pieces
2 eggs	(6 ounces)
1 teaspoon baking powder	Powdered sugar
½ teaspoon salt	½ cup preserves, jam, or jelly (such as
½ teaspoon ground cinnamon	cherry, mint, peach, apricot, or
½ teaspoon almond extract	raspberry)

1989

Cyndi Hight
Conroe, TX

Fruit preserves of your choice contribute to the great flavor of these pretty sandwich cookies.

1 In a large mixing bowl beat butter with an electric mixer on medium to high speed for 30 seconds. Add granulated sugar; beat until fluffy. Beat in eggs, baking powder, salt, cinnamon, and almond extract. Gradually beat in as much of the flour as you can. Stir in any remaining flour. Divide dough in half. Cover; chill dough for 1 hour or until firm.

2 On a lightly floured surface, roll half of the dough to ⅛-inch thickness. (Keep remaining dough in refrigerator until ready to roll.) Cut into shapes with a 2- to 2½-inch cookie cutter. Place on ungreased cookie sheets. With a 1-inch cookie cutter, cut out centers from half of the unbaked cookies. Bake in a 375° oven about 7 minutes or until edges are firm and bottoms are very light brown; cool on a wire rack. Repeat with dough scraps and remaining chilled dough.

3 In a heavy, small saucepan melt chocolate pieces over low heat, stirring constantly. Spread about 1 teaspoon of the melted chocolate on the bottom of each cookie with cutout center. Immediately place each chocolate-coated cookie, chocolate side down, on an uncut cookie to form a sandwich. Sift powdered sugar over cookies. Spoon about ½ teaspoon preserves, jam, or jelly into the center cutout of each cookie sandwich. Makes about 40 sandwich cookies.

Nutrition Facts per cookie: 111 calories, 5 g total fat (3 g saturated fat), 20 mg cholesterol, 81 mg sodium, 14 g carbohydrate, 1 g fiber, 1 g protein. Daily Values: 4% vit. A, 1% vit. C, 1% calcium, 2% iron.

Brownie Meringues

Prep: 15 minutes **Stand:** 30 minutes **Bake:** 10 minutes per batch

1965

Unknown

Letting egg whites stand at room temperature allows them to gain greater volume when beaten with sugar than if they were cold.

2 egg whites
½ teaspoon vinegar
½ teaspoon vanilla
   Dash salt
½ cup sugar

1 cup semisweet chocolate pieces
   (6 ounces), melted and cooled
¾ cup chopped walnuts
½ cup semisweet chocolate pieces
1 teaspoon shortening

1 Grease cookie sheets; set aside. For meringue, place egg whites in a large mixing bowl; let stand at room temperature for 30 minutes. Add the vinegar, vanilla, and salt. Beat with an electric mixer on medium speed until soft peaks form (tips curl). Add the sugar, 1 tablespoon at a time, beating on high speed about 4 minutes or until stiff peaks form (tips stand straight) and the sugar is almost dissolved. Fold in the melted chocolate and nuts.

2 Drop mixture from teaspoons onto prepared cookie sheets. Bake in a 350° oven for 10 to 12 minutes or until edges are firm. Transfer cookies to wire racks; let cool. In a small saucepan heat the ½ cup semisweet chocolate pieces and the shortening until melted. Drizzle over cookies. Makes 24 cookies.

Nutrition Facts per cookie: 95 calories, 5 g total fat (2 g saturated fat), 0 mg cholesterol, 11 mg sodium, 8 g carbohydrates, 2 g fiber, 1 g protein. Daily Values: 1% iron.

chocolate chips catch on

The idea of stirring tiny pieces of chocolate into cookie dough began in the early 1930s with a recipe from the Toll House Cookbook. The cookbook featured a cookie recipe that used bars of Nestlé chocolate bars cut into tiny pieces. With the publication of the Toll House Cookie recipe, sales of Nestlé chocolate in the Boston area rose dramatically. When Nestlé investigated the trend, they discovered the recipe and the reason for the increase of sales. Before long, Nestlé began packaging its semisweet chocolate bars with a chopper designed to break them up. Then, in 1939, Nestlé introduced "chocolate morsels." Since then, cooks have relied on semisweet chocolate pieces when making countless recipes, such as Brownie Meringues, above.

Lemonade **Cookies**

Prep: 20 minutes **Bake:** 6 minutes per batch

1965

Unknown

These cakey cookies get their tangy citrus flavor from frozen lemonade concentrate. They're marvelous with ice cream or as a snack.

1 cup butter
1 cup granulated sugar
1 teaspoon baking soda
2 eggs

1 6-ounce can (¾ cup) frozen
   lemonade concentrate, thawed
3 cups all-purpose flour
   Granulated sugar or coarse sugar

1 In a medium mixing bowl beat butter with an electric mixer on medium speed for 30 seconds. Add the 1 cup granulated sugar and the baking soda. Beat until combined. Beat in eggs and ½ cup of the lemonade concentrate. Beat in as much of the flour as you can. Stir in any remaining flour.

2 Drop dough by rounded teaspoons 2 inches apart on ungreased cookie sheets. Bake in a 400° oven for 6 to 7 minutes or until lightly brown around the edges. Cool on baking sheet for 1 minute. Transfer cookies to a wire rack. Brush hot cookies lightly with remaining lemonade concentrate; sprinkle with granulated or coarse sugar. Let cool. Makes about 48 cookies.

Nutrition Facts per cookie: 90 calories, 4 g total fat (3 g saturated fat), 20 mg cholesterol, 70 mg sodium, 12 g carbohydrate, 0 g fiber, 1 g protein. Daily Values: 4% vit. A, 1% vit. C, 2% iron.

cookies aplenty

As the number of cookie recipes in this chapter attests, cookies have been a popular recipe entry through decades of our contests. With categories ranging from Cookie Jar Favorites to Holiday Cookies and Best-Ever Bars, home bakers send in their ideas, hoping to win a prize and to see their recipes featured in *Better Homes and Gardens*® magazine. Lemonade Cookies, above, was the winner of the drop cookies category in our May 1965 Prize Tested Recipes contest.

Fudgy Fruitcake Drops

Prep: 30 minutes **Bake:** 10 minutes per batch

¼ cup butter, softened
½ cup granulated sugar
1 egg
½ cup grape jelly
1 teaspoon vanilla
1 cup all-purpose flour
¼ cup unsweetened cocoa powder

2 teaspoons baking powder
2 cups chopped walnuts (8 ounces)
1½ cups raisins (8 ounces)
1 cup semisweet chocolate pieces
   (6 ounces)
Powdered sugar (optional)

1985

Samuel Mancuso
East Meadow, NY

The exquisite flavor of this cocoa-rich cookie—filled with nuts, raisins, and chocolate pieces—explodes in your mouth when you take a bite.

1 Grease cookie sheets; set aside. In a large mixing bowl beat butter with an electric mixer on medium speed for 30 seconds. Add granulated sugar; beat until combined. Add egg, grape jelly, and vanilla; beat until combined. In another bowl stir together flour, cocoa powder, and baking powder. Stir flour mixture into beaten mixture. Stir in the nuts, raisins, and chocolate pieces.

2 Drop dough by rounded teaspoons onto prepared cookie sheets. Bake in a 350° oven about 10 minutes or just until set. Cool on cookie sheets for 1 minute. Transfer to wire racks; let cool. If desired, sift powdered sugar over cookies. Makes about 50 cookies.

Nutrition Facts per cookie: 97 calories, 5 g total fat (1 g saturated fat), 7 mg cholesterol, 30 mg sodium, 11 g carbohydrate, 1 g fiber, 1 g protein. Daily Values: 1% vit. A, 1% vit. C, 2% calcium, 3% iron.

Orange-Macadamia Nut Cookies

Prep: 45 minutes **Bake:** 12 minutes per batch

Margaret Pache
Mesa, AZ

Don't be alarmed by the amount of cornstarch called for in these cookies. It helps in making a cookie that will melt in your mouth.

4 cups all-purpose flour
2 cups sifted powdered sugar
1 cup cornstarch
2 cups butter
1 cup chopped macadamia nuts or
   toasted walnuts
2 egg yolks

1 tablespoon finely shredded
   orange peel
4 to 6 tablespoons orange juice
   Granulated sugar
1 recipe Orange Frosting
   Finely shredded orange peel
   (optional)

1 In a large bowl combine flour, powdered sugar, and cornstarch. Using a pastry blender or two knives, cut in butter until mixture resembles coarse crumbs. Stir in nuts. In a small bowl combine egg yolks, the 1 tablespoon orange peel, and 4 tablespoons of the orange juice; add to flour mixture, stirring until moistened. If necessary, add enough of the remaining orange juice to moisten.

2 On a lightly floured surface, knead dough until it forms a ball. Shape dough into 1¼-inch balls. Arrange balls on an ungreased cookie sheet; flatten to ¼-inch thickness by pressing with the bottom of a glass, dipping glass into granulated sugar for each cookie.

3 Bake in a 350° oven for 12 to 15 minutes or until edges begin to brown. Transfer cookies to a wire rack; let cool. Frost with Orange Frosting. If desired, sprinkle with additional finely shredded orange peel. Makes 72 cookies.

Orange Frosting: In a small bowl stir together 2 cups sifted powdered sugar, 3 tablespoons softened butter, 1 teaspoon finely shredded orange peel, and enough orange juice (2 to 3 tablespoons) to make icing of spreading consistency.

Nutrition Facts per cookie: 117 calories, 7 g total fat (4 g saturated fat), 20 mg cholesterol, 58 mg sodium, 13 g carbohydrate, 0 g fiber, 1 g protein. Daily Values: 6% vit. A, 1% vit. C, 2% iron.

Birds' Nests

Prep: 25 minutes **Bake:** 10 minutes per batch

Mrs. B. A. Haggen
Bellington, WA

This early version of jam thumbprints makes a colorful addition to any cookie tray. To change the look—and flavor—of the cookies, try several different flavors of jam or preserves.

½ cup butter
¼ cup packed brown sugar
1 egg yolk
1 cup all-purpose flour

1 slightly beaten egg white
1 cup finely chopped walnuts
   or pecans
¼ cup raspberry jam or preserves

1 Grease cookie sheets; set aside. In a medium mixing bowl beat butter with an electric mixer on medium speed for 30 seconds. Add the brown sugar; beat until combined, scraping sides of bowl occasionally. Beat in egg yolk until combined. Beat in as much of the flour as you can. Stir in any remaining flour.

2 Shape dough into 1-inch balls. Dip each ball in egg white; roll in chopped nuts. Place balls 1 inch apart on prepared cookie sheets. Press your thumb into the center of each ball. Bake in a 375° oven for 10 to 12 minutes or until edges are lightly brown. Transfer cookies to a wire rack; let cool. Before serving, fill centers with jam or preserves (about ½ teaspoon each). Makes about 18 cookies.

Nutrition Facts per cookie: 140 calories, 10 g total fat (4 g saturated fat), 26 mg cholesterol, 62 mg sodium, 12 g carbohydrate, 1 g fiber, 2 g protein. Daily Values: 6% vit. A, 1% vit. C, 1% calcium, 3% iron.

bet on butter

During the war in the 1940s, margarine became a cheaper substitute for butter, which was scarce and expensive. Today, butter is no longer scarce and, for best results and flavor, The Better Homes and Gardens® Test Kitchen recommends using butter, not margarine, for cookie recipes in this book. Only margarines that contain at least 80 percent vegetable oil or fat (these have 100 calories per tablespoon) should be used in place of butter. However, with so many different margarine products available at the supermarket, it can be confusing to know which is which. If you choose margarine or a similar product with less than 80 percent vegetable oil or fat, it will contain additional water and milk solids that may make your cookies either soggy or hard.

Molasses Crinkles

Prep: 20 minutes **Bake:** 10 minutes per batch

¾ cup shortening
1 cup packed brown sugar
1 teaspoon baking soda
1 teaspoon ground cinnamon
1 teaspoon ground ginger
¼ teaspoon salt

¼ teaspoon ground cloves
1 beaten egg
¼ cup light-flavored molasses
2¼ cups all-purpose flour
¼ cup granulated sugar

1948

Perle Hinshaw
St. Louis, MO

Although they start out as smooth, sugared balls of dough, these old-fashioned spice cookies come out of the oven covered with delightful cracks and crinkles, which give them their name.

1 In a large mixing bowl beat shortening with an electric mixer on medium speed for 30 seconds. Add the brown sugar, baking soda, cinnamon, ginger, salt, and cloves; beat until combined. Beat in egg and molasses. Beat in as much of the flour as you can. Stir in any remaining flour. (If necessary, cover dough with plastic wrap and chill for 30 minutes to 1 hour or until easy to handle.)

2 Shape dough into 1½-inch balls. Roll balls in the granulated sugar to coat. Place balls 2 inches apart on an ungreased cookie sheet. Bake in a 375° oven about 10 minutes or until edges are set and tops are crackled. Transfer cookies to a wire rack; let cool. Makes about 30 cookies.

Nutrition Facts per cookie: 121 calories, 5 g total fat (1 g saturated fat), 7 mg cholesterol, 68 mg sodium, 17 g carbohydrate, 0 g fiber, 1 g protein. Daily Values: 2% calcium, 4% iron.

Mocha Truffle Cookies

Prep: 20 minutes **Bake:** 10 minutes per batch

1992

*Donna Higgins
Halfway, OR*

These double-chocolate cookies have a soft trufflelike center, a crispy outside, and a delectable coffee flavor. For the ultimate indulgence, serve them with cups of rich hot chocolate or flavored coffee.

½ cup butter
½ cup semisweet chocolate pieces
1 tablespoon instant coffee crystals
¾ cup granulated sugar
¾ cup packed brown sugar
2 eggs
2 teaspoons vanilla

2 cups all-purpose flour
⅓ cup unsweetened cocoa powder
½ teaspoon baking powder
¼ teaspoon salt
1 cup semisweet chocolate pieces
   (6 ounces)

1 Lightly grease cookie sheets; set aside. In a large saucepan melt butter and the ½ cup chocolate pieces over low heat. Remove from heat. Stir in coffee crystals; cool 5 minutes. Stir in sugars, eggs, and vanilla.

2 In a medium bowl combine flour, cocoa powder, baking powder, and salt. Stir into coffee mixture. Stir in the 1 cup chocolate pieces. Drop dough by rounded teaspoons 2 inches apart onto prepared cookie sheets. Bake in a 350° oven about 10 minutes or until edges are firm. Cool cookies on cookie sheet for 1 minute. Transfer cookies to a wire rack; let cool. Makes about 36 cookies.

Nutrition Facts per cookie: 123 calories, 5 g total fat (3 g saturated fat), 19 mg cholesterol, 55 mg sodium, 16 g carbohydrate, 1 g fiber, 1 g protein. Daily Values: 3% vit. A, 1% calcium, 4% iron.

Exquisite Almond Truffles

Prep: 1 hour **Freeze:** 2½ hours

16 ounces white chocolate baking pieces
¼ cup whipping cream
¼ cup cream of coconut
1 cup sliced almonds, toasted and chopped
2 tablespoons amaretto

18 ounces semisweet chocolate pieces (3 cups)
3 tablespoons shortening
4 ounces white chocolate baking pieces
2 tablespoons shortening

*Mary King
Concordia, KS*

Let your imagination run when you make these coconut delights. If you like, instead of the melted semisweet chocolate dip the truffles in melted white chocolate baking pieces and dust them in cocoa powder. Or, skip the white chocolate drizzle and roll them in chopped toasted pecans. (Pictured on page 194.)

1 For filling, in a medium saucepan heat and stir the 16 ounces white chocolate, the whipping cream, and cream of coconut just until white chocolate is melted. Remove from heat. Stir in chopped almonds and amaretto. Cover; freeze 2 hours or until firm. Divide filling into 48 portions; shape each portion into a ball. Freeze 15 minutes.

2 Meanwhile, in a 4-cup glass measure combine the semisweet chocolate pieces and the 3 tablespoons shortening. In a large glass bowl pour very warm tap water (100° to 110°) to a depth of 1 inch. Place measure with semisweet chocolate inside large bowl. (Water should cover bottom half of the glass measure.) Stir semisweet chocolate constantly with a rubber spatula until chocolate is completely melted and smooth. This takes about 20 minutes; don't rush. If water cools, remove glass measure. Discard cool water; add warm water. Return glass measure to bowl with water.

3 Using a fork, dip frozen balls, one at a time, into melted chocolate; place on a waxed-paper-lined baking sheet. Freeze for 15 minutes.

4 Meanwhile, in a 1-cup glass measure combine the 4 ounces white chocolate and the 2 tablespoons shortening; melt over hot water. Drizzle over truffles. Chill for a few minutes before serving until set. Makes 48 truffles.

Nutrition Facts per truffle: 159 calories, 10 g total fat (5 g saturated fat), 6 mg cholesterol, 13 mg sodium, 11 g carbohydrate, 2 g fiber, 2 g protein. Daily Values: 1% vit. A, 2% calcium, 1% iron.

White Chocolate Fudge

Prep: 15 minutes **Cook:** 15 minutes

1972

Val Jean Fredrickson
Sioux City, IA

Looking for an special gift to give for a birthday or the holidays? Make a batch of this light-colored fudge loaded with coconut and toasted almonds. Anyone with a sweet tooth will be delighted.

2 cups sugar
1 cup evaporated milk
½ cup butter
8 ounces white chocolate baking
    squares, cut up
1 cup tiny marshmallows

1 teaspoon vanilla
½ cup flaked coconut
½ cup chopped unblanched almonds,
    toasted
Unblanched almonds, toasted and
    chopped (optional)

1 Line an 8×8×2-inch baking pan with foil, extending foil over edges of pan. Butter the foil; set pan aside.

2 Butter sides of a heavy, 3-quart saucepan. In the saucepan combine the sugar, evaporated milk, and butter. Cook and stir over medium heat until mixture boils. Clip a candy thermometer to side of pan. Cook until thermometer registers 234°, soft-ball stage (about 15 minutes), stirring frequently. Remove from heat. Add white chocolate, marshmallows, and vanilla; beat until melted. Quickly stir in coconut and the ½ cup chopped almonds. Pour into prepared pan. If desired, sprinkle with additional chopped almonds. Score into squares while warm.

3 When fudge is firm, use foil to lift it out of pan. Cut into squares. Store tightly covered. Makes about 2 pounds or 36 pieces.

Nutrition Facts per piece: 132 calories, 7 g total fat (4 g saturated fat), 10 mg cholesterol, 43 mg sodium, 17 g carbohydrate, 0 g fiber, 1 g protein. Daily Values: 3% vit. A, 2% vit. C, 3% calcium, 1% iron.

white chocolate mania

Although it had been around for years, the fascination with white chocolate peaked with the introduction of white chocolate mousse in the late 1970s and early 1980s. Before long, cooks were using white chocolate in all sorts of delicacies from candies and cakes to cookies and ice creams. Val Jean Fredrickson was ahead of the pack by winning with her recipe for White Chocolate Fudge, above, back in 1972.

White chocolate isn't true chocolate at all, but rather a mixture of sugar, cocoa butter, and milk solids. When shopping for it in the store, you'll also find white baking bars that do not contain cocoa butter. The two products can be used interchangeably.

Dotted Coffee Fudge

Prep: 30 minutes **Cool:** 1 hour **Chill:** overnight

Mrs. Roland Gorham
La Grande, OR

This smooth, coffee-flavored candy, with crunchy chocolate bits and nuts scattered throughout, is slightly softer than classic chocolate fudge.

3 cups sugar
1¼ cups half-and-half, light cream, or milk
2 tablespoons instant coffee crystals
1 tablespoon light-colored corn syrup
Dash salt

3 tablespoons butter
1 teaspoon vanilla
½ cup miniature semisweet chocolate pieces
½ cup chopped pecans
Pecan halves (optional)

1 Line an 8×8×2-inch pan with foil, extending foil over edges of pan. Butter the foil; set aside. Butter sides of a heavy, 3-quart saucepan. In the saucepan combine sugar, half-and-half, coffee crystals, corn syrup, and salt. Heat over medium-high heat, stirring constantly, until sugar dissolves and mixture comes to boiling. Clip candy thermometer to pan. Reduce heat to medium; continue boiling at a moderate, steady rate, stirring frequently, until thermometer registers 234°, soft-ball stage (about 10 minutes).

2 Immediately remove saucepan from heat; add the 3 tablespoons butter, but do not stir. Cool to lukewarm (110°) without stirring (60 to 65 minutes). Add vanilla. Beat vigorously until fudge becomes very thick and starts to lose its gloss (about 10 minutes). Immediately stir in chocolate pieces and the chopped pecans. Quickly spread into prepared pan. Score in squares while warm and, if desired, top each square with a pecan half. Cover and chill overnight. Cut into squares. Makes 2 pounds or 36 pieces.

Nutrition Facts per piece: 106 calories, 4 g total fat (2 g saturated fat), 6 mg cholesterol, 19 mg sodium, 18 g carbohydrate, 0 g fiber, 0 g protein. Daily Values: 2% vit. A, 1% calcium.

Orange and Walnut Fudge

Prep: 25 minutes **Cook:** 5 minutes **Chill:** 2 hours

3 cups sugar
½ cup water
2 teaspoons finely shredded orange peel (set aside)

½ cup orange juice
1 12-ounce package semisweet chocolate pieces (2 cups)
4 cups coarsely chopped walnuts

1992

Erma Falusi
Tempe, AZ

Rich and chocolaty with a hint of orange, this no-beat fudge is easy to make and delicious to eat.

1 Line a 13×9×2-inch baking pan with foil, extending foil over edges of pan; butter the foil and set aside. Butter the sides of a heavy, 3-quart saucepan. In the saucepan combine sugar, water, and orange juice. Cook and stir over medium-high heat until sugar dissolves and mixture comes to boiling. Clip candy thermometer to side of pan; reduce heat to medium and continue cooking to 234°, soft-ball stage (about 5 minutes), stirring occasionally. Remove from heat.

2 Immediately stir in chocolate pieces and orange peel. Stir in walnuts. Spread candy into prepared pan. Chill for 2 to 3 hours or until set. To serve, cut into small pieces. Store tightly covered. Makes about 3 pounds or 56 pieces.

Nutrition Facts per piece: 126 calories, 7 g total fat (1 g saturated fat), 0 mg cholesterol, 1 mg sodium, 14 g carbohydrate, 1 g fiber, 1 g protein. Daily Values: 2% vit. C, 1% calcium, 1% iron.

oh fudge!

Visit a fudge shop and you'll be amazed at the variety of flavors available. However, for most people, fudge conjures up an image of a rich, chocolate candy. How do contest entrants improve on perfection? One way is to enhance the chocolate with such flavors as coffee and orange. Old-fashioned fudge was always beaten, as is Dotted Coffee Fudge, page 212, a 1961 prizewinner. By the 1990s, entrants were often using a streamlined method, such as no-beat Orange and Walnut Fudge, above, or Microwave Candy-Bar Fudge, page 214.

Microwave **Candy-Bar Fudge**

Prep: 15 minutes **Microwave:** 7¾ minutes **Chill:** 1 hour

1991

Irene Mullenbach
Little Cedar, IA

It is essential that you use butter, rather than margarine or a spread, in this ultimate fudge. See tip on page 206 regarding margarines. Margarine can adversely effect the outcome of some candies.

½ cup butter
⅓ cup unsweetened cocoa powder
¼ cup packed brown sugar
¼ cup milk
3½ cups sifted powdered sugar
1 teaspoon vanilla

30 vanilla caramels (about 10 ounces)
1 tablespoon water
2 cups unsalted peanuts
½ cup semisweet chocolate pieces
½ cup milk chocolate pieces

1 Line a 9×9×2-inch pan with foil, extending the foil over edges of pan. Butter the foil; set pan aside.

2 In a large microwave-safe bowl microwave the butter, uncovered, on 100% power (high) for 1 minute or until melted. Stir in cocoa powder, brown sugar, and milk. Microwave, uncovered, on high for 1 to 2 minutes or until mixture comes to a boil, stirring once. Stir again. Microwave for 30 seconds more. Stir in powdered sugar and vanilla. Spread into prepared pan.

3 In a medium microwave-safe bowl combine unwrapped caramels and water. Microwave, uncovered, on 50% power (medium) for 2½ to 3 minutes or until caramels are melted, stirring once. Stir in nuts. Microwave on medium power for 45 to 60 seconds more or until softened. Gently but quickly spread over fudge layer.

4 In a 2-cup glass measure combine semisweet and milk chocolate pieces. Microwave, uncovered, on 50% power (medium) for 2 to 3 minutes or until melted, stirring once. Spread over caramel layer. Cover and chill 1 to 2 hours or until firm. Remove from pan; cut into squares. Serve fudge at room temperature. Store, covered, in the refrigerator. Makes 64 pieces.

Nutrition Facts per piece: 98 calories, 5 g total fat (2 g saturated fat), 4 mg cholesterol, 29 mg sodium, 12 g carbohydrate, 0 g fiber, 2 g protein. Daily Values: 1% vit. A, 2% calcium, 1% iron.

Nutty Pudding Bars

Prep: 30 minutes **Freeze:** 1 hour

½ of a 24-ounce package chocolate-flavored candy coating
1 10-ounce package butterscotch pieces
1 cup peanut butter
1 ounce unsweetened chocolate
1 cup butter

½ cup evaporated milk
1 4-serving-size package cook-and-serve vanilla pudding mix
1 2-pound package powdered sugar (about 7½ cups, unsifted)
1 teaspoon vanilla
1½ cups chopped peanuts

Mrs. Vern Olson
Duluth, MN

Tempt the candy lovers you know with this tri-level chocolate-and-peanut-butter treat. They won't be able to resist coming back for seconds, or maybe even thirds.

1 Line a 15×10×1-inch baking pan with foil, extending over edges of pan; set aside. In a large saucepan combine candy coating, butterscotch pieces, peanut butter, and unsweetened chocolate. Cook and stir over low heat until melted and smooth. Spread 1⅓ cups of the chocolate mixture in a thin, even layer in the prepared pan; freeze while making next layer. (Keep remaining melted mixture at room temperature.)

2 In a medium saucepan melt the butter over low heat; stir in evaporated milk. Stir in pudding mix. Cook, stirring constantly, until mixture is just slightly thickened and just begins to bubble around the edge. (Do not boil or mixture may separate.) Remove from heat.

3 Place powdered sugar in a very large mixing bowl. Add pudding mixture and vanilla. Stir until smooth. Spread over chilled layer; spread remaining chocolate mixture over all. Sprinkle nuts on top. Freeze about 1 hour or until firm.

4 To serve, lift candy out of pan using the foil. Remove foil and place candy on a large cutting board. Cut into 1-inch pieces to serve. Store in an airtight container in refrigerator or at room temperature for 1 week, or freeze for up to 4 months. Makes about 108 pieces.

Nutrition Facts per piece: 112 calories, 6 g total fat (3 g saturated fat), 5 mg cholesterol, 47 mg sodium, 14 g carbohydrate, 0 g fiber, 1 g protein. Daily Values: 2% vit. A, 1% calcium, 1% iron.

Chocolate-Praline Squares

Prep: 35 minutes **Bake:** 35 minutes **Chill:** 1 hour

1995

Darci Truax
Billings, MT

These nutty caramel squares will remind you of a cross between bar cookies and pecan pie. If you like, next time serve them without the Orange Cream.

1½ cups all-purpose flour
½ cup sifted powdered sugar
¾ cup butter
1½ cups chopped pecans, toasted
¾ cup light-colored corn syrup
½ cup dark-colored corn syrup
1 cup packed brown sugar
¼ cup butter
4 eggs

2 cups coarsely chopped pecans
1 teaspoon finely shredded orange peel
1 teaspoon vanilla
1½ cups miniature semisweet chocolate pieces
1 recipe Orange Cream
Shredded orange peel (optional)

1 Lightly grease a 13×9×2-inch baking pan; set aside. For crust, stir together flour and powdered sugar. Using a pastry blender or two knives, cut in the ¾ cup butter until pieces are the size of small peas. Stir in the 1½ cups pecans. Press evenly into prepared pan. Bake in a 325° oven about 25 minutes or until light brown.

2 For the filling, in a medium saucepan combine corn syrups, brown sugar, and the ¼ cup butter. Cook over medium heat just until mixture begins to bubble around edges and butter is melted, stirring constantly. Remove from heat; cool for 10 minutes. In a large mixing bowl beat eggs with an electric mixer on medium speed until combined. Gradually add syrup mixture, beating until smooth. Stir in the 2 cups pecans, the 1 teaspoon orange peel, and the vanilla.

3 Pour the filling over crust. Sprinkle with chocolate pieces. Bake in a 350° oven for 35 to 40 minutes or until center is set. Cool in pan on a wire rack; chill about 1 hour or until firm enough to cut. Serve with Orange Cream and, if desired, shredded orange peel. Store in the refrigerator. Makes 48 squares.

Orange Cream: In a chilled medium mixing bowl combine 1 cup whipping cream, 2 tablespoons granulated sugar, and 2 tablespoons dairy sour cream; beat with the chilled beaters of an electric mixer on low to medium speed until the mixture starts to thicken. Add 1 tablespoon orange liqueur or ½ teaspoon orange extract, ½ teaspoon finely shredded orange peel, and ½ teaspoon vanilla. Beat on low speed just until soft peaks form.

Nutrition Facts per square: 200 calories, 13 g total fat (5 g saturated fat), 36 mg cholesterol, 61 mg sodium, 19 g carbohydrate, 1 g fiber, 2 g protein. Daily Values: 7% vit. A, 1% calcium, 3% iron.

Crisp Toffee Bars

Prep: 15 minutes **Bake:** 20 minutes

1959

Mrs. David G. Murray
Syracuse, NY

Reminiscent of old-fashioned toffee candy, these bar cookies are rich, crunchy, and delicious.

1 cup butter, softened
1 cup packed brown sugar
1 teaspoon vanilla
2 cups all-purpose flour

1 cup semisweet chocolate pieces
   (6 ounces)
1 cup chopped walnuts

1 In a large mixing bowl beat butter with an electric mixer on medium speed for 30 seconds. Add brown sugar and vanilla; beat until fluffy. Beat in as much of the flour as you can. Stir in any remaining flour, the chocolate pieces, and walnuts.

2 Press mixture into an ungreased 15×10×1-inch baking pan. Bake in a 350° oven about 20 minutes or until brown. While warm, cut into bars or squares. Cool in pan on a wire rack. Makes about 48 bars.

Nutrition Facts per bar: 104 calories, 7 g total fat (3 g saturated fat), 11 mg cholesterol, 43 mg sodium, 10 g carbohydrate, 1 g fiber, 1 g protein. Daily Values: 4% vit. A, 1% calcium, 2% iron.

bars: cookies made easy

Like the history of many all-time favorite foods, the who, when, and where of the first bar cookie is lost in time. Our best guess is that resourceful cooks figured instead of shaping, rolling, or dropping, it was easier to spread the dough in one pan. Although Crisp Toffee Bars, above, first appeared more than 40 years ago, this bar cookie recipe fits right into today's cooking trends—it's quick to fix, uses only a few ingredients, and appeals to anyone with a sweet tooth.

Hazelnut Toffee

Prep: 30 minutes **Cook:** 10 minutes

1 cup chopped hazelnuts, toasted	1 tablespoon hazelnut liqueur
½ cup butter	1 cup semisweet chocolate pieces
1 cup packed brown sugar	(6 ounces)
1 tablespoon water	

1 Line a large baking sheet with foil, extending foil over the edges. Sprinkle ½ cup of the nuts in an 8-inch square on the prepared baking sheet. Set aside.

2 Butter the sides of a heavy, 1-quart saucepan. In the saucepan melt the butter. Add brown sugar and water. Cook and stir over medium-high heat to boiling. Clip a candy thermometer to the side of the pan. Cook and stir over medium heat to 280°, soft-crack stage (about 10 minutes). Remove pan from heat; remove thermometer.

3 Immediately stir in liqueur; pour over nuts on prepared baking sheet. Sprinkle with chocolate. Let stand for 2 minutes or until chocolate is soft; spread to cover. Sprinkle with remaining nuts. Cool. (If necessary, chill several minutes to harden chocolate.) Holding onto foil, lift candy from baking sheet. Break into pieces. Store in refrigerator for up to 2 weeks. Makes about 1½ pounds or 48 servings.

Nutrition Facts per serving: 63 calories, 4 g total fat (1 g saturated fat), 5 mg cholesterol, 21 mg sodium, 6 g carbohydrate, 0 g fiber, 0 g protein. Daily Values: 1% vit. A, 1% iron.

1995

Maureen Biro
Pleasant Hill, CA

Stack this toffee in a tissue-paper-lined tin to create a prized gift.

Peanut Butter Peanut Brittle

Prep: 10 minutes **Cook:** 20 minutes

2 cups peanut butter	2 tablespoons butter
1½ cups sugar	2 cups raw peanuts
1½ cups light-colored corn syrup	1 teaspoon baking soda, sifted
¼ cup water	1 teaspoon vanilla

2000

Kris White
Gig Harbor, WA

It is worth your while to search out raw peanuts for this brittle; they are less likely to burn when stirred into the hot syrup. Check out a health food market if your supermarket doesn't carry them.

1 In the top of double boiler warm peanut butter over low heat. (Or, warm peanut butter in a heatproof bowl set over a pan of warm water over low heat.) Meanwhile, butter two large baking sheets. Set aside.

2 Butter sides of a heavy, 3-quart saucepan. In the saucepan combine the sugar, corn syrup, and water. Cook and stir over medium-high heat until mixture boils. Clip candy thermometer to side of saucepan. Cook and stir over medium-high heat until thermometer registers 275°, soft-crack stage (about 15 minutes).

3 Reduce heat to medium. Add the 2 tablespoons butter, stirring until melted. Add peanuts. Cook and stir for 5 minutes more or until candy starts turning brown and thermometer registers 295°, hard-crack stage. Remove pan from heat. Remove thermometer from saucepan.

4 Quickly sprinkle baking soda over mixture, stirring constantly. Stir in vanilla. Gently stir in warm peanut butter until combined.

5 Immediately pour candy onto prepared baking sheets. Working quickly, spread as thin as possible with a spatula or stretch using two forks to lift and pull candy as it cools. When cool, break into serving-size pieces. Makes about 3 pounds or 48 servings.

Nutrition Facts per serving: 156 calories, 9 g total fat (2 g saturated fat), 1 mg cholesterol, 91 mg sodium, 17 g carbohydrate, 1 g fiber, 4 g protein. Daily Values: 1% calcium, 5% iron.

Mocha and Pecan Divinity

Prep: 25 minutes **Cook:** 20 minutes

1985

D. R. Sarkisian
Inman, SC

Instant Swiss-style coffee powder adds a delightful flavor to this creamy, rich divinity. To assure that the candy gets stiff enough, beat it with a heavy-duty freestanding electric mixer.

2½ cups sugar	¼ cup instant Swiss-style coffee powder
½ cup light-colored corn syrup	2 egg whites
½ cup water	1 cup chopped pecans

1 In a heavy, 2-quart saucepan combine sugar, corn syrup, water, and coffee powder. Cook and stir over medium-high heat until mixture boils (5 to 7 minutes). Clip a candy thermometer to the side of the pan. Reduce heat to medium; continue cooking, without stirring, until the thermometer registers 260°, hard-ball stage (about 15 minutes). Remove from heat; remove thermometer.

2 In a large mixing bowl immediately beat egg whites with a free-standing electric mixer on medium speed until stiff peaks form (tips stand straight). Gradually pour hot mixture in a thin stream over egg whites, beating on high speed and scraping the sides of the bowl occasionally (this will take about 3 minutes). Continue beating on high speed just until candy starts to lose its gloss (5 to 6 minutes). When beaters are lifted, mixture should fall in a ribbon that mounds on itself. Drop a spoonful of candy mixture onto waxed paper. If it stays mounded, the mixture has been beaten sufficiently. If mixture flattens, beat ½ to 1 minute more; check again. If mixture is too stiff to spoon, beat in a few drops hot water until candy is a softer consistency.

3 Immediately fold in nuts. Quickly drop remaining candy onto waxed paper. Store tightly covered. Makes about 36 pieces.

Nutrition Facts per piece: 90 calories, 2 g total fat (0 g saturated fat), 0 mg cholesterol, 12 mg sodium, 18 g carbohydrate, 0 g fiber, 0 g protein.

dos (and don'ts) of divinity

If your visions of sugarplums include mounds of fluffy white divinity, here are some tips that will help you achieve your dream. Select a relatively dry day to make divinity. If the humidity is above 60 percent, the sugar will absorb moisture, making the candy too runny to set up. Allow the egg whites to come to room temperature before beating so they'll whip up to maximum volume. Use a sturdy freestanding electric mixer because making divinity requires heavy beating, which puts a strain on mixer motors. Portable mixers and some lightweight freestanding mixers don't have enough power. Finally, follow recipe directions precisely and pay close attention to visual tips.

Orange-Cappuccino Creams

Prep: 30 minutes **Chill:** 20 minutes

About 72 small paper or foil candy
cups (1¼- to 1½-inch size)
1½ pounds white chocolate, chopped
½ cup whipping cream
1 tablespoon finely shredded
orange peel
1 tablespoon orange liqueur or
orange juice

1 teaspoon orange extract
½ cup finely chopped walnuts
¼ cup whipping cream
4 teaspoons instant espresso coffee
powder or instant coffee crystals
8 ounces semisweet chocolate
White chocolate curls (optional)
Shredded orange peel (optional)

Miriam Baroga
Fircrest, WA

These sweet bites of coffee,
orange, and chocolate
flavors make any holiday
candy platter a success.

1 Place candy cups on a large baking sheet; set aside. For filling, in a large saucepan combine the 1½ pounds white chocolate, the ½ cup whipping cream, the orange peel, orange liqueur or juice, and orange extract. Stir over low heat until white chocolate is just melted. Remove from heat; stir in walnuts. Cool slightly.

2 Place the white chocolate mixture in a self-sealing plastic bag. Make a small opening by snipping off a bottom corner of the bag. Squeeze mixture through hole to fill each candy cup about two-thirds full. Chill for 20 minutes.

3 In a medium saucepan heat the ¼ cup whipping cream and espresso powder or coffee crystals over low heat until dissolved. Add semisweet chocolate, stirring over low heat for 3 to 4 minutes or until chocolate melts. Spoon ½ teaspoon of the semisweet chocolate mixture onto white chocolate in each candy cup. Chill for a few minutes before serving until set. If desired, garnish with white chocolate curls and orange peel. Serve at room temperature. Store, covered, in the refrigerator. Makes about 72 candies.

Nutrition Facts per candy: 84 calories, 5 g total fat (3 g saturated fat), 7 mg cholesterol, 11 mg sodium, 8 g carbohydrate, 0 g fiber, 1 g protein. Daily Values: 1% vit. A, 1% calcium.

Coconut-Orange Cake page 252

Pies & Cakes

CHAPTER INDEX

Lemon-Sour Cream Pie

Prep: 40 minutes **Bake:** 15 minutes **Cool:** 1 hour **Chill:** 3 to 6 hours

1966

Mrs. John W. Loucks
Commack, NY

You'll savor every forkful of Mrs. Loucks' creamy, yet tart, meringue pie. Be sure to finely shred real lemon peel and squeeze fresh lemon juice for fabulous made-from-scratch flavor.

1 recipe Pastry Shell (page 227)	¼ cup butter or margarine
3 egg whites	1 teaspoon finely shredded lemon peel
1 cup sugar	¼ cup lemon juice
3 tablespoons cornstarch	1 8-ounce carton dairy sour cream
Dash salt	½ teaspoon vanilla
1 cup milk	¼ teaspoon cream of tartar
3 slightly beaten egg yolks	6 tablespoons sugar

1 Prepare and bake Pastry Shell; set aside. Let egg whites stand at room temperature for 30 minutes.

2 Meanwhile, for filling, in a medium saucepan stir together the 1 cup sugar, the cornstarch, and salt. Stir in milk. Cook and stir over medium heat until thickened and bubbly. Cook and stir for 2 minutes more. Remove from heat. Gradually stir about 1 cup of the hot filling into egg yolks. Pour egg yolk mixture into remaining hot filling in saucepan. Bring to a gentle boil. Cook and stir for 2 minutes more. Remove from heat. Stir in butter or margarine, lemon peel, and lemon juice. Gradually stir hot mixture into sour cream. Keep warm.

3 For meringue, in a large mixing bowl combine egg whites, vanilla, and cream of tartar. Beat with an electric mixer on medium speed about 1 minute or until soft peaks form (tips curl). Gradually add the 6 tablespoons sugar, 1 tablespoon at a time, beating on high speed about 4 minutes more or until mixture forms stiff, glossy peaks (tips stand straight) and sugar dissolves.

4 Spoon hot filling into pastry shell. Immediately spread meringue over hot filling, carefully sealing to edge of pastry to prevent shrinkage.

5 Bake in a 350° oven for 15 minutes. Cool on a wire rack for 1 hour. Chill for at least 3 hours or up to 6 hours before serving. Cover for longer storage. Makes 8 servings.

Nutrition Facts per serving: 442 calories, 23 g total fat (11 g saturated fat), 111 mg cholesterol, 201 mg sodium, 53 g carbohydrate, 1 g fiber, 6 g protein. Daily Values: 17% vit. A, 7% vit. C, 9% calcium, 6% iron.

Double-Coconut Cream Pie

Prep: 40 minutes **Bake:** 15 minutes **Cool:** 1 hour **Chill:** 3 to 6 hours

1 recipe Pastry Shell	2 tablespoons butter or margarine
3 egg whites	1 cup flaked coconut
¼ cup cornstarch	2 teaspoons vanilla
¼ teaspoon salt	½ teaspoon vanilla
2 cups milk	¼ teaspoon cream of tartar
¾ cup cream of coconut	⅓ cup sugar
3 beaten egg yolks	2 tablespoons flaked coconut

Teresa Cicchella
Englewood, FL

Coconut fans will adore this exquisite pie that has both cream of coconut and flaked coconut in the filling.

1 Prepare and bake Pastry Shell; set aside. Let egg whites stand at room temperature for 30 minutes. Meanwhile, for filling, in a medium saucepan combine cornstarch and salt; stir in ¼ cup of the milk until smooth. Stir in remaining milk and the cream of coconut. Cook and stir over medium heat until thickened. Cook and stir for 2 minutes more. Remove from heat. Gradually stir about 1 cup of the hot filling into egg yolks, stirring constantly. Pour yolk mixture into remaining hot filling in saucepan. Bring to a gentle boil. Cook and stir 2 minutes more. Remove from heat. Stir in butter or margarine until melted. Stir in the 1 cup coconut and the 2 teaspoons vanilla. Keep warm.

2 For meringue, in a large mixing bowl combine egg whites, the ½ teaspoon vanilla, and cream of tartar. Beat with an electric mixer on medium speed about 1 minute or until soft peaks form. Gradually add the ⅓ cup sugar, 1 tablespoon at a time, beating on high speed 4 minutes more or until mixture forms stiff peaks and sugar dissolves.

3 Spoon hot filling into pastry shell. Immediately spread meringue over hot filling, carefully sealing to edge of pastry to prevent shrinkage. Sprinkle with the 2 tablespoons coconut. Bake in a 350° oven for 15 minutes. Cool 1 hour. Chill for at least 3 hours or up to 6 hours before serving. Makes 8 servings.

Pastry Shell: Combine 1¼ cups all-purpose flour and ¼ teaspoon salt. Using a pastry blender, cut in ⅓ cup shortening until pieces are pea-size. Sprinkle 1 tablespoon cold water over part of flour mixture; gently toss with a fork. Push moistened dough to one side of the bowl. Repeat, using 1 tablespoon cold water at a time, until all of flour mixture is moistened (4 to 5 tablespoons water). Form dough into a ball. On a lightly floured surface, slightly flatten dough. Roll dough from center to edge into a 12-inch circle. Ease pastry to a 9-inch pie plate, being careful not to stretch pastry. Trim pastry to ½ inch beyond edge of pie plate. Fold under extra pastry. Crimp edge as desired. Do not prick pastry. Line with a double thickness of foil. Bake in a 450° oven for 8 minutes. Remove foil. Bake 5 to 6 minutes more or until golden.

Nutrition Facts per serving: 399 calories, 26 g total fat (15 g saturated fat), 92 mg cholesterol, 229 mg sodium, 35 g carbohydrate, 2 g fiber, 7 g protein. Daily Values: 10% vit. A, 2% vit. C, 9% calcium, 10% iron.

Chocolate-Hazelnut Pie

Prep: 25 minutes **Bake:** 8 minutes **Chill:** Several hours or overnight

*Sally Cracroft
Paonia, CO*

Chocolate lovers take note! Sally drizzles melted chocolate drizzled over a rich chocolate filling for this scrumptious pie. To drizzle the melted chocolate mixture, let it cool slightly, transfer it to a plastic sandwich bag, snip off a corner, and squeeze.

¾ cup all-purpose flour
⅓ cup very finely chopped hazelnuts
3 tablespoons brown sugar
⅓ cup butter or margarine, melted
1 8-ounce package cream cheese, softened
¾ cup semisweet chocolate pieces, melted and cooled
⅓ cup granulated sugar

2 tablespoons milk
1 cup whipping cream
¼ cup semisweet chocolate pieces
2 tablespoons butter or margarine
1 cup frozen loose-pack unsweetened red raspberries, thawed
2 tablespoons light-colored corn syrup
Fresh mint (optional)

1 For crust, in a small bowl stir together the flour, hazelnuts, and brown sugar. Stir in melted butter or margarine; toss to mix. Spread crust mixture evenly into a 9-inch pie plate. Press onto bottom and sides to form a firm, even crust. Bake in a 425° oven for 8 to 10 minutes or until brown. Cool.

2 For filling, in a medium mixing bowl combine cream cheese, melted chocolate, granulated sugar, and milk; beat with an electric mixer on medium speed until smooth. In a chilled small mixing bowl beat whipping cream with chilled beaters of an electric mixer until soft peaks form (tips curl); fold into cream cheese mixture. Spread into the cooled crust. Cover loosely; chill for several hours or overnight.

3 Before serving, in a small saucepan melt the ¼ cup chocolate pieces and the 2 tablespoons butter or margarine; drizzle onto pie. For sauce, in a blender container or food processor bowl combine the thawed raspberries and the corn syrup; cover and blend or process until nearly smooth. If desired, press sauce through a sieve to remove seeds. Serve sauce with pie. If desired, garnish with mint. Makes 10 servings.

Nutrition Facts per serving: 428 calories, 33 g total fat (16 g saturated fat), 80 mg cholesterol, 168 mg sodium, 34 g carbohydrate, 1 g fiber, 5 g protein. Daily Values: 28% vit. A, 5% vit. C, 5% calcium, 10% iron.

White Chocolate-Banana Cream Pie

Prep: 30 minutes **Chill:** 4 hours

40	chocolate wafers
1/3	cup butter or margarine, melted
1/2	cup granulated sugar
1/4	cup cornstarch
1/4	teaspoon salt
2 1/2	cups milk
3	slightly beaten egg yolks

4	ounces white chocolate baking squares, finely chopped
1 1/4	teaspoons vanilla
4	medium bananas
1	cup whipping cream
2	tablespoons sifted powdered sugar
	Milk chocolate curls (optional)
	White chocolate curls (optional)

1997

Bernice V. Janowski
Stevens Point, WI

Treat yourself to a piece of Bernice's dazzling delight. She layers a white chocolate filling, banana slices, and chocolate wafers in a chocolate wafer crust and tops it all off with sweetened whipped cream and chocolate curls.

1 Crush 30 of the chocolate wafers into fine crumbs (1½ cups). In a small bowl combine wafer crumbs and melted butter or margarine; toss to mix well. Spread into a 9-inch pie plate. Press onto the bottom and up the sides to form a firm, even crust; cover and chill.

2 For filling, in a saucepan combine granulated sugar, cornstarch, and salt. Stir in milk. Cook and stir over medium heat until thickened and bubbly. Cook and stir for 2 minutes more. Remove from heat. Gradually stir about 1 cup of the hot filling into the egg yolks, stirring constantly. Pour egg yolk mixture into remaining hot filling in saucepan. Bring to a gentle boil. Cook and stir for 2 minutes more. Remove saucepan from heat. Stir in chopped white chocolate and 1 teaspoon of the vanilla. Stir until chocolate has melted.

3 Slice 2 bananas onto the chilled crust. Spread with half of the filling. Layer remaining chocolate wafers on filling. Chop the remaining bananas; sprinkle over chocolate wafers. Spread with remaining filling. Cover and chill for at least 4 hours.

4 Before serving, combine whipping cream, powdered sugar, and remaining vanilla in a chilled medium mixing bowl. Beat with the chilled beaters of an electric mixer on medium speed until soft peaks form (tips curl). Spread whipped cream over pie. If desired, top with milk chocolate and white chocolate curls. Makes 10 servings.

Nutrition Facts per serving: 422 calories, 24 g total fat (13 g saturated fat), 131 mg cholesterol, 210 mg sodium, 47 g carbohydrate, 1 g fiber, 6 g protein. Daily Values: 30% vit. A, 8% vit. C, 10% calcium, 4% iron.

Praline and Pumpkin Pie

Prep: 30 minutes **Chill:** 5 hours

1	recipe Pastry Shell (page 227)
6	tablespoons butter
½	cup packed brown sugar
¾	cup chopped toasted pecans
1	2.9-ounce package custard-flavored dessert mix

⅓	cup granulated sugar
1¼	teaspoons pumpkin pie spice
1	cup evaporated milk
2	beaten eggs
1	15-ounce can pumpkin
	Whipped cream (optional)
	Chopped toasted pecans (optional)

1976

Mrs. L. L. Greene
Houma, LA

Pumpkin, custard-flavored dessert mix, and toasted pecans team up for Mrs. Greene's first-rate Southern variation on a Thanksgiving Day classic.

1 Prepare and bake Pastry Shell. In a small saucepan melt butter; stir in brown sugar. Cook over medium heat, stirring constantly, for 1 to 2 minutes or until bubbly and mixture does not separate. Remove from heat. Stir in the ¾ cup pecans. Immediately spread over bottom of pastry shell; cool.

2 In a medium saucepan combine dessert mix, granulated sugar, and pumpkin pie spice. Stir in evaporated milk. Cook and stir over medium heat until thickened and mixture comes to a full boil. Remove from heat. Gradually stir hot mixture into beaten eggs. Return mixture to saucepan. Cook and stir over low heat for 2 minutes more. Do not boil.

3 Remove from heat. Stir in pumpkin. Pour into prepared pastry shell, spreading evenly. Chill about 5 hours or until thoroughly chilled (filling will not be firm). If desired, top with whipped cream and additional toasted pecans. Makes 8 servings.

Nutrition Facts per serving: 490 calories, 28 g total fat (9 g saturated fat), 80 mg cholesterol, 284 mg sodium, 55 g carbohydrate, 3 g fiber, 8 g protein. Daily Values: 131% vit. A, 13% vit. C,

pumpkin pie, please

Pumpkin pie took a giant leap forward in popularity when canned pumpkin was introduced in 1929. Before then, making pumpkin pie was a laborious process because fresh pumpkin had to be cooked down to pie-filling consistency. The evaporated-milk version of the pie that many adults grew up eating first appeared on the Libby's can in 1950. In the years since, cooks have continued to experiment with the classic dessert. Praline and Pumpkin Pie, above, is an innovative version from 1976 that starts with custard-flavored dessert mix.

Peanut Butter-Cream Cheese Pie

Prep: 15 minutes **Chill:** 5 to 24 hours

1976

Betty Behrendt
Two Rivers, WI

Betty's fluffy peanut butter filling piled into a purchased graham cracker crust makes a remarkably easy refrigerator dessert that will bring compliments galore.

2 3-ounce packages cream cheese, softened
¾ cup sifted powdered sugar
½ cup peanut butter
2 tablespoons milk

1 1.3-ounce envelope dessert topping mix
1 6-ounce purchased graham cracker crumb pie shell
   Coarsely chopped peanuts (optional)

1 In a medium mixing bowl beat cream cheese and powdered sugar with an electric mixer on low to medium speed until light and fluffy. Add peanut butter and milk, beating until smooth and creamy.

2 Prepare dessert topping mix according to package directions; fold into peanut butter mixture. Spoon into pie shell. Chill for at least 5 hours or up to 24 hours. If desired, sprinkle with coarsely chopped peanuts. Makes 8 servings.

Nutrition Facts per serving: 395 calories, 25 g total fat (9 g saturated fat), 24 mg cholesterol, 320 mg sodium, 37 g carbohydrate, 1 g fiber, 7 g protein. Daily Values: 14% vit. A, 3% calcium, 7% iron.

protein-packed peanut butter

Peanut butter was one of the original health foods. In 1890, a St. Louis doctor invented it for his patients who had bad teeth and thus needed an easily eaten, high-protein diet. By 1903, a patent for a peanut butter-making machine was issued. And at the St. Louis Universal Exposition in 1904, peanut butter was promoted as a health food. It took until 1922 for J. L. Rosefield to develop a process that kept the oil from separating out of peanut butter, and by the mid-1930s, commercial peanut butters were available. It didn't take cooks long to develop an extensive repertoire of peanut butter delights. Peanut Butter-Cream Cheese Pie, above, and Peanutty Ice Cream Pie, right, are two additions to the list.

Peanutty Ice Cream Pie

Prep: 30 minutes **Freeze:** 6 hours

1½ cups coarsely ground peanuts
3 tablespoons butter or margarine, melted
2 tablespoons sugar
¼ cup flaked coconut
¼ cup light-colored corn syrup

¼ cup peanut butter
3 tablespoons chopped peanuts
1 quart vanilla ice cream
Chopped candy-coated milk chocolate pieces or peanuts (optional)

Hyacinth Rizzo
Snyder, NY

Hyacinth's kid-appeal pie features a peanut-butter-swirled ice cream filling enhanced by a crunchy peanut crust. To get a head start, make the pie several days in advance and tuck it into your freezer.

1 Lightly grease a 9-inch pie plate. In a medium bowl combine ground peanuts, butter or margarine, and sugar. Press mixture firmly onto bottom and up sides of the prepared pie plate. Chill for 15 minutes.

2 Meanwhile, for filling, in a small bowl stir together coconut, corn syrup, peanut butter, and the 3 tablespoons chopped peanuts. Place ice cream in a large chilled bowl; stir ice cream just to soften. Stir in the coconut mixture just until combined. Spoon into chilled crust. If desired, sprinkle chopped chocolate pieces or peanuts over pie. Cover; freeze about 6 hours or until firm. Remove from freezer and place the pie on a warm, damp towel for a few minutes before cutting into wedges. Makes 8 servings.

Nutrition Facts per serving: 493 calories, 36 g total fat (14 g saturated fat), 57 mg cholesterol, 269 mg sodium, 36 g carbohydrate, 3 g fiber, 13 g protein. Daily Values: 18% vit. A, 1% vit. C, 12% calcium, 4% iron.

Banana Split Pie

Prep: 40 minutes   **Freeze:** 3 hours   **Stand:** 30 minutes

Eleanor Osmond
Jackson Heights, NY

A rich chocolate-and-marshmallow-creme sauce bedecks this soda fountain treat in a crust. Serve any leftover sauce over ice cream, pound cake, or angel food cake.

1 recipe Pastry Shell (page 227)
3 medium bananas
1 tablespoon lemon juice
1 pint strawberry ice cream (2 cups)
½ of an 8-ounce container frozen
    whipped dessert topping, thawed
    (about 1½ cups)

1 cup fresh strawberries, halved
2 tablespoons finely chopped walnuts
1 cup semisweet chocolate pieces
    (6 ounces)
1 5-ounce can (⅔ cup) evaporated
    milk
1 cup marshmallow creme

1 Prepare and bake Pastry Shell; set aside. Thinly slice the bananas; sprinkle with lemon juice. Arrange banana slices on bottom of pastry shell. Stir ice cream to soften slightly; spread over bananas. Freeze about 2 hours or until firm.

2 Spread whipped topping over ice cream. Top with strawberry halves; sprinkle with walnuts. Freeze about 1 hour or until firm. Let stand at room temperature for 30 minutes before serving.

3 Meanwhile, for sauce, in small saucepan combine semisweet chocolate pieces and evaporated milk. Cook and stir over low heat until chocolate is melted. Stir in marshmallow creme until smooth. Serve warm or cooled sauce over pie.* Makes 8 servings.

*Note: Store leftover sauce, covered, in refrigerator for up to 5 days.

Nutrition Facts per serving: 478 calories, 26 g total fat (14 g saturated fat), 12 mg cholesterol, 112 mg sodium, 56 g carbohydrate, 4 g fiber, 5 g protein. Daily Values: 7% vit. A, 30% vit. C, 8% calcium, 7% iron.

Secret Strawberry-Rhubarb Pie

Prep: 30 minutes **Bake:** 50 minutes

1 recipe Pastry for Double-Crust Pie	½ teaspoon ground nutmeg
⅔ cup sugar	¼ teaspoon salt
¼ cup cornstarch	3 cups fresh or frozen sliced rhubarb
½ of a 12½-ounce can (about ½ cup) almond cake-and-pastry filling (not almond paste)	2½ cups sliced fresh strawberries
	1 tablespoon margarine or butter
1 tablespoon lemon juice	1 slightly beaten egg white
	2 tablespoons sliced almonds

1999

Michelle Toth
Redmond, WA

What is Michelle's secret? She uses almond cake-and-pastry filling to add a pleasing hint of nuttiness to her double-fruit filling.

1 Prepare Pastry for Double-Crust Pie. On a lightly floured surface, roll half of the pastry into a 12-inch circle. Line a 9-inch pie plate with the pastry; set aside.

2 In a large bowl stir together sugar, cornstarch, almond filling, lemon juice, nutmeg, and salt. Stir in the rhubarb and strawberries. (If using frozen fruit, let the mixture stand about 30 minutes or until fruit is partially thawed, but still icy.) Transfer mixture to the pastry-lined pie plate. Trim the pastry to the edge of pie plate. Dot filling with margarine or butter.

3 For top crust, roll remaining pastry into a 12-inch circle. Cut slits in top crust; place on filling. Seal and flute the edge. To prevent overbrowning, cover edge with foil. Place pie plate on a baking sheet to catch any drips.

4 Bake in a 375° oven for 25 minutes for fresh fruit (50 minutes for frozen fruit). Remove foil. Bake pie for 25 to 30 minutes more or until top is golden brown. Before last 10 minutes of baking, quickly brush top with egg white; sprinkle with almonds. Cool on a wire rack. Makes 8 servings.

Pastry for Double-Crust Pie: In a medium bowl stir together 2 cups all-purpose flour and ½ teaspoon salt. Using a pastry blender or two knives, cut in ⅔ cup shortening until pieces are pea-size. Sprinkle 1 tablespoon cold water over part of the mixture; gently toss with a fork. Push moistened dough to sides of bowl. Repeat, using 1 tablespoon cold water at a time, until all of the dough is moistened (6 to 7 tablespoons water total). Divide in half. Form each half into a ball.

Nutrition Facts per serving: 461 calories, 22 g total fat (5 g saturated fat), 4 mg cholesterol, 253 mg sodium, 62 g carbohydrate, 5 g fiber, 5 g protein. Daily Values: 1% vit. A, 51% vit. C, 4% calcium, 13% iron.

Rhubarb-Raspberry-**Apple Pie**

Prep: 45 minutes **Bake:** 25 minutes

Mae M. Clark
Coeur d'Alene, ID

Mae's trio of fruit flavors makes a delicious combination in this winning pie. Using pastry cutouts in lieu of a top crust gives the pie a festive appearance. (Also pictured on the cover.)

1 recipe Pastry for Double-Crust Pie (page 235)
1¼ cups sugar
3 tablespoons cornstarch
2 tablespoons all-purpose flour
4 cups chopped fresh rhubarb or frozen rhubarb

2 cups fresh raspberries
1 medium cooking apple, peeled and shredded (about ¾ cup)
1 to 2 tablespoons milk
2 to 3 teaspoons sugar (optional)

1 Prepare Pastry for Double-Crust Pie. On a lightly floured surface, roll half of the pastry into a 12-inch circle. Line a 9-inch pie plate with pastry. Trim pastry ½ inch beyond edge of pie plate. Fold under extra pastry. Line pastry with double thickness of foil. Bake in a 450° oven for 8 minutes. Remove foil. Bake for 5 to 6 minutes more or until golden brown. Cool on a wire rack. On a lightly floured surface, roll remaining pastry into a 12-inch circle. Using a 2- to 3-inch cutter, cut pastry into desired shapes. Cover cutouts loosely; set aside.

2 Meanwhile, in a large saucepan stir together the sugar, cornstarch, and flour. Stir in rhubarb, raspberries, and apple. Cook over low heat, stirring frequently, until fruit begins to juice out. Increase heat to medium. Cook and stir over medium heat until thickened and bubbly. Transfer to the baked pie shell. Brush edge of pie with milk. Place pastry cutouts over fruit filling and around the edge of the pie. Brush pastry cutouts with milk and, if desired, sprinkle with sugar. Bake in a 375° oven about 25 minutes or until pastry is golden brown. Cool on a wire rack. Makes 8 servings.

For a double-crust pie: For a conventional pie with a filling that doesn't require precooking, line pie plate with half of the pastry, as directed above, except do not trim pastry or fold under. Omit the prebaking step. Set pie plate aside. To prepare filling, omit the cornstarch and reduce the raspberries to 1 cup. In a large mixing bowl stir together the sugar and, if using fresh rhubarb, 6 tablespoons of all-purpose flour. (If using frozen rhubarb, increase the all-purpose flour to ½ cup.) Stir in the rhubarb, raspberries, and apple. Transfer filling to the pastry-lined plate. Trim pastry even with rim of pie plate. Cut slits in top crust; place crust over filling. Seal; flute edge. Cover edges with foil. Bake in a 375° oven for 25 minutes. Remove foil; bake 20 to 25 minutes more or until top is golden and fruit is tender. Cool on a wire rack.

Nutrition Facts per serving: 429 calories, 18 g total fat (4 g saturated fat), 0 mg cholesterol, 138 mg sodium, 65 g carbohydrate, 5 g fiber, 4 g protein. Daily Values: 1% vit. A, 23% vit. C, 7% calcium, 10% iron.

Festive Cranberry-Apricot Pie

Prep: 30 minutes **Bake:** 50 minutes

1998

Arnold Espinosa
Santa Ana, CA

Arnold's intriguing combination of canned apricots and dried cranberries captured top honors in the 1998 Pies Aplenty category. A taste of this two-fruit pie may just convince you to start a delicious new holiday dessert tradition.

1 15-ounce package (2 crusts) folded refrigerated unbaked piecrust
½ cup sugar
3 tablespoons cornstarch
1½ teaspoons pumpkin pie spice
¼ teaspoon salt

3 15¼-ounce cans apricot halves, drained and cut into quarters
½ cup dried cranberries, snipped
1 egg white
1 tablespoon milk
1 tablespoon sugar
¼ teaspoon pumpkin pie spice

1 Using one of the piecrusts, line a 9-inch pie plate according to package directions. Fold edge under. Set aside.

2 In a large bowl combine the ½ cup sugar, the cornstarch, the 1½ teaspoons pumpkin pie spice, and the salt. Stir in apricots and cranberries. Spoon into prepared crust.

3 Place remaining piecrust on a lightly floured surface. Cut with a 2-inch-long leaf-shaped cutter or other desired cutter to make 18 to 20 shapes. In a small bowl stir together egg white and milk. Brush egg white mixture over pastry shapes; reserve remaining egg white mixture. Combine the 1 tablespoon sugar and the ¼ teaspoon pumpkin pie spice. Sprinkle half of the pastry shapes with the sugar mixture. Arrange six to eight of the shapes, alternating brushed and sprinkled shapes, in a circle in center of the top of pie filling. Brush edge of crust with remaining egg white mixture. Evenly distribute the remaining pastry shapes around edge of crust. Cover edge lightly with foil. Bake in a 375° oven for 35 minutes. Remove foil. Bake for 15 minutes more. Cool on a wire rack. Makes 8 servings.

Nutrition Facts per serving: 394 calories, 14 g total fat (6 g saturated fat), 10 mg cholesterol, 285 mg sodium, 65 g carbohydrate, 3 g fiber, 2 g protein. Daily Values: 24% vit. A, 12% vit. C, 2% calcium, 3% iron.

Sour Cream and Berry Pie

Prep: 30 minutes **Chill:** 5 to 24 hours

1   cup finely crushed graham crackers
¼   cup finely chopped walnuts
2   tablespoons all-purpose flour
1   tablespoon sugar
⅓   cup butter or margarine, melted
½   cup sugar
3   tablespoons cornstarch
1   teaspoon unflavored gelatin

1⅓   cups milk
1½   cups dairy sour cream
1   tablespoon vanilla
1½   teaspoons finely shredded orange, lemon, or lime peel
3   cups fresh blueberries, raspberries, and/or small whole strawberries, quartered

1994

*Susan Brinskele
Petaluma, CA*

The tanginess of sour cream partners perfectly with juicy, sweet berries. Let summer's best blueberries, raspberries, or strawberries take center stage or use a combination of fresh berries for this versatile pie.

1 For crust, in a small bowl combine the crushed graham crackers, walnuts, flour, and the 1 tablespoon sugar. Stir in the melted butter or margarine. Toss to mix well. Press mixture onto the bottom and up sides of a 9-inch pie plate. Bake in a 375° oven for 8 minutes. Cool on a wire rack.

2 For filling, in a medium saucepan combine the ½ cup sugar, the cornstarch, and gelatin; stir in milk. Cook and stir over medium heat until thickened; cook and stir for 2 minutes more. Place sour cream in a medium bowl. Gradually stir milk mixture into sour cream; stir in vanilla and citrus peel. Gently fold the 3 cups berries into sour cream mixture. Spoon into cooled crust. Cover; chill for at least 5 hours or up to 24 hours. Makes 8 servings.

Nutrition Facts per serving: 339 calories, 20 g total fat (11 g saturated fat), 41 mg cholesterol, 182 mg sodium, 36 g carbohydrate, 3 g fiber, 5 g protein. Daily Values: 17% vit. A, 29% vit. C, 11% calcium, 5% iron.

piecrust possibilities

When it comes to making pastry for a pie, there are quite a few options. You can make your own piecrust (see recipes on pages 227 and 235). Or, you can purchase refrigerated pastry, piecrust mix, or frozen piecrusts. Look for refrigerated pastry in your supermarket's dairy case. Each package contains two 12-inch crusts that are enough for two 9-inch single-crust pies or one 9-inch double-crust pie. Piecrust mix, available in the baking aisle of the supermarket, is sold in one-crust and two-crust sizes. And, in the frozen food case, you'll find deep-dish and shallow piecrusts. A deep-dish crust is the equivalent of a homemade pie shell. The shallow piecrusts are too small for the recipes in this cookbook.

Double-Cherry Pie

Prep: 20 minutes **Bake:** 45 minutes

1995

Bernice Janowski
Stevens Point, WI

A chocolate-oat crust, tart cherries, cherry pie filling, and a chocolate-brown sugar topping add up to pastry perfection in this easy-to-make dessert.

½ cup miniature semisweet chocolate
    pieces
5 tablespoons butter
¾ cup rolled oats
¾ cup all-purpose flour
¼ cup packed brown sugar
1 20-ounce can reduced-calorie cherry
    pie filling

1 16-ounce can pitted tart red cherries
    (water pack), drained
¼ teaspoon almond extract
½ cup all-purpose flour
2 tablespoons brown sugar
2 tablespoons rolled oats
3 tablespoons butter, softened
¼ cup miniature semisweet
    chocolate pieces

1 Grease a 10-inch pie plate; set aside. For crust, in a medium saucepan melt the ½ cup chocolate pieces and the 5 tablespoons butter over low heat. Remove from heat; stir in the ¾ cup oats, the ¾ cup flour, and the ¼ cup brown sugar. Press oat mixture onto bottom and sides of prepared pie plate to form a firm, even crust. Bake in a 350° oven for 10 minutes.

2 Meanwhile, for filling, in a medium bowl combine pie filling, cherries, and almond extract. Pour filling into the baked crust.

3 For topping, in a small bowl stir together the ½ cup flour, the 2 tablespoons brown sugar, and the 2 tablespoons oats. Using a pastry blender or two knives, cut in the 3 tablespoons butter until mixture resembles coarse crumbs. Stir in the ¼ cup chocolate pieces. Sprinkle over filling. Bake in a 350° oven for 35 minutes. Cool on a wire rack. Makes 10 servings.

Nutrition Facts per serving: 296 calories, 13 g total fat (7 g saturated fat), 34 mg cholesterol, 99 mg sodium, 43 g carbohydrate, 1 g fiber, 4 g protein. Daily Values: 12% vit. A, 4% vit. C, 1% calcium, 13% iron.

Cream Cheese-Filled Cupcakes

Prep: 20 minutes **Bake:** Per package directions

1 8-ounce package cream cheese, softened
⅓ cup sugar
1 egg
   Dash salt

1 cup semisweet chocolate pieces (6 ounces)
1 package 2-layer-size chocolate cake mix
   Favorite frosting (optional)

1969

*Mrs. Conrad Stanley
Kansas City, MO*

Break open one of these chocolaty treats and you'll discover a cream cheese filling dotted with semisweet chocolate pieces. Kids of all ages will love 'em, whether unadorned or crowned with your favorite frosting.

1 In a medium mixing bowl beat the cream cheese and sugar with an electric mixer on medium-high speed until combined. Beat in egg and salt. Stir in chocolate pieces; set aside.

2 Prepare cake mix according to package directions. Line thirty 2½-inch muffin cups with paper bake cups. Divide batter among muffin cups, filling each about half full. Drop a rounded teaspoon of the cream cheese mixture into each muffin cup. Bake as directed on package. Cool on wire racks. If desired, frost with favorite frosting. Makes about 30 cupcakes.

Nutrition Facts per cupcake: 165 calories, 9 g total fat (4 g saturated fat), 29 mg cholesterol, 141 mg sodium, 18 g carbohydrate, 1 g fiber, 2 g protein. Daily Values: 3% vit. A, 1% calcium, 2% iron.

modernizing the cake

Cake baking advanced in the 1920s and 1930s when gas and electric ranges replaced wood and petroleum stoves and the electric mixer was perfected. Cakes could be baked higher and lighter than ever before. During the 1940s, traditional two-step creamed cakes gave way to one-bowl "dump" or muffin-method cakes. Out of this cake-making innovation was born the cake mix. In the late 1940s, cake mixes were introduced. Time-conscious homemakers eagerly embraced the new products. Over the next 50 years, recipes that adapted and enhanced mixes, such as Cream Cheese-Filled Cupcakes, above, abounded. Cake mixes revolutionized cake baking so much that there are many contemporary cooks who have never baked a cake from scratch.

Peanut Butter Cupcakes

Prep: 25 minutes   **Bake:** 18 minutes

2 cups all-purpose flour
2½ teaspoons baking powder
½ teaspoon salt
2 eggs
½ cup packed brown sugar
1 cup packed brown sugar
⅓ cup shortening

½ cup creamy peanut butter
1 teaspoon vanilla
¾ cup milk
1½ cups purchased creamy chocolate or fudge frosting
Chopped peanuts (optional)

1939

Mrs. George Waterhouse
Pittsford, NY

Some things never go out of style. Perfect for lunch box treats or after-school snacks, these chocolate-frosted peanut butter cupcakes from 1939 will be a surefire hit even with today's kids.

1 Grease twenty-four 2½-inch muffin cups or line with paper bake cups; set aside. In a small bowl combine flour, baking powder, and salt; set aside.

2 In a medium mixing bowl beat eggs and the ½ cup brown sugar with an electric mixer on medium-high speed about 5 minutes or until thick and smooth; set aside.

3 In a large mixing bowl beat the 1 cup brown sugar and shortening with an electric mixer on low to medium speed until well mixed. Beat in the peanut butter and vanilla. Add the egg mixture, beating on low speed until combined. Add flour mixture and milk alternately to beaten mixture, beating on low speed after each addition just until combined.

4 Spoon into prepared muffin cups, filling each about two-thirds full. Bake in a 350° oven for 18 to 20 minutes or until cupcakes spring back when lightly touched. Cool in pans on wire racks for 5 minutes. Remove cupcakes to a wire rack; cool thoroughly. Spread tops with chocolate or fudge frosting. If desired, sprinkle with chopped peanuts. Makes 24 cupcakes.

Nutrition Facts per cupcake: 219 calories, 9 g total fat (2 g saturated fat), 18 mg cholesterol, 177 mg sodium, 33 g carbohydrate, 1 g fiber, 3 g protein. Daily Values: 1% vit. A, 5% calcium, 7% iron.

Mocha **Pound Cake**

Prep: 25 minutes **Bake:** 1 hour 5 minutes

*Marjorie Johnson
Omaha, NE*

The mocha flavor of Marjorie's velvety pound cake is irresistible. The coffee-flavored icing isn't required, of course, but adds a special touch.

3 eggs
2 cups sifted cake flour or 1¾ cups sifted all-purpose flour
½ teaspoon salt
½ teaspoon cream of tartar
¼ teaspoon baking soda
½ cup water
1 tablespoon instant espresso coffee powder or 4 teaspoons instant coffee crystals

⅔ cup shortening
1¼ cups sugar
1 teaspoon vanilla
2 ounces unsweetened chocolate, melted and cooled
1 recipe Coffee Icing

1 Let eggs stand at room temperature for 30 minutes. Meanwhile, grease and lightly flour a 9×5×3-inch loaf pan; set aside. In a medium bowl combine flour, salt, cream of tartar, and baking soda; set aside. Combine water and espresso powder or coffee crystals; set aside.

2 In a large mixing bowl beat shortening with an electric mixer on medium to high speed for 30 seconds. Gradually add sugar, beating about 10 minutes or until very light and fluffy. Beat in vanilla. Add eggs, one at a time, beating 1 minute after each addition and scraping sides of bowl frequently. Beat in chocolate. Add flour mixture and espresso mixture alternately to beaten mixture, beating on low to medium speed after each addition just until combined. Pour batter into prepared pan, spreading evenly.

3 Bake in a 325° oven for 65 to 70 minutes or until a toothpick inserted in center comes out clean. Cool in pan on a wire rack for 10 minutes. Remove from pan. Cool thoroughly on rack. Drizzle with Coffee Icing. Makes 10 servings.

Coffee Icing: In a small bowl dissolve ½ teaspoon instant espresso coffee powder or 1 teaspoon instant coffee crystals in 2 teaspoons milk. Stir in ½ cup sifted powdered sugar until smooth. If necessary, stir in additional milk, 1 teaspoon at a time, to make icing of drizzling consistency.

Nutrition Facts per serving: 369 calories, 19 g total fat (6 g saturated fat), 64 mg cholesterol, 169 mg sodium, 48 g carbohydrate, 1 g fiber, 4 g protein. Daily Values: 3% vit. A, 2% calcium, 12% iron.

Mocha and Cherry Cake

Prep: 50 minutes **Bake:** 25 minutes **Chill:** 1 to 24 hours

Unsweetened cocoa powder
2 cups granulated sugar
1¾ cups all-purpose flour
¾ cup unsweetened cocoa powder
2 teaspoons baking soda
1 teaspoon baking powder
½ teaspoon salt
2 eggs
1 cup buttermilk
1 cup strong coffee, cooled
½ cup cooking oil
2 teaspoons vanilla
2½ cups ricotta cheese

½ cup granulated sugar
½ cup miniature semisweet chocolate
    pieces
½ cup maraschino cherries, well
    drained and chopped
1 teaspoon instant coffee crystals
½ cup milk
⅔ cup butter
7½ cups sifted powdered sugar
½ cup unsweetened cocoa powder
2 teaspoons vanilla
    Chocolate shavings (optional)
    Edible flower petals (optional)

1994

Brenda Vernon
East Hartford, CT

Filled with a combination of ricotta cheese, chocolate, and cherries, this elegant cake will tempt even the most determined dessert dodger.

1 Grease two 9x1½-inch round baking pans; sprinkle with cocoa powder. Set aside. In a very large mixing bowl combine the 2 cups granulated sugar, the flour, the ¾ cup cocoa powder, the baking soda, baking powder, and salt. Add eggs, buttermilk, strong coffee, oil, and 2 teaspoons vanilla. Beat with an electric mixer on low speed for 30 seconds or until combined; beat on medium speed for 2 minutes. Spread batter evenly into prepared pans.

2 Bake in a 350° oven for 25 to 30 minutes or until toothpick inserted near the centers comes out clean. Cool in pans on wire racks for 10 minutes. Remove from pans. Cool thoroughly on racks. Split each cake layer horizontally to make 4 layers.

3 For filling, combine ricotta cheese, the ½ cup granulated sugar, and chocolate pieces. Gently stir in cherries. Place one cake layer, cut side up, on a serving plate; carefully spread with one-third of the filling. Top with another cake layer. Continue layering filling and cake layers, ending with a cake layer, top side up.

4 For frosting, stir coffee crystals into the milk until dissolved; set aside. In a large mixing bowl beat butter with an electric mixer on medium speed until fluffy. Gradually add half of the powdered sugar and the ½ cup cocoa powder. Slowly beat in half of milk mixture and 2 teaspoons vanilla. Beat in remaining powdered sugar. Beat in remaining milk mixture. If necessary, beat in additional milk, 1 teaspoon at a time, to make frosting of spreading consistency. Frost top and sides of cake. If desired, garnish with chocolate shavings and edible flowers. Cover; chill for at least 1 hour or up to 24 hours. Makes 14 to 16 servings.

Nutrition Facts per serving: 628 calories, 23 g total fat (10 g saturated fat), 69 mg cholesterol, 401 mg sodium, 96 g carbohydrate, 1 g fiber, 9 g protein. Daily Values: 14% vit. A, 19% calcium, 10% iron.

Pumpkin-Praline Cake

Prep: 30 minutes **Bake:** 20 minutes

Norma J. Keleher
Pacific Grove, CA

Ground pecans and vanilla wafer crumbs replace the flour in this is unique pumpkin cake that's filled with vanilla pudding and frosted with brown sugar-sweetened whipped cream.

- 6 egg yolks
- ½ cup granulated sugar
- ⅔ cup canned pumpkin
- 1 teaspoon vanilla
- 2 cups pecan pieces, finely ground
- ⅓ cup finely crushed vanilla wafers (7 wafers)
- 2 teaspoons shredded orange peel
- 1 teaspoon baking powder
- 6 egg whites
- ½ cup granulated sugar
  Sifted powdered sugar
- 1 package 4-serving-size cook-and-serve vanilla pudding mix
- 1½ cups milk
- 2 tablespoons rum (optional)
- 1 cup whipping cream
- 2 tablespoons brown sugar
  Chopped pecans (optional)
  Orange peel curls (optional)

1 Grease and flour a 15×10×1-inch baking pan; set aside. In a large mixing bowl beat egg yolks with an electric mixer on high speed about 5 minutes or until thick and lemon colored. Gradually add ½ cup granulated sugar, beating at low speed until combined. Increase speed to medium; beat until mixture thickens slightly and doubles in volume (about 5 minutes). Stir in pumpkin and vanilla. Stir together ground pecans, vanilla wafers, orange peel, and baking powder; stir into pumpkin mixture. Set aside.

2 Wash and dry beaters thoroughly. In another large mixing bowl beat egg whites with an electric mixer on medium speed until soft peaks form. Gradually add ½ cup granulated sugar; beat on high speed until stiff peaks form. Fold about 1 cup beaten egg white mixture into pumpkin mixture; fold pumpkin mixture into remaining egg white mixture. Spread evenly into prepared pan. Bake in a 350° oven for 20 to 25 minutes or until cake springs back when lightly touched. Immediately loosen edges. Turn out onto a towel sprinkled generously with powdered sugar; cool completely.

3 Meanwhile, cook pudding according to package directions, except decrease milk to 1½ cups. Remove from heat. If desired, stir in rum. Cover surface with plastic wrap. Cool without stirring.

4 Cut cake crosswise into three 10×5-inch pieces. Place one piece of cake on serving plate. Spread with half of the pudding mixture; top with second cake piece and remaining pudding mixture. Top with third cake piece.

5 In a chilled medium mixing bowl combine whipping cream and brown sugar. Beat with chilled beaters of an electric mixer on medium speed just until soft peaks form. Spread top and sides of cake with whipped cream mixture. If desired, garnish with chopped pecans and orange peel curls. Makes 10 servings.

Nutrition Facts per serving: 439 calories, 28 g total fat (8 g saturated fat), 163 mg cholesterol, 174 mg sodium, 42 g carbohydrate, 2 g fiber, 8 g protein. Daily Values: 55% vit. A, 4% vit. C, 12% calcium, 7% iron.

Chocolate Fleck **Cake**

Prep: 20 minutes **Bake:** per package directions **Chill:** 1 hour

Mrs. Orville H. Warwick, Jr.
Northbrook, IL

Cap off a special evening by serving this luscious cake mix fix-up with steaming cups of coffee or tea.

1 package 2-layer-size white or yellow
   cake mix
⅓ cup chocolate-flavored sprinkles
1½ cups whipping cream
⅔ cup presweetened cocoa powder
¼ cup finely chopped pecans or
   walnuts

1 Grease and lightly flour two 8×1½- or 9×1½-inch round baking pans; set aside. Prepare batter from cake mix according to package directions; fold in chocolate sprinkles. Divide batter evenly between prepared pans; bake as directed on package. Cool in pans for 10 minutes. Remove from pans. Cool thoroughly on wire racks.

2 For frosting, in a medium mixing bowl combine whipping cream and cocoa powder; chill for 1 hour. Beat cream mixture with chilled beaters of an electric mixer on medium speed until soft peaks form (tips curl).

3 Fill and frost cooled cake with whipped cream mixture; sprinkle nuts over top. Serve immediately or chill for up to 2 hours. Store leftover cake, covered, in the refrigerator. Makes 12 servings.

Nutrition Facts per serving: 395 calories, 21 g total fat (10 g saturated fat), 41 mg cholesterol, 339 mg sodium, 46 g carbohydrate, 1 g fiber, 3 g protein. Daily Values: 13% vit. A, 6% calcium, 5% iron.

chocolate takes the cake

The true origins of chocolate cake are buried in the recipe boxes of yesteryear, but cookbooks have been giving instructions for this delightful confection since the late 1800s. Recipes for devil's food cake, one of the earliest favorites, began appearing around the turn of the 20th century. While there's no strict definition for devil's food cake, the consensus seems to be that it must be as dark and rich as angel food cake is white and light. Over the decades, recipes such as chocolate fudge cake, German chocolate cake, Texas sheet cake, and Mississippi mud cake have all taken their turns on top of the chocolate cake hit parade. In the 1980s and 1990s, extremely dense, almost flourless chocolate creations, such as Truffle Cake with Raspberry Sauce, right, topped the best-loved list.

Truffle Cake with Raspberry Sauce

Prep: 25 minutes **Bake:** 25 minutes **Chill:** 4 to 24 hours

16 ounces semisweet chocolate, cut up
½ cup butter
1 tablespoon granulated sugar
1½ teaspoons all-purpose flour
4 egg yolks
4 egg whites

1 12-ounce jar seedless raspberry jam
1 tablespoon raspberry liqueur or
   orange juice
   Whipped cream or powdered sugar
   (optional)
   Fresh raspberries (optional)

1993

Melissa Luebkemann
Tallahassee, FL

You use very little flour—1½ teaspoons—in this superb cake. Don't worry if it seems soft after baking. It becomes firmer upon chilling.

1 Grease and flour an 8-inch springform pan; set aside. In a heavy, large saucepan stir chocolate and butter over low heat just until chocolate melts. Remove from heat; cool slightly (about 5 minutes). Stir in granulated sugar and flour. Using a wooden spoon, beat in egg yolks, one at a time, just until combined. Set aside.

2 In a medium mixing bowl beat egg whites with an electric mixer on high speed until stiff peaks form (tips stand straight). Fold into chocolate mixture. Pour into the prepared pan. Bake in a 350° oven for 25 to 30 minutes or until edges puff (toothpick will not come out clean). Cool in pan on a wire rack for 30 minutes. Remove side of pan; cool completely. Cover and chill for at least 4 hours or up to 24 hours.

3 To serve, cut cake into wedges.* In a small saucepan heat and stir jam and liqueur or orange juice over low heat just until jam is melted. Drizzle jam on dessert plates; top each with a cake wedge. If desired, top with whipped cream or dust with powdered sugar and garnish with fresh raspberries. Makes 12 servings.

*Note: If the cake sticks to the bottom of the pan when serving, place the pan bottom on a warm, moist dish cloth for one minute before cutting.

Nutrition Facts per serving: 363 calories, 22 g total fat (12 g saturated fat), 93 mg cholesterol, 115 mg sodium, 42 g carbohydrate, 3 g fiber, 5 g protein. Daily Values: 11% vit. A, 4% vit. C, 2% calcium, 13% iron.

Blueberry-Citrus Cake

Prep: 20 minutes **Bake:** 35 minutes

1 package 2-layer-size lemon cake mix
1 tablespoon finely shredded orange peel (set aside)
½ cup orange juice
½ cup water
⅓ cup cooking oil

3 eggs
1½ cups fresh or frozen blueberries
1 tablespoon finely shredded lemon peel
1 recipe Citrus Frosting
Orange peel curls (optional)

Donna Isler
Clarksville, IN

This dessert is '90s-style cooking at its best. Blueberries and citrus peel transform a simple lemon cake mix into a delectable treat. A cream cheese-citrus frosting complements the moist cake.

1 Grease and lightly flour two 8×1½-inch or 9×1½-inch round baking pans; set aside. In a large mixing bowl combine cake mix, orange juice, water, oil, and eggs. Beat with an electric mixer on low speed for 30 seconds. Beat for 2 minutes on medium speed. Gently fold in blueberries, lemon peel, and finely shredded orange peel. Divide batter evenly between prepared pans.

2 Bake in a 350° oven for 35 to 40 minutes or until a toothpick inserted near the centers comes out clean. Cool in pans on wire racks for 10 minutes. Remove from pans. Cool thoroughly on wire racks. Fill and frost with Citrus Frosting. If desired, garnish with orange peel curls. Store frosted cake in the refrigerator. Makes 12 servings.

Citrus Frosting: Finely shred 2 tablespoons orange peel and 1 tablespoon lemon peel; set aside. In a medium mixing bowl beat one 3-ounce package softened cream cheese and ¼ cup softened butter with an electric mixer on low to medium speed until fluffy. Add 3 cups sifted powdered sugar and 2 tablespoons orange juice. Beat until combined. In a small chilled mixing bowl beat 1 cup whipping cream with chilled beaters of an electric mixer on medium speed until soft peaks form (tips curl); add to cream cheese mixture. Add the orange peel and lemon peel. Beat on low speed until combined.

Nutrition Facts per serving: 493 calories, 25 g total fat (11 g saturated fat), 98 mg cholesterol, 345 mg sodium, 66 g carbohydrate, 1 g fiber, 4 g protein. Daily Values: 18% vit. A, 12% vit. C, 9% calcium, 5% iron.

Coconut-Orange **Cake**

Prep: 30 minutes **Bake:** 30 minutes

1969

Mrs. Charles Scott
Indianapolis, IN

**When we published
Mrs. Scott's recipe in 1969,
we included the ingredients
for her homemade fluffy
frosting. Today's version of
this company-pleasing cake
substitutes a frosting mix to
give the same luscious
results in less time. (Pictured
on page 224.)**

1 package 2-layer-size white cake mix
1 cup milk
2 egg whites
½ of a 6-ounce can (⅓ cup) frozen
   orange juice concentrate, thawed

½ cup flaked coconut
1 7.2-ounce package fluffy white
   frosting mix (for a 2-layer cake)
⅓ cup flaked coconut or large coconut
   flakes, toasted

1 Grease and flour two 9×1½-inch round baking pans; set aside. In a large mixing bowl combine cake mix, milk, egg whites, and orange juice concentrate. Beat with an electric mixer on medium speed for 2 minutes. Fold in the ½ cup coconut.

2 Divide batter evenly between prepared pans. Bake in a 350° oven for 30 to 35 minutes or until a toothpick inserted near the center comes out clean. Cool in pans on wire racks for 10 minutes. Remove from pans. Cool thoroughly on wire racks.

3 Prepare frosting according to package directions. Fill and frost cake. Sprinkle toasted coconut on top of cake. Store cake, covered, in refrigerator. Makes 12 servings.

Nutrition Facts per serving: 291 calories, 6 g total fat (3 g saturated fat), 2 mg cholesterol, 361 mg sodium, 57 g carbohydrate, 0 g fiber, 3 g protein. Daily Values: 1% vit. A, 18% vit. C, 7% calcium, 5% iron.

facts about fluffy frostings

Home bakers have been embellishing their cakes with fluffy white frostings since the 19th century. The earliest versions were called boiled frostings because boiling-hot sugar mixtures were beaten into egg whites until fluffy marshmallow-like frostings formed. (Today, these types of frosting pose a safety concern because the egg whites are not thoroughly cooked.) In the 1930s and 1940s, seven-minute icing became the fluffy frosting of choice. The frosting gets its name from the fact that the egg whites are beaten for seven minutes while the mixture cooks in the top of a double boiler. Although many cooks take pride in their homemade seven-minute frostings, other cooks prefer to simply prepare a fluffy white frosting mix. Either choice is a delicious way to crown cakes of all flavors.

Lemonade Roll

Prep: 25 minutes **Bake:** 12 minutes **Chill:** 1 hour

¾ cup all-purpose flour
1 teaspoon baking powder
½ teaspoon salt
4 egg yolks
¾ cup granulated sugar
½ cup frozen lemonade concentrate, thawed

4 egg whites
Sifted powdered sugar
1 teaspoon finely shredded lemon peel
½ of an 8-ounce container frozen whipped dessert topping, thawed (about 1½ cups)

1971

Mrs. James L. Stube
Des Plaines, IL

Light and refreshing, this tender cake roll filled with lemon-spiked whipped topping is a great finalé for a warm-weather dinner.

1 Lightly grease a 15×10×1-inch baking pan. Line pan with waxed paper; grease and flour paper. Set aside. In a small bowl stir together flour, baking powder, and salt; set aside.

2 In a medium mixing bowl beat egg yolks with an electric mixer on high speed about 5 minutes or until thick and lemon colored. Gradually add ½ cup of the granulated sugar, beating on high speed until sugar is almost dissolved. Add flour mixture and lemonade concentrate alternately to beaten mixture, beating after each addition just until combined.

3 Wash beaters with warm, soapy water; dry beaters. In a large mixing bowl beat egg whites with electric mixer on medium speed until soft peaks form (tips curl); gradually add the remaining granulated sugar, beating until stiff peaks form (tips stand straight). Fold egg yolk mixture into beaten egg whites.

4 Spread batter evenly into prepared pan. Bake in a 375° oven for 12 to 15 minutes or until cake springs back when lightly touched. Immediately loosen the edges of cake from pan and turn onto a towel sprinkled with powdered sugar. Remove waxed paper. Starting from one of the short sides, roll up cake and towel together; cool cake on a wire rack.

5 Fold lemon peel into dessert topping. Unroll cake; remove towel. Spread dessert topping mixture to within 1 inch of edges. Roll up cake. Chill at least 1 hour before serving. Makes 10 servings.

Nutrition Facts per serving: 178 calories, 4 g total fat (3 g saturated fat), 85 mg cholesterol, 182 mg sodium, 31 g carbohydrate, 0 g fiber, 3 g protein. Daily Values: 4% vit. A, 5% vit. C, 4% calcium, 4% iron.

Tropical Isle Chiffon Cake

Prep: 30 minutes **Bake:** 1 hour

1965

Mary Burkhart
Tucson, AZ

Nothing beats old-fashioned chiffon cake—especially when it's flavored with orange juice and dressed up with coconut.

2¼ cups sifted cake flour or 2 cups sifted
    all-purpose flour
1½ cups sugar
 1 tablespoon baking powder
¼ teaspoon salt
½ cup cooking oil
 5 egg yolks

1 teaspoon finely shredded
    orange peel
¾ cup orange juice
 8 egg whites (1 cup)
½ teaspoon cream of tartar
 1 3½-ounce can (1⅓ cups) flaked
    coconut

1 In a large mixing bowl combine flour, sugar, baking powder, and salt. Make a well in the center of flour mixture. Add oil, egg yolks, orange peel, and orange juice. Beat with an electric mixer on low speed until combined. Beat on high speed about 5 minutes more or until smooth. Wash and dry beaters thoroughly.

2 In an extra-large mixing bowl beat egg whites and cream of tartar with an electric mixer on medium speed until stiff peaks form (tips stand straight). Pour egg yolk-flour mixture in a thin stream over beaten egg whites. Sprinkle with coconut; fold in gently. Pour into an ungreased 10-inch tube pan, spreading evenly.

3 Bake in a 325° oven for 60 to 65 minutes or until top springs back when lightly touched. Immediately invert cake (leave in pan); cool thoroughly. Loosen side of cake from pan; remove cake. Makes 12 servings.

Nutrition Facts per serving: 328 calories, 14 g total fat (4 g saturated fat), 89 mg cholesterol, 191 mg sodium, 46 g carbohydrate, 1 g fiber, 6 g protein. Daily Values: 4% vit. A, 13% vit. C, 8% calcium, 11% iron.

celebrating chiffon cake

Heralded as the first new cake innovation in a century, chiffon cake burst onto the baking scene in the late 1940s. This cross between a butter cake and a sponge cake uses oil instead of butter or shortening. Originally invented by an insurance salesman in the late 1920s, the cake became a Hollywood sensation when he began making it for celebrity gatherings. The salesman hung on to his secret until 1947 when he sold the recipe to a large food company, which then published the cake recipe in 1948, using it to boost the sale of cake flour. Since then, chiffon cakes have appeared in many flavors.

Banana Cream Cake

Prep: 20 minutes **Bake:** 35 minutes

2 cups all-purpose flour
1⅓ cups granulated sugar
1½ teaspoons baking powder
1 teaspoon baking soda
½ teaspoon salt
½ teaspoon ground nutmeg
1 cup mashed ripe banana (about 3)
½ cup shortening

¼ cup milk
1 teaspoon vanilla
2 eggs
½ cup finely chopped walnuts
1 8-ounce carton dairy sour cream
⅓ cup packed brown sugar
¼ cup broken walnuts

1961

Alvina DuVall
Santa Clara, CA

A nifty sour cream frosting bakes right on top of Alvina's feathery cake. The can't-miss combo offers the perfect ending to any special or everyday meal.

1 Grease and flour a 9×9×2-inch baking pan; set aside. In a large mixing bowl stir together flour, granulated sugar, baking powder, baking soda, salt, and nutmeg. Add banana, shortening, milk, and vanilla. Beat with an electric mixer on low speed until combined. Add eggs; beat with an electric mixer on medium speed for 2 minutes. Stir in finely chopped nuts.

2 Pour batter into prepared pan, spreading evenly. Bake in a 350° oven for 35 to 40 minutes or until a toothpick inserted near the center comes out clean.

3 Meanwhile, for frosting, in a small bowl stir together sour cream and brown sugar. Spoon evenly over warm cake in pan. Sprinkle with broken nuts. Bake about 5 minutes more or until frosting is set. Cool cake in pan on a wire rack. Cover and chill leftovers within 2 hours. Makes 9 servings.

Nutrition Facts per serving: 511 calories, 25 g total fat (7 g saturated fat), 59 mg cholesterol, 372 mg sodium, 69 g carbohydrate, 2 g fiber, 7 g protein. Daily Values: 8% vit. A, 7% vit. C, 11% calcium, 10% iron.

Chocolate-Raspberry Cheesecake, page 265

Desserts

Four-Flavor **Freeze**

Prep: 25 minutes **Freeze:** 6 hours + 1 to 24 hours

*Mrs. Joseph D. Weber
Houston, TX*

Bananas, black walnuts, vanilla ice cream, and chocolate are the four flavors in this delightful dessert that will make any dinner special.

1¼ cups finely crushed chocolate wafers	¾ cup chopped black walnuts
2 tablespoons sugar	1 cup whipping cream
⅓ cup butter or margarine, melted	1 tablespoon sugar
1 pint vanilla ice cream	3 tablespoons shaved semisweet
1 cup mashed ripe banana	chocolate

1 For crust, in a small bowl combine finely crushed cookies, the 2 tablespoons sugar, and the melted butter or margarine. Press onto the bottom of an 8×8×2-inch baking pan. Chill crust while preparing filling.

2 Place ice cream in a chilled, medium bowl; stir to soften. Stir in banana and walnuts. Pour into crust; cover and freeze about 6 hours or until firm.

3 In a chilled bowl combine whipping cream and the 1 tablespoon sugar. Beat with chilled beaters of an electric mixer on medium speed until soft peaks form. Spread over ice cream layer. Sprinkle shaved chocolate over whipped cream layer; freeze until firm (about 1 hour) or for up to 24 hours. To serve, place pan on a warm, damp cloth for a few minutes to loosen crust; cut into squares. Makes 9 servings.

Nutrition Facts per serving: 428 calories, 31 g total fat (15 g saturated fat), 77 mg cholesterol, 215 mg sodium, 36 g carbohydrate, 2 g fiber, 6 g protein. Daily Values: 25% vit. A, 8% vit. C, 7% calcium, 6% iron.

irresistible ice cream

Ever since Dolly Madison introduced the United States to ice cream by serving it at the White House in the early 1800s, it has been adored by many. Young and old alike love ice cream in many forms—pressed into bars and dipped in chocolate, scooped, whipped, blended into a drink, spiraled into a cake, as the main ingredient in sundaes and pies, and more. The favorite flavors have long been vanilla, chocolate, strawberry, and butter pecan. The recipes on these two pages, Four-Flavor Freeze, above, and Butterscotch Crunch Squares, right, feature top-favorite flavors and illustrate how cooks can be creative with the cool, creamy confection.

Butterscotch Crunch Squares

Prep: 40 minutes **Freeze:** 4 hours **Stand:** 10 minutes

1 cup all-purpose flour
¼ cup quick-cooking rolled oats
¼ cup packed brown sugar
½ cup butter
½ cup chopped pecans or walnuts

½ cup butterscotch-flavored or caramel
   ice cream topping
1 quart chocolate or your favorite
   flavor ice cream

1971

Barbara Schenke
Caruthersville, MO

**This fix-and-freeze dessert
is like eating an ice cream
sandwich that's covered
with a crunchy nut-and-
oatmeal coating.**

1 In a medium bowl combine the flour, oats, and brown sugar; cut in butter until mixture resembles coarse crumbs. Stir in nuts. Pat mixture into a 13×9×2-inch baking pan. Bake in a 400° oven for 15 minutes. Remove from oven. Stir nut mixture while still warm to crumble; cool.

2 Spread half of the crumbs in a 9×9×2-inch pan; drizzle about half of the ice cream topping over crumbs in pan. Place ice cream in a chilled, medium bowl; stir to soften. Spoon softened ice cream carefully over crumbs drizzled with topping. Drizzle with remaining topping; sprinkle with the remaining crumbs. Cover and freeze about 4 hours or until firm. Let stand at room temperature for 10 to 15 minutes before serving. Makes 12 servings.

Nutrition Facts per serving: 291 calories, 16 g total fat (8 g saturated fat), 37 mg cholesterol, 166 mg sodium, 35 g carbohydrate, 1 g fiber, 4 g protein. Daily Values: 13% vit. A, 1% vit. C, 7% calcium, 6% iron.

Blueberry Cream **Dessert**

Prep: 1 hour 5 minutes   **Chill:** 4 hours

1977

Mrs. Robert E. Huber
Dowagiac, MI

Ideal for a backyard
barbecue, these creamy
fruit-and-yogurt squares will
win you high praise.

1¼ cups finely crushed graham crackers
¼ cup sugar
⅓ cup butter or margarine, melted
½ cup sugar
1 envelope unflavored gelatin
¾ cup cold water

1 cup dairy sour cream
1 8-ounce carton blueberry yogurt
½ teaspoon vanilla
½ cup whipping cream
1 cup fresh or frozen blueberries
   Fresh blueberries (optional)

1 In a medium bowl combine crushed graham crackers, the ¼ cup sugar, and the melted butter or margarine. Reserve ¼ cup of the crumb mixture; press remaining crumbs in bottom of a 2-quart square baking dish.

2 In a small saucepan stir together the ½ cup sugar and the gelatin; stir in the water. Heat and stir until gelatin and sugar dissolve. In a large bowl combine sour cream and yogurt; gradually stir in gelatin mixture. Stir in vanilla. Chill about 45 minutes or until partially set (consistency of egg whites).

3 In a chilled small mixing bowl beat whipping cream with chilled beaters of an electric mixer on medium speed until soft peaks form. Fold whipped cream into yogurt mixture. Stir in the 1 cup blueberries. Spoon into crust, spreading evenly. Chill about 4 hours or until set. Cut into squares. Sprinkle some of the reserved crumbs on top of each serving. If desired, garnish with additional blueberries. Makes 9 servings.

Nutrition Facts per serving: 310 calories, 18 g total fat (11 g saturated fat), 49 mg cholesterol, 173 mg sodium, 34 g carbohydrate, 1 g fiber, 4 g protein. Daily Values: 17% vit. A, 5% vit. C, 8% calcium, 3% iron.

Strawberry-White Chocolate Dessert

Prep: 30 minutes **Chill:** 3 to 4 hours

Lisa Molnar
Kissimmee, FL

This showy dessert features an easy ladyfinger shell, a rich white-chocolate-and-cream-cheese filling, and fresh strawberries.

2 6-ounce packages white chocolate baking squares, cut up
1½ cups whipping cream
1 cup brewed espresso or strong coffee
2 tablespoons brandy (optional)

1 3-ounce package cream cheese, softened
30 ladyfingers (2½ three-ounce packages), split
3 cups sliced fresh strawberries
2 cups halved fresh strawberries

1 In a medium saucepan combine white chocolate and ¼ cup of the whipping cream; heat and stir over low heat until white chocolate is melted. Cool slightly. Stir together espresso or strong coffee and, if desired, brandy; set aside.

2 For filling, in a chilled medium mixing bowl beat remaining whipping cream with the chilled beaters of an electric mixer on medium speed until soft peaks form. Set aside. In a large mixing bowl beat cream cheese until fluffy. Add cooled white chocolate mixture to cream cheese; beat on medium speed until smooth. Fold whipped cream into cream cheese mixture; set aside.

3 To assemble, line the side of a 9-inch springform pan with some of the ladyfinger halves, flat sides in. Arrange half of the remaining ladyfingers on the bottom of the pan. Drizzle half of the espresso or coffee mixture over ladyfingers in the bottom of the pan. Spoon a third of the filling over ladyfingers. Top with sliced strawberries. Top with remaining ladyfingers. Drizzle with remaining espresso or coffee mixture. Top with remaining filling. Cover; chill for 3 to 4 hours.

4 Before serving, arrange halved strawberries on top of filling. To serve, carefully remove side of pan. Cut into wedges. Makes 10 to 12 servings.

Nutrition Facts per serving: 434 calories, 29 g total fat (17 g saturated fat), 137 mg cholesterol, 101 mg sodium, 40 g carbohydrate, 1 g fiber, 6 g protein. Daily Values: 23% vit. A, 72% vit. C, 10% calcium, 8% iron.

Sweet Potato Torte

Prep: 70 minutes **Bake:** 65 minutes **Cool:** 1¾ hours **Chill:** 4 hours

1 cup all-purpose flour	3 tablespoons all-purpose flour
2 cups sugar	1 tablespoon finely shredded lemon peel
1½ teaspoons finely shredded lemon peel	1 tablespoon finely shredded orange peel
1½ teaspoons finely shredded orange peel	¾ to 1 teaspoon ground nutmeg
½ cup cold butter	½ teaspoon ground cinnamon
½ cup flaked coconut	2 cups mashed, cooked sweet potatoes*
1 beaten egg yolk	4 eggs
1 tablespoon water	¼ cup whipping cream
3 8-ounce packages cream cheese, softened	Sweetened whipped cream (optional)

2000

*Pamala M. Brown
Tacoma, WA*

Pamela adores cheesecake and her mother's memorable sweet potato pie. She captured the best of both when she merged pie and cheesecake to create this elegant torte.

1 For crust, in a medium bowl stir together the 1 cup flour, ¼ cup of the sugar, the 1½ teaspoons lemon peel, and the 1½ teaspoons orange peel. Using a pastry blender, cut in butter until mixture resembles coarse crumbs. Stir in coconut. Stir together egg yolk and water; stir into flour mixture. Form into a ball. Press slightly less than half of the mixture onto bottom of a 9-inch springform pan with sides removed. Place on a baking sheet. Bake in a 350° oven for 14 to 15 minutes or until lightly browned. Cool. Attach sides of pan. Press remaining crust mixture up the sides of pan; set aside.

2 In a large mixing bowl beat cream cheese, the remaining 1¾ cups sugar, the 3 tablespoons flour, the 1 tablespoon lemon peel, the 1 tablespoon orange peel, the nutmeg, and cinnamon with an electric mixer on medium speed until smooth. Beat in mashed sweet potatoes. Add eggs, beating on low speed just until mixed. Do not overbeat. Stir in whipping cream. Pour into prepared crust. Place springform pan in a shallow baking pan. Bake in the 350° oven for 65 to 70 minutes or until a 3-inch circle in the center appears nearly set when gently shaken.

3 Cool in pan on a wire rack for 15 minutes. Using a small spatula loosen crust from sides of pan; cool 30 minutes more. Remove side of pan; cool for 1 hour. Cover; chill for at least 4 hours or until thoroughly chilled. Makes 16 servings.

*Note: To make 2 cups mashed sweet potatoes, peel and cut up 1 pound plus 6 ounces sweet potatoes. In a large saucepan cook potatoes, covered, in a moderate amount of boiling water for 25 to 30 minutes or until very tender. Cool. Process or blend potatoes, a portion at a time, in a food processor bowl or covered blender container until smooth.

Nutrition Facts per serving: 417 calories, 25 g total fat (15 g saturated fat), 135 mg cholesterol, 212 mg sodium, 43 g carbohydrate, 1 g fiber, 7 g protein. Daily Values: 97% vit. A, 14% vit. C, 6% calcium, 8% iron.

White Chocolate-**Hazelnut Cheesecake**

Prep: 25 minutes **Bake:** 55 minutes **Cool:** 1¾ hours **Chill:** 4 hours

Mary L. Erickson
Madison, WI

Cracks in the top of a cheesecake are often inevitable, no matter how closely you follow the rules to avoid them. Don't worry too much about it. They're the badge of honor that shows everyone you care enough to make your own cheesecake.

1 8-ounce package hazelnut shortbread or shortbread cookies, crushed

3 tablespoons butter or margarine, melted

1 pound white chocolate baking squares or white baking bar

4 8-ounce packages cream cheese, softened

¼ cup butter or margarine, softened

¼ cup hazelnut liqueur or milk

1 tablespoon vanilla
Dash ground nutmeg

4 eggs

1 egg yolk

2 3-ounce bars milk chocolate with hazelnuts or four 1.45-ounce bars milk chocolate with almonds, chopped

Chocolate curls (optional)

1 For crust, combine the crushed cookies and melted butter in a medium bowl; press evenly onto the bottom only of a 10-inch springform pan. Place springform pan in a shallow baking pan; set aside.

2 For filling, in a medium saucepan stir baking squares or bar over low heat until melted. In a large mixing bowl beat melted baking bar, cream cheese, ¼ cup butter or margarine, liqueur or milk, vanilla, and nutmeg with an electric mixer until combined. Add eggs and egg yolk all at once; beat on low speed just until combined. Stir in milk chocolate. Pour into crust.

3 Bake in a 350° oven for 55 to 60 minutes or until center appears nearly set when shaken. Cool in pan on a wire rack for 15 minutes. Loosen cheesecake from sides of pan. Cool for 30 minutes more. Remove sides of pan; cool cheesecake completely. Cover; chill for at least 4 hours before serving. If desired, garnish with chocolate curls. Makes 16 servings.

Nutrition Facts per serving: 567 calories, 43 g total fat (27 g saturated fat), 166 mg cholesterol, 315 mg sodium, 32 g carbohydrate, 0 g fiber, 10 g protein. Daily Values: 33% vit. A, 11% calcium, 7% iron.

Chocolate-Raspberry Cheesecake

Prep: 40 minutes **Bake:** 50 minutes **Cool:** 1¾ hours **Chill:** 4 hours

1½ cups finely crushed graham crackers
¼ cup sifted powdered sugar
⅓ cup butter, melted
2 cups fresh or frozen loose-pack
    raspberries, thawed
½ teaspoon granulated sugar
3 8-ounce packages cream cheese,
    softened

1 14-ounce can (1¼ cups) sweetened
    condensed milk
4 eggs
1 teaspoon vanilla
1 cup semisweet chocolate pieces
    (6 ounces), melted and cooled

*Nicole Coriaty-Trovato
Eden Prairie, MN*

Two favorite flavors—chocolate and raspberry—meld exquisitely in this two-layer dessert. It's so rich and creamy that one cheesecake will serve 16 people. (Pictured on page 256.)

1 For crust, combine crushed graham crackers and powdered sugar; stir in melted butter. Press onto the bottom and 2 inches up the sides of a 9-inch springform pan; set aside.

2 For filling, in a small bowl combine 1 cup of the raspberries and the granulated sugar; set aside. In a large mixing bowl beat cream cheese and sweetened condensed milk with an electric mixer on low speed until combined. Add eggs and vanilla; beat just until combined. Divide batter in half. Stir melted chocolate into half of the batter. Pour chocolate batter into the crust-lined pan. Stir raspberry-sugar mixture into remaining batter. Spoon raspberry batter over chocolate batter.

3 Place springform pan on a shallow baking pan. Bake in a 350° oven for 50 to 60 minutes or until center appears nearly set when pan is gently shaken. Cool in pan on wire rack for 15 minutes. Loosen crust from sides of pan. Cool 30 minutes. Remove side of pan; cool 1 hour on wire rack. Cover; chill for at least 4 hours before serving. Serve with remaining raspberries. Makes 16 servings.

Nutrition Facts per serving: 382 calories, 26 g total fat (14 g saturated fat), 119 mg cholesterol, 257 mg sodium, 32 g carbohydrate, 1 g fiber, 8 g protein. Daily Values: 27% vit. A, 7% vit. C, 10% calcium, 9% iron.

Candy Crème Tart

Prep: 30 minutes **Bake:** 30 minutes **Cool:** 1 hour **Chill:** 4 hours

1999

Samantha Mitchell
Conyers, GA

When 10-year-old Samantha's grandmother suggested she create a cake, the delightful result was this cream cheese dessert loaded with bits of chocolate-covered toffee, white chocolate, and malted milk balls.

¾ cup finely crushed shortbread
    cookies (about 12 cookies)
¼ cup finely crushed graham crackers
1 tablespoon butter, melted
1 8-ounce package cream cheese,
    softened
3 tablespoons butter, softened
½ cup half-and-half or light cream
3 eggs
¼ cup sugar

1 teaspoon vanilla
3 1.4-ounce bars chocolate-covered
    English toffee, coarsely chopped
1 1.55-ounce bar white chocolate with
    crunchy chocolate cookie bits,
    coarsely chopped
15 malted milk balls, coarsely chopped
    (about ⅓ cup)
    Additional chopped candy

1 For the crust, in a small bowl stir together crushed cookies, crushed graham crackers, and the 1 tablespoon melted butter (mixture will be crumbly). Press onto the bottom and up the sides of a 9×1-inch tart pan with removable sides. Bake in a 350° oven about 10 minutes or until lightly browned. Set aside to cool.

2 For the filling, in a blender container or food processor bowl combine the cream cheese, the 3 tablespoons softened butter, the half-and-half or light cream, eggs, sugar, and vanilla. Cover and blend or process until smooth. In a large bowl place chopped candy; stir in the cream cheese mixture. Place crust-lined pan in a shallow baking pan. Pour filling into crust-lined pan. (Pan will be full.)

3 Bake about 30 minutes or until center appears nearly set when tart is shaken. Cool on a wire rack for 1 hour. Loosen and remove sides of tart pan. Place on a serving plate. Cover and chill for at least 4 hours before serving. If desired, garnish with additional chopped candy. Makes 12 servings.

Nutrition Facts per serving: 285 calories, 20 g total fat (9 g saturated fat), 94 mg cholesterol, 213 mg sodium, 22 g carbohydrate, 0 g fiber, 5 g protein. Daily Values: 16% vit. A, 5% calcium, 5% iron.

Ginger-Pear **Galette**

Prep: 25 minutes **Bake:** 18 minutes

1995

Edwina Gadsby
Great Falls, MT

Frozen puff pastry makes a flaky crust for this delectable pear dessert, which resembles a French tart or galette (gah-LEHT).

½ of a 17¼-ounce package (1 sheet) frozen puff pastry
1 slightly beaten egg white
2 tablespoons all-purpose flour
2 tablespoons granulated sugar
2 tablespoons brown sugar
1 tablespoon finely chopped crystallized ginger

1 teaspoon finely shredded lemon peel
2 tablespoons butter
3 large pears, halved, cored, peeled, and thinly sliced
  Whipped cream (optional)
  Crystallized ginger (optional)

1 Line a baking sheet with parchment paper; set aside. Thaw puff pastry according to package directions. Roll pastry into a 14×11-inch rectangle. Trim to a 12×10-inch rectangle. Place on the parchment-lined baking sheet. Prick pastry with a fork. Build up the sides slightly by folding in about ½ inch of pastry on each edge. Brush edges with egg white. Crimp edges or decorate edges with cutouts from the pastry trimmings. Brush pastry again with the egg white.

2 In a small bowl stir together the flour, granulated sugar, brown sugar, the 1 tablespoon ginger, and the lemon peel. Using a pastry blender or two knives, cut in the butter until pieces are the size of small peas. Sprinkle half of the ginger mixture over pastry. Arrange pear slices on top, overlapping slightly. Sprinkle with the remaining ginger mixture.

3 Bake, uncovered, in a 400° oven for 18 to 20 minutes or until the pastry is golden brown and the pears are tender. Serve warm. If desired, top each serving with whipped cream and additional crystallized ginger. Makes 8 servings.

Nutrition Facts per serving: 247 calories, 13 g total fat (11 g saturated fat), 61 mg cholesterol, 156 mg sodium, 33 g carbohydrate, 2 g fiber, 2 g protein. Daily Values: 3% vit. A, 4% vit. C, 2% iron.

Strawberry-Nut Shortcake

Prep: 15 minutes **Bake:** 12 minutes

1½ cups all-purpose flour
¼ cup sugar
1 teaspoon baking powder
¼ teaspoon salt
¼ teaspoon baking soda
⅓ cup butter
½ cup chopped walnuts

½ cup dairy sour cream
2 tablespoons milk
1 egg
3 cups sliced fresh strawberries
1 tablespoon sugar
1 cup whipping cream

*Anna Schmidt
Newton, KS*

Showcase summer's first plump strawberries in this rich walnut-and-sour-cream shortcake, then relish the rave reviews.

1 Grease a large baking sheet; set aside. In a medium bowl stir together the flour, the ¼ cup sugar, the baking powder, salt, and baking soda. Using a pastry blender or two knives, cut in butter until mixture resembles coarse crumbs. Stir in walnuts. In a small bowl combine sour cream, milk, and egg; add to flour mixture, stirring just until moistened. Drop by ⅓-cup portions onto prepared baking sheet. Bake in a 400° oven for 12 to 15 minutes or until golden brown.

2 Meanwhile, stir together the strawberries and the 1 tablespoon sugar; let stand for 15 minutes. In a chilled medium mixing bowl beat whipping cream with chilled beaters of an electric mixer on medium speed until soft peaks form. Split warm shortcakes; fill and top with strawberry mixture and whipped cream. Makes 6 servings.

Nutrition Facts per serving: 512 calories, 37 g total fat (19 g saturated fat), 127 mg cholesterol, 365 mg sodium, 41 g carbohydrate, 3 g fiber, 8 g protein. Daily Values: 32% vit. A, 69% vit. C, 12% calcium, 11% iron.

the quintessential american dessert

Apple pie is commonly touted as the favorite American dessert, but a strong case can be built for strawberry shortcake. Originally made only when strawberries were at their peak, shortcake now can be enjoyed almost all year long. As with many traditional favorites, cooks don't agree on how it should be made. Some insist the shortcake be fresh-from-the-oven baking powder biscuits that are split and buttered while warm and layered with fresh berries and sweetened whipped cream. Others prefer fresh berries ladled over sponge-cake cups. Strawberry-Nut Shortcake, above, takes the baking powder biscuit version to award-winning heights.

Banana-Pecan Streusel **Bread Pudding**

Prep: 20 minutes **Bake:** 40 minutes **Stand:** 30 minutes

Veronica Betancourt
Antioch, CA

Bananas add even more appeal to an old-fashioned dessert. In this version croissants substitute for bread, increasing the rich flavor. Top each serving with whipped cream, French vanilla ice cream, or butter brickle ice cream for the ultimate dessert.

1 12-ounce can (1½ cups) evaporated milk
1⅓ cups mashed ripe banana (4 medium)
3 beaten eggs
½ cup granulated sugar
1 tablespoon vanilla
1 teaspoon ground cinnamon
¼ to ½ teaspoon almond extract

2 large croissants, cut or torn into 1-inch pieces (5 ounces total)
¼ cup packed brown sugar
2 tablespoons all-purpose flour
1 tablespoon margarine or butter, melted
1 teaspoon ground cinnamon
½ cup chopped pecans
   Whipped cream or ice cream (optional)

1 Lightly grease a 2-quart rectangular baking dish; set aside. Stir together evaporated milk, banana, eggs, granulated sugar, vanilla, 1 teaspoon cinnamon, and the almond extract. Place croissant pieces in prepared baking dish. Pour egg mixture evenly over croissants, pressing pieces down to be sure they are all moistened.

2 In a small bowl combine brown sugar, flour, melted margarine or butter, and 1 teaspoon cinnamon. Stir in pecans. Sprinkle over croissant mixture. Bake in a 350° oven for 40 to 45 minutes or until a knife inserted near center comes out clean. Let stand for 30 minutes. Serve warm. If desired, top with whipped cream or ice cream. Makes 10 to 12 servings.

Nutrition Facts per serving:
280 calories, 12 g total fat
(5 g saturated fat),
93 mg cholesterol, 141 mg sodium,
38 g carbohydrate, 1 g fiber,
7 g protein. Daily Values: 9% vit. A,
8% vit. C, 9% calcium, 8% iron.

Chocolate Chip-Peanut Butter Bread Pudding

Prep: 15 minutes **Bake:** 40 minutes

3 cups dry white bread cubes*
½ cup semisweet chocolate pieces
½ cup flaked coconut (optional)
⅔ cup sugar
½ cup peanut butter

2 eggs
1 teaspoon vanilla
  Dash salt
2 cups milk

1978

Mrs. P. L. Browns
Denver, CO

On a cold winter evening, bread pudding is the perfect comfort food. Delight your family with this delectable version; serve it with a little fudge ice cream topping for an especially tasty treat.

1 Place bread cubes in a grease a 2-quart square baking dish. Sprinkle with chocolate pieces and, if desired, coconut. In a medium mixing bowl beat sugar and peanut butter with an electric mixer on medium speed until well mixed. Beat in eggs, vanilla, and salt. Gradually stir in milk. Pour over bread, pressing bread down to be sure it is all moistened.

2 Bake in a 350° oven for 40 to 45 minutes or until a knife inserted halfway between the edge and the center comes out clean. Serve warm. Makes 8 servings.

*Note: To dry bread cubes, measure 3½ cups fresh bread cubes. Spread in a single layer in a shallow pan; cover with waxed paper and let stand overnight.

Nutrition Facts per serving: 298 calories, 14 g total fat (4 g saturated fat), 58 mg cholesterol, 214 mg sodium, 33 g carbohydrate, 3 g fiber, 9 g protein. Daily Values: 6% vit. A, 1% vit. C, 10% calcium, 5% iron.

comfort food comes of age

During the late 1970s and early 1980s, people found themselves leading more and more hectic lives. When the economy took a downturn, many frazzled people said, "Enough!" They started to slow down to spend more time at home. Along with the return to home came a longing for more basic foods—dishes like Grandma made in the '30s and '40s. Suddenly, foods such as meat loaf, mashed potatoes, and macaroni and cheese were back in fashion and became known as comfort foods. One favorite that has gained new life is bread pudding. Today many restaurants serve it as a signature dessert. At home, cooks have tinkered with the classic recipe and have come up with innovative adaptations. Chocolate Chip-Peanut Butter Bread Pudding, above, and Banana-Pecan Streusel Bread Pudding, left, are two examples of how traditional favorites have inspired new creations.

Peanut Butter Parfaits

Prep: 15 minutes **Chill:** 2 hours

1 cup packed brown sugar	¼ cup peanut butter
⅓ cup milk	3 pints vanilla ice cream
¼ cup light-colored corn syrup	Crushed peanut brittle or peanuts
1 tablespoon butter or margarine	(optional)

1 For caramel sauce, in a medium saucepan combine the brown sugar, milk, corn syrup, and butter or margarine. Cook and stir over medium heat until sugar dissolves and butter or margarine melts; remove from heat. Add peanut butter. Beat with rotary beater or wire whisk until smooth. Cover and chill thoroughly, about 2 hours.

2 In 12 parfait glasses alternate layers of the ice cream and the caramel sauce, beginning and ending with ice cream. If desired, top with crushed peanut brittle or peanuts. Makes 12 servings.

Nutrition Facts per serving: 310 calories, 16 g total fat (9 g saturated fat), 48 mg cholesterol, 95 mg sodium, 41 g carbohydrate, 0 g fiber, 4 g protein. Daily Values: 15% vit. A, 1% vit. C, 11% calcium, 3% iron.

1967

Mrs. Leslie E. Dunkin
Bremen, IN

Remember this scrumptious caramel sauce next time you make banana splits. Or, try drizzling it over pound cake slices for an easy-to-fix dessert. You can make the sauce up to five days ahead; store it, covered, in the refrigerator.

perfect french

While *parfait* means "perfect" in French, the technical definition of the dessert depends on where you live. In France, a parfait is a rich frozen custard made with cream and eggs and often flavored with a fruit puree. In the United States, a parfait is usually a type of ice cream sundae, such as Peanut Butter Parfaits, above, that includes ice cream layered with a sauce or syrup. It also can be a chilled layered dessert made with pudding. No matter what the ingredients, parfaits are usually served in tall, slender glasses. To minimize the mess when assembling parfaits, use long-handled iced-tea spoons to gently place the layers in the glasses. To keep from mixing the layers, use a separate spoon for each mixture.

Brownie **Pudding**

Prep: 15 minutes **Bake:** 40 minutes

Mrs. D. B. Allen
Des Moines, IA

Treat your family to a delicious home-baked dessert. This eggless baked pudding stirs together in a jiffy and makes its own delectable fudge sauce as it bakes.

1 cup all-purpose flour
¾ cup granulated sugar
2 tablespoons unsweetened cocoa powder
2 teaspoons baking powder
½ teaspoon salt
½ cup milk

2 tablespoons cooking oil
1 teaspoon vanilla
¾ cup chopped walnuts
¾ cup packed brown sugar
¼ cup unsweetened cocoa powder
1¾ cups hot water

1 Grease an 8×8×2-inch baking pan; set aside. In a medium bowl combine flour, granulated sugar, the 2 tablespoons cocoa powder, the baking powder, and salt. Add milk, oil, and vanilla; stir until smooth. Stir in walnuts. Spread batter into prepared pan.

2 In a small bowl combine brown sugar and the ¼ cup cocoa powder; sprinkle evenly over batter. Pour hot water over entire surface of batter. Bake in a 350° oven for 40 to 45 minutes or until a toothpick inserted near the center comes out clean. Serve warm. Makes 8 servings.

Nutrition Facts per serving: 329 calories, 11 g total fat (1 g saturated fat), 1 mg cholesterol, 263 mg sodium, 54 g carbohydrate, 1 g fiber, 5 g protein. Daily Values: 1% vit. A, 1% vit. C, 11% calcium, 10% iron.

pudding cake craze

Pudding cakes captured the imagination of many cooks in the 1940s. They were popular because the batter stirred together quickly and baked into a tender cake topper with a rich, saucy bottom— eliminating the need to make a separate sauce. Although recipes for lemon, orange, and pineapple pudding cakes appeared throughout the '40s, it was chocolate pudding cakes, such as Brownie Pudding, above, that were the rage. Today, new generations of time-conscious cooks are rediscovering how marvelous pudding cakes can be.

Perfect Pecan Pudding

Prep: 15 minutes **Bake:** 30 minutes

3 eggs
1 cup dark-colored corn syrup
½ cup granulated sugar
2 tablespoons butter or margarine, melted
1 teaspoon vanilla

½ cup all-purpose flour
⅛ teaspoon cream of tartar
1 cup chopped pecans
Sifted powdered sugar
Half-and-half, light cream, or ice cream (optional)

Melicia Montemayor
Santa Maria, CA

If you really love pecans, top this homey pudding with a scoop of butter pecan ice cream.

1 Grease a 2-quart square baking dish; set aside. In a small mixing bowl beat eggs with an electric mixer on high speed about 5 minutes or until thick and lemon colored. Add corn syrup, granulated sugar, butter or margarine, and vanilla; mix well.

2 In a small bowl stir together flour and cream of tartar; fold into egg mixture. Stir in ½ cup of the pecans. Pour into prepared baking dish. Sprinkle with remaining pecans. Bake in a 375° oven for 30 minutes. Cool slightly. To serve, spoon into dessert dishes. Sprinkle powdered sugar over top. If desired, serve warm with half-and-half, light cream, or ice cream. Makes 6 to 8 servings.

Nutrition Facts per serving: 447 calories, 19 g total fat (4 g saturated fat), 117 mg cholesterol, 138 mg sodium, 69 g carbohydrate, 2 g fiber, 6 g protein. Daily Values: 9% vit. A, 1% vit. C, 2% calcium, 7% iron.

Choclava

1985

*Deborah Jordan
Tacoma, WA*

This chocolate version of baklava—a classic Greek pastry—will surely attract quite a following of enthusiasts whenever you make it. Bake a batch to share with friends and savor the compliments.

Prep: 45 minutes **Bake:** 45 minutes

4 cups walnuts, finely chopped (1 pound)	¾ cup orange juice
1 cup miniature semisweet chocolate pieces	½ cup sugar
	½ cup water
¾ cup sugar	½ cup honey
1½ teaspoons ground cinnamon	2 tablespoons lemon juice
1¼ cups butter, melted	2 ounces semisweet chocolate (optional)
1 16-ounce package frozen phyllo dough, thawed	2 tablespoons water (optional)

1 For filling, in a large bowl stir together walnuts, the 1 cup chocolate pieces, the ¾ cup sugar, and the cinnamon; set aside.

2 Brush the bottom of a 15×10×1-inch baking pan with some of the melted butter. Unfold phyllo. Layer 8 of the phyllo sheets in the pan, brushing each sheet with butter and allowing the phyllo to extend up sides of pan. (To prevent phyllo from drying out, keep sheets covered with a slightly moistened cloth until ready to use.) Sprinkle about 2 cups of the nut mixture over phyllo in pan.

3 Top with another 4 sheets of the phyllo, brushing each with more of the melted butter. Sprinkle with 2 more cups of the nut mixture and top with 4 more phyllo sheets, brushing each sheet with butter. Top with remaining nut mixture and remaining phyllo sheets, brushing each sheet with butter. Drizzle any remaining butter over top layer. Trim edges of phyllo to fit pan. Using a sharp knife, cut into diamond- or triangle-shape pieces, cutting to but not through the bottom layer.

4 Bake in a 325° oven for 45 to 50 minutes or until golden brown. Immediately finish cutting diamonds or triangles. Cool slightly in pan on a wire rack.

5 Meanwhile, in a medium saucepan combine orange juice, the ½ cup sugar, the ½ cup water, the honey, and lemon juice. Bring to boiling; reduce heat. Simmer, uncovered, for 20 minutes. Pour over warm choclava in pan. Cool completely.

6 To serve, if desired, in a heavy, small saucepan heat and stir the 2 ounces chocolate and the 2 tablespoons water over low heat until smooth. Drizzle some of the chocolate mixture over each piece of choclava. Store in the refrigerator. Makes about 60 pieces.

Nutrition Facts per piece: 147 calories, 10 g total fat (3 g saturated fat), 11 mg cholesterol, 79 mg sodium, 13 g carbohydrate, 1 g fiber, 2 g protein. Daily Values: 4% vit. A, 3% vit. C, 1% calcium, 3% iron.

Polenta-Pecan **Apple Cobbler**

Prep: 30 minutes **Bake:** 35 minutes

Helen Wolt
Colorado Springs, CO

If you're used to serving polenta only in savory dishes, here's a new way to try it. Polenta, made from cornmeal, makes a great-tasting topping for this apple-cherry cobbler.

½ cup all-purpose flour
⅓ cup quick-cooking polenta mix or yellow cornmeal
2 tablespoons granulated sugar
1 teaspoon baking powder
⅛ teaspoon salt
3 tablespoons butter
½ cup chopped pecans
2 tablespoons brown sugar
¼ teaspoon ground cinnamon

8 cups cubed, cored, peeled cooking apples (8 medium)
½ cup dried tart red cherries
⅓ cup packed brown sugar
1 tablespoon lemon juice
¼ teaspoon ground cinnamon
¼ cup cold water
1 tablespoon cornstarch
⅓ cup half-and-half or light cream
Half-and-half or light cream

1 For topping, in a small bowl stir together flour, polenta mix or cornmeal, granulated sugar, baking powder, and salt. Using a pastry blender or two knives, cut in butter until mixture resembles coarse crumbs; set aside.

2 In another small bowl combine the pecans, the 2 tablespoons brown sugar, and ¼ teaspoon cinnamon; set aside.

3 For filling, in a large saucepan combine the apples, cherries, the ⅓ cup brown sugar, the lemon juice, and ¼ teaspoon cinnamon. Bring to boiling, stirring constantly; reduce heat. Cover and simmer about 5 minutes or until fruit is almost tender, stirring occasionally. Combine cold water and cornstarch; add to saucepan. Cook and stir until thickened and bubbly. Keep hot.

4 Add the ⅓ cup half-and-half or light cream to topping mixture, stirring just to moisten. Transfer filling to a 2-quart square baking dish. Using a spoon, immediately drop topping into small mounds onto filling. Sprinkle with pecan mixture.

5 Bake in a 375° oven about 35 minutes or until a toothpick inserted into topping comes out clean. If desired, serve with additional half-and-half or light cream. Makes 6 servings.

Nutrition Facts per serving: 448 calories, 15 g total fat (6 g saturated fat), 24 mg cholesterol, 180 mg sodium, 78 g carbohydrate, 5 g fiber, 4 g protein. Daily Values: 15% vit. A, 14% vit. C, 9% calcium, 9% iron.

Rhubarb-Pineapple Crumble

Prep: 10 minutes **Stand:** 1 hour **Bake:** 45 minutes

1994

Carmela M. Meely
Walnut Creek, CA

This crumble is simply irresistible! Crystallized ginger in the rich crumb topping complements the spunky fruit filling. It is equally delicious with fresh or frozen rhubarb.

- 7 cups fresh or frozen rhubarb, cut into 1-inch pieces
- 1 8-ounce can crushed pineapple (juice pack), drained
- 1 cup packed brown sugar
- 2 tablespoons cornstarch
- 2 teaspoons finely shredded lemon peel
- ⅔ cup all-purpose flour
- ¼ cup packed brown sugar
- 1 tablespoon granulated sugar
- 1 tablespoon chopped crystallized ginger
- Dash salt
- ⅓ cup butter
- Vanilla ice cream (optional)

1 Thaw rhubarb, if frozen; drain well. In a large bowl combine rhubarb, pineapple, and the 1 cup brown sugar. Let stand for 1 hour. Drain mixture, reserving juices. If necessary, add water to reserved juices to equal ⅔ cup liquid. Place juices in a small saucepan. Stir in cornstarch. Cook and stir over medium heat until thickened and bubbly. Remove from heat. Stir into rhubarb mixture; stir in lemon peel. Spoon into a 2-quart square baking dish; set aside.

2 In a small bowl combine flour, the ¼ cup brown sugar, the granulated sugar, ginger, and salt. Using a pastry blender or two knives, cut in butter until mixture resembles coarse crumbs. Spoon over top of fruit. Bake in a 350° oven for 45 to 50 minutes or until lightly browned and bubbly. Serve warm. If desired, serve with ice cream. Makes 6 to 8 servings.

Nutrition Facts per serving: 391 calories, 11 g total fat (7 g saturated fat), 29 mg cholesterol, 158 mg sodium, 73 g carbohydrate, 3 g fiber, 3 g protein. Daily Values: 12% vit. A, 27% vit. C, 17% calcium, 11% iron.

keeping cobblers and crumbles crisp

To make crisp, inviting cobblers and crumbles, such as Polenta-Pecan Apple Cobbler, left, and Rhubarb-Pineapple Crumble, above, the Test Kitchen recommends using only butter—not margarine. Why? Many margarine or similar products with less than 80 percent vegetable oil contain additional water and milk solids that make the topping of cobblers and crumbles soggy. If you prefer margarine, only use those brands that contain 80 percent vegetable oil (these will have about 100 calories per tablespoon).

Cherry **Puff**

1952

Elizabeth Howser
Colorado Springs, CO

Bake this versatile dessert in small individual casseroles or in a large casserole. Either choice results in a tart cherry sauce nestled under airy sponge cake.

Prep: 25 minutes **Bake:** 35 minutes

1 16-ounce can pitted tart red cherries (water pack)	¼ teaspoon cream of tartar
½ cup sugar	⅛ teaspoon salt
2 tablespoons quick-cooking tapioca	2 egg yolks
2 egg whites	⅓ cup sugar
	⅓ cup all-purpose flour

1 Drain cherries, reserving ½ cup liquid. Transfer cherries to a medium saucepan. Add reserved cherry liquid, the ½ cup sugar, and the tapioca. Cook and stir over medium heat until mixture boils; reduce heat. Simmer, uncovered, for 5 minutes, stirring constantly; keep warm.

2 In a medium mixing bowl beat egg whites, cream of tartar, and salt with an electric mixer on medium speed until stiff peaks form (tips stand straight); set aside. In a small mixing bowl beat egg yolks for 2 to 3 minutes or until thick and lemon colored; add the ⅓ cup sugar. Beat 1 minute more. Stir a small amount of egg white mixture into egg yolk mixture to lighten. Fold remaining egg yolk mixture into egg white mixture. Sprinkle flour over egg mixture; fold in.

3 Pour hot cherry mixture into a 1½-quart casserole or into six 6- to 8-ounce casseroles or custard cups. Pour batter over cherry mixture. Bake in a 325° oven for 35 to 40 minutes for the 1½-quart casserole or about 30 minutes for the small casseroles or custard cups or until top springs back when lightly touched. Serve warm. Makes 6 servings.

Nutrition Facts per serving: 216 calories, 2 g total fat (1 g saturated fat), 71 mg cholesterol, 72 mg sodium, 48 g carbohydrate, 1 g fiber, 3 g protein. Daily Values: 4% vit. A, 5% vit. C, 2% calcium, 4% iron.

INDEX

Photographs: Page indicated in **bold**.

A-B

Metric Cooking Hints

By making a few conversions, cooks in Australia, Canada, and the United Kingdom can use the recipes in this book with confidence. The charts on this page provide a guide for converting measurements from the U.S. customary system, which is used throughout this book, to the imperial and metric systems. There also is a conversion table for oven temperatures to accommodate the differences in oven calibrations.

Product Differences: Most of the ingredients called for in the recipes in this book are available in English-speaking countries. However, some are known by different names. Here are some common U.S. American ingredients and their possible counterparts:
- Sugar is granulated or castor sugar.
- Powdered sugar is icing sugar.
- All-purpose flour is plain household flour or white four. When self-rising flour is used in place of all-purpose flour in a recipe that calls for leavening, omit the leavening agent (baking soda or baking powder) and salt.
- Light-colored corn syrup is golden syrup.
- Cornstarch is cornflour.
- Baking soda is bicarbonate of soda.
- Vanilla is vanilla essence.
- Green, red, or yellow sweet peppers are capsicums.
- Golden raisins are sultanas.

Volume and Weight: U.S. Americans traditionally use cup measures for liquid and solid ingredients. The chart, below, shows the approximate imperial and metric equivalents. If you are accustomed to weighing solid ingredients, the following approximate equivalents will help.
- 1 cup butter, castor sugar, or rice = 8 ounces = about 230 grams
- 1 cup flour = 4 ounces = about 115 grams
- 1 cup icing sugar = 5 ounces = about 140 grams

Spoon measures are used for smaller amounts of ingredients. Although the size of the tablespoon varies slightly in different countries, for practical purposes and for recipes in this book, a straight substitution is all that's necessary.

Measurements made using cups or spoons always should be level unless stated otherwise.

Equivalents: U.S. = Australia/U.K.

⅛ teaspoon = 1 ml
¼ teaspoon = 1.25 ml
½ teaspoon = 2.5 ml
1 teaspoon = 5 ml
1 tablespoon = 15 ml
1 fluid ounce = 30 ml
¼ cup = 60 ml
⅓ cup = 80 ml
½ cup = 120 ml
⅔ cup = 160 ml
¾ cup = 180 ml
1 cup = 240 ml
2 cups = 475 ml
1 quart = 1 liter
½ inch = 1.25 cm
1 inch = 2.5 cm

Baking Pan Sizes

U.S.	Metric
8×1½-inch round baking pan	20×4-cm cake tin
9×1½-inch round baking pan	23×4-cm cake tin
11×7×1½-inch baking pan	28×18×4-cm baking tin
13×9×2-inch baking pan	32×23×5-cm baking tin
2-quart rectangular baking dish	28×18×4-cm baking tin
15×10×1-inch baking pan	38×25.5×2.5-cm baking tin (Swiss roll tin)
9-inch pie plate	22×4- or 23×4-cm pie plate
7- or 8-inch springform pan	18- or 20-cm springform or loose-bottom cake tin
9×5×3-inch loaf pan	23×13×8-cm or 2-pound narrow loaf tin or pâté tin
1½-quart casserole	1.5-liter casserole
2-quart casserole	2-liter casserole

Oven Temperature Equivalents

Fahrenheit Setting	Celsius Setting*	Gas Setting
300°F	150°C	Gas mark 2 (very low)
325°F	170°C	Gas mark 3 (low)
350°F	180°C	Gas mark 4 (moderate)
375°F	190°C	Gas mark 5 (moderately hot)
400°F	200°C	Gas mark 6 (hot)
425°F	220°C	Gas mark 7 (hot)
450°F	230°C	Gas mark 8 (very hot)
475°F	240°C	Gas mark 9 (very hot)
Broil		Grill

*Electric and gas ovens may be calibrated using Celsius. However, for an electric oven, increase the Celsius setting 10 to 20 degrees when cooking above 160°C. For convection or forced-air ovens (gas or electric), lower the temperature setting 10°C when cooking at all heat levels.